# DESTROYING A NATION

## THE CIVIL WAR IN SYRIA

### NIKOLAOS VAN DAM

I.B. TAURIS

LONDON · NEW YORK

Copyright © 2017 Nikolaos van Dam

The right of Nikolaos van Dam to be identified as the author of this work has been asserted by the author in accordance with the Copyright, Designs and Patents Act 1988.

All rights reserved. Except for brief quotations in a review, this book, or any part thereof, may not be reproduced, stored in or introduced into a retrieval system, or transmitted, in any form or by any means, electronic, mechanical, photocopying, recording or otherwise, without the prior written permission of the publisher.

References to websites were correct at the time of writing.

ISBN: 978 1 78453 797 5
eISBN: 978 1 78672 248 5
ePDF: 978 1 78673 248 4

A full CIP record for this book is available from the British Library
A full CIP record is available from the Library of Congress

Library of Congress Catalog Card Number: available

Cover image: A Syrian man carries a baby in the Maadi district of eastern Aleppo after regime aircrafts reportedly dropped explosive-packed barrel bombs on 27 August 2016. (Photo: AMEER ALHALBI/AFP/Getty Images)

Typeset by Riverside Publishing Solutions
Printed and bound by CPI Group (UK) Ltd, Croydon, CR0 4YY

MIX
Paper from
responsible sources
FSC® C020471
www.fsc.org

*To Marinka*

# CONTENTS

# PREFACE

When I first visited Syria in 1964, more than half a century ago, I was free to travel almost anywhere I wanted. In the fascinating *suqs* of Aleppo, I had an unexpected encounter with a Syrian student from a picturesque nearby rural village who invited me to stay overnight to be his guest under the open summer sky, next to his traditional beehive mud-brick house. Inside the mud-brick cupola it was too hot to sleep comfortably, but it was a different kind of comfort that I grew accustomed to. In his tiny rural village, I, for the first time, enjoyed the great hospitality of a Syrian family.

What struck me most during my frequent visits to Syria over the years was the kindness and great hospitality of the Syrian people, wherever I went. I got to know the Syrians as friendly and charming, open-minded and tolerant, and respectful heirs of rich civilisations. I enjoyed the fascinating historical cities of Aleppo and Damascus, with their industrious people, the smells of oriental spices and the busy sounds of market life; the ingenious architectural splendour of beautifully decorated palaces and traditional houses, with their treasures surprisingly hidden behind anonymous walls; all this next to the cosmopolitan buzz of the modern city quarters, where people remained attached to their valuable traditions. The soft-spoken Syrian Arabic sounded like harmonious music to my ears. I visited the fertile

Alawi Mountains near the Mediterranean coast with their strategically located Crusader and Assassin castles; the city of Hama with its elegant Azm Palace and its chirping large water wheels (*norias*) from which enthusiastic children jumped from high up, plunging joyfully into the Orontes river; and the various museums with their spectacular mosaics made by Syrians in Roman times. I travelled across the occasionally blooming deserts with their impressive ancient Umayyad castles and cities like Palmyra, justly called 'the pearl of the desert'. There is hardly any place in Syria I did not visit.

The beautiful picture that once existed has now been destroyed to such an extent that Syria can never be the same again. In 2010, just before the start of the Syrian Revolution, Syria still seemed to be a quiet and peaceful country. What was less visible on the surface then – although it was well known – was that Syria had been ruled for almost half a century by the same Ba'thist dictatorship, which severely suppressed those people who did not accept its views or opposed it.

Many of the beautiful places I visited in the past now conjure up images of fierce battles and bloody war; of a country buried to a large extent under a pile of growing rubble. Aleppo with its burnt-out *suqs* and mosques and richly ornamented notable houses being destroyed; Hama with its bloodbath of 1982 and repeated heavy destruction during the Syrian Revolution; Homs with its embattled district of al-Wa'r; Palmyra with the destruction of its ancient temples and public executions by the barbaric Islamic State (Da'ish). The so-called 'forgotten villages' in northern Syria with their magnificent ancient Byzantine monasteries, where some of the best olive oil was produced, have been disrupted by fierce battles in places like Kafr Nubul. Bosra with its spectacular Roman theatre close to Deraa, where the Syrian Revolution started in 2011, has become part of the Southern Front. The border I crossed from Syria to Iraq by train in 1965 was eradicated by the Islamic State during the Syrian War, and Raqqa and Dayr al-Zur, with their splendid views over the majestic Euphrates river, were occupied and terrorised by them.

When last visiting Damascus in September 2010, I – like many others – could hardly ever have imagined that several months later a revolution would start all over the country, leading to a devastating bloody war. The Syrian dictatorship and its unwillingness and inability to reform finally caused Syria's seemingly peaceful life to explode, and the subsequent war led to the destruction of great parts of the country, with immense and profound social consequences. By 2017, more than 400,000 Syrians had been killed, while many millions of people tried to escape from the conflict, becoming refugees or internally displaced persons. All this was accompanied by an immense amount of destruction in the refined social fabric of what used to be the Syrian nation.

This book deals with various aspects of the Syrian Revolution that started in March 2011. It explains why the Syrian War that followed the revolution was inevitable, taking into account the earlier behaviour (and misbehaviour) of the Syrian regime as described in detail in my earlier book *The Struggle for Power in Syria*.[1]

The regime of President Bashar al-Asad had imagined that it could suppress the Syrian Revolution in 2011 with brute force, just as it had succeeded in doing on earlier occasions. But this time the situation was completely different. The wall of fear and silence in Syria had been broken and many peaceful Syrian demonstrators were inspired by Arab Spring developments elsewhere in the region, which still looked promising in the beginning. Both the Syrian regime and the Syrian opposition groups started to receive political, military and financial support from a number of foreign countries that thereby began to interfere in Syria's internal affairs. All this gave rise to a combination of a bloody war among Syrians themselves, and a war by proxy between other countries to the detriment of the Syrian people.

The violent confrontation between the regime and opposition was bound to take on a sectarian dimension, given the highly visible and disproportionate number of Alawi minority sect members in the army's elite units, as well as in other repressive institutions that were mobilised to quell the revolution. This factor strengthened the perception amongst many that the war also had the character of a sectarian-tinted minority-majority Alawi-Sunni conflict. Radical Sunni Islamist military groups hijacked the initially peaceful revolution, and contributed to pushing Syria further into the violent quagmire.

Various Western and regional parties, that originally intended to support the Syrian opposition against the regime, occasionally created false expectations that fuelled the Syrian War, rather than contributing to a solution as apparently intended.

This book is not meant to be a repetition of the various books that have already been published on the Syrian Revolution since 2011 (and can be found in the bibliography), but is intended as an analysis that purports to explain some of the deeper backgrounds to what has been happening in Syria since the start of the revolution in 2011. It also deals with the prospects for a solution to the conflict.

Over the past two years I have worked as the Dutch Special Envoy for Syria, operating from Istanbul, with the support of an expert Dutch Syria team. I had intensive contact with most of the parties involved in the Syria conflict: in Moscow, Teheran, Riyadh, Ankara, Cairo, Geneva, Vienna, Beirut, Amman, Istanbul, Antakya, Gaziantep and many other places. I had meetings with representatives of almost all opposition organisations and associated movements. I also had meetings with the UN Special Envoys for Syria, Kofi Annan, Lakhdar Brahimi and Staffan de Mistura, as well as with most of the Special Envoys for Syria of individual other countries. People close to the regime provided me with insights from Damascus. All this gave me numerous opportunities to witness the Syrian conflict, and the attempts at its resolution, at a very close range, including during the various intra-Syrian talks in Geneva and elsewhere.

My experiences are reflected in this book.

Without mentioning specific names for reasons of confidentiality, I want to sincerely thank all those Syrians and others with whom I had the opportunity to exchange views on the conflict, and who helped me tremendously in gaining a deeper understanding of the developments during the years since 2011.

I hope this book will contribute to further understanding the conflict in Syria and will possibly be of some help in finding a solution.

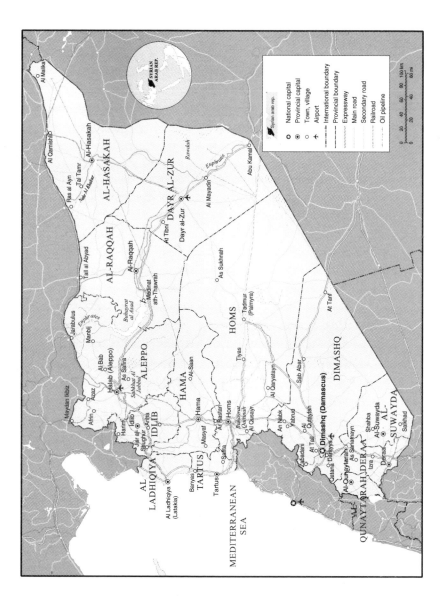

# INTRODUCTION
## GREATER SYRIA OR BILAD AL-SHAM

In Arab nationalist literature Syria has often been described as a country which has been severed from the hinterland of Greater Syria, and has thereby become a 'limbless trunk'. The northern city of Aleppo is a clear example of this phenomenon. Whoever looks at the political map of today's Syria considers it as self-evident that inside the country there are intensive north–south contacts between Aleppo and Damascus, both socially and in the field of trade or economics. But when looking at older maps and reports, it turns out that in the past trade routes ran quite differently and that, as a result, west–east contact between, for instance, Aleppo in the north and Mosul (in contemporary northern Iraq) were even more intensive than those between Aleppo and Damascus.

And towns like Mardin, 'Ayntab (Gaziantep) and Harran – all located just north of present-day Syria – and now part of south-eastern Turkey, were still part of the natural Aleppo network.

But what exactly is the territory of Greater Syria or Bilad al-Sham?[1] It is rather convenient to define it as 'the territory of Syria, Jordan, Lebanon and Palestine which could be viewed as geographically, culturally and historically having been a united entity that was separated by the colonial powers'. This is the way in which it was described in an introduction to the Conference of 'Bilad al-Sham in the Ottoman Era', which was held in Damascus in 2005. But is this really correct? Greater Syria is indeed a clearly identifiable predominantly Arab region with certain geographic, social and linguistic specifics. In the cities of Syria, Lebanon, Jordan, Palestine and southern Turkey west of the Euphrates river, various types of so-called 'Syrian Arabic' are being spoken with common characteristics, which can generally not be found outside Greater Syria.

But it can also be argued that certain areas of north-eastern Syria, east of the river Euphrates, are not really part of Greater Syria, because they constitute a natural part of Mesopotamia, or Bilad al-Rafidayn, the land between the Euphrates and Tigris rivers in present-day Iraq, which is equally clearly identifiable as an Arab region with its own specifics. In this (now Syrian) area, the Mesopotamian (Iraqi) Arabic dialects show their influence, well into the Syrian city of Dayr al-Zur and into southern Turkey, east of the river Euphrates.[2]

Seen from the Syrian side, the dividing line between Greater Syria and Mesopotamia can be located at the eastern end of the Badiyat al-Sham ('The Desert of Greater Syria') and somewhere at the shores of the Euphrates River. Several ancient maps of the Ottoman Empire indicate that the eastern border of Greater Syria ran along the river Euphrates.

This means that today's Syrian Arab Republic covers an area which is on the one hand much smaller than Greater Syria – because it does not include Palestine, Lebanon, Jordan and parts which now fall within the Republic of Turkey – but on the other hand also covers areas which fall outside geographic Greater Syria, notably some north-eastern parts of the Syrian Arab Republic which start somewhere at the Euphrates river, which is the al-Jazirah area in the wider sense.

It is not clear whether the British and French colonial powers drew the borderlines between Iraq and Syria on purpose in such a way that not only Greater Syria was cut into various so-called artificial parts, but also parts of Mesopotamia between Syria and Iraq were divided; or whether other practical factors played a role. But does it really matter? The Sykes–Picot boundaries in the Fertile Crescent area (being Greater Syria and Mesopotamia together) may indeed be considered artificial and imposed, and those imposed under French Mandate inside part of Greater Syria equally so. But earlier boundaries in the region could in that sense also be seen as artificial, as long as they did not follow clear geographical and ethnic lines. Often they just reflected the zones of influence among rival powers. Under the dynasties of the Umayyads, Abbasids, Fatimids, Nizari Isma'ilis (or Assassins), Mamluks, Hamdanids and several others, the boundaries of and within Greater Syria also shifted repeatedly.[3] And before, under the Romans, the boundaries of the province of Syria were different as well.

Nevertheless, Greater Syria can be considered as constituting a 'geographic and cultural entity', with some internal varieties. The concept of the Western colonial powers having separated it on purpose into different pieces for various reasons is also valid. But Greater Syria as 'historically a united entity' beforehand seems to be a rather idealistic way of looking at things, one that does not conform to historic reality.

It appears to be a way of saying that 'if the colonial powers would not have split up the Arab Fertile Crescent region as they did, then this area would now have been united as far as Greater Syria is concerned'.[4] Most of it was a matter of colonial divide-and-rule and power politics. The fact that the Arab countries since their independence did not succeed in their unity plans can, however, not all be blamed on former colonial powers and Western imperialism. At least as important a factor was the fact that most Arab rulers wanted to monopolise power for themselves, instead of sharing it with others for the sake of Arab unity.

In due course, it turned out that former colonial boundaries had a resistant durability, even though they had, at first, been rejected by Arab nationalist Syrians in general. Another phenomenon is that states generally fully accept their original territory as defined by their former colonial rulers, albeit that they would like to claim a larger area if this, in their view, could be justified on historic grounds.

Changes would only be accepted if these would imply obtaining additional territory, not losing part of their original state territory.

People grow up, or are educated in such a way that they have a particular political geographical map in mind, which may differ from the geographical maps in the minds of other people in different regions. It took the Syrian Government some 75 years to accept de facto that the former north-western Syrian district (Sanjaq) of Iskenderun, that was ceded by the French to Turkey in 1939, does now belong to the latter country. It is no longer shown on official Syrian maps as being part of the Syrian Arab Republic, but many Syrians still consider it to be part of Syria, and keep calling it the 'illegally seized province' (*al-Liwa' al-Mughtasab*).[5] Arab inhabitants of former Iskenderun (now called Hatay, named after the Hittites) in the meantime focus much more on Turkey than on Syria, even if they have family connections with, for instance, people from Aleppo. They generally have adopted the Turkish national identity, although many have maintained Arabic as their mother tongue.[6]

It can be concluded that, after more than 70 years of Syrian independence, the Syrian national identity has taken root, whatever its earlier history, including the arguments that present-day Syria used to be seen for some time as an artificial entity.

Almost all Syrian parties involved in the war in Syria since 2011 are united in the principle that the territorial integrity and unity of Syria should be preserved. This applies to both the Ba'th regime and the opposition groups, with the exception of some of the Kurds.

As far as the present-day population is concerned, the peaceful demonstrators at the beginning of the Syrian Revolution in 2011 stressed that all Syrians were one and united. One of the slogans was that they were Syrians, rather than members of religious groups like the Alawis, Druzes, Isma'ilis, Sunnis or Kurds; and that they were all 'one'. This was the sincere wish, expressed by the demonstrators. But events took a different turn, and, as will be explained later, the Syrian War moved in the direction of a sectarian-tinted conflict that most Syrians did not want, but nevertheless became a reality, as a result of dynamics in Syrian society.

## SYRIAN NATIONAL IDENTITY AND LOYALTY TOWARDS THE SYRIAN STATE

By the end of the French Mandate in 1946, the Syrian identity, linked to the new Syrian state, was not yet well developed. Syria was in many respects a state without being a nation-state, and a political entity without being a political community.

In the Ottoman Empire there was Bilad al-Sham, the 'Country of Greater Syria', which was composed of a much bigger geographical area, including present-day Syria, Lebanon, Jordan, Palestine/Israel and parts of present-day southern Turkey. But Bilad al-Sham, under Ottoman rule, had also been divided into various administrative districts.

In 1864, the Ottomans created the Vilayet (administrative district) of Syria ('Vilayet-i Suriye'), using the name of Syria for the first time for such a district in contemporary history.

The name 'Syria' has been coined by the Greeks by erroneously deriving it from Assyria sometime in the sixth century BC, thereby initiating a confusion regarding the name and its geographic and political connotation that would last until the present. The name stuck from ancient times through the period of Byzantine rule and was still in use during the first century of Arab Muslim rule, but then disappeared for more than a thousand years until the nineteenth century, when the Ottomans started using it again.[7] The Arabs only used the name Bilad al-Sham.

The Ottoman Vilayet of Syria, also known as the Vilayet of Damascus, was only one of the seven districts in Greater Syria at the time.

These districts did not imply that the respective administrative boundaries were a kind of obstacle like today's international borders. Local inhabitants could easily travel all over Greater Syria: between Damascus and Jerusalem, between Beirut and Haifa, between Mosul and Aleppo or between Aleppo and Urfa. It was an area that could be travelled across without political obstacles.[8]

Arab nationalists considered the new Syrian Arab Republic, which gained independence after the French had left in 1946, as an artificial entity that should be seen as a truncated part of Greater Syria.

During the French Mandate, the area of today's modern Syria was 'truncated' even more, because it was divided into four different states and an additional administrative entity: the State of Damascus, the State of Aleppo, the Alawi State, the State of the Jabal al-Duruz, and the Sanjaq of Alexandretta.

In general, the Syrians strongly opposed the French Mandate, which they saw as a foreign occupation, and there were various uprisings against the French all over the country. Some uprisings were Arab nationalist in character, whereas those which involved compact minorities were more often inspired by local considerations or, at least, non-ideological ones. Alawi leaders at the time were mainly interested in protecting the Alawi districts from all external interference.

The Arab nationalists rejected the country being divided into separate states, but they were challenged at the time by movements in the Alawi region, the Jabal al-Duruz and the northeastern Jazirah region, which had their own considerations. Such developments hindered the crystallisation of a Syrian national identity.[9]

Later, Arab nationalists, like the Ba'thists, maintained that they should not focus on a loyalty towards the Syrian state, but rather on the bigger Arab nation, stretching from Iraq to Morocco and from Syria to Oman. The Ba'th Party at first even rejected the Arab League Charter, because it stated that the Arab states should mutually respect their state boundaries, whereas the Ba'thists considered those national boundaries as an official obstacle to Arab unification. Since there was no larger Arab union to focus on, the main focal point became the smaller regional identity, based on the region of birth or residence.

## WHO IS A SYRIAN?

If one would ask a Syrian Arab several decades ago from which area he hailed, or to which religious community he belonged, the standard – and evading – answer would generally be: 'we are all Arabs'. Arab nationalists in Syria usually disliked the use of geographical names that indicated the religious background of the local inhabitants. Thus, stressing that all Arabs are equal irrespective of their religion, they preferred the name of Jabal al-'Arab ('Mountain of the Arabs') to that of Jabal al-Duruz

('Mountain of the Druzes'). 'The Mountains of the Alawis' or 'Nusayris' (Jibal al-'Alawiyin or Jibal al-Nusayriyah) are now given the more neutral name of Jibal al-Sahil ('The Coastal Mountains'), and the Wadi al-Nasara ('Valley of the Christians') in the Homs region is nowadays called Wadi al-Nadara ('Blooming Valley'). The introduction of this more neutral terminology did not mean, however, that people were not just as fully aware of the religion of the inhabitants concerned. In that respect giving different names did not make much difference, except that people tended to be more aware that talking about sectarianism was surrounded by a kind of taboo in Syria.

It may be questioned whether trying to obliterate the original identity of these regions has not even been counterproductive. Leila Al-Shami and Robin Yassin-Kassab have argued that 'silencing the issue made it more salient. What Syria needed was a national conversation about historical fears and resentments aiming towards greater mutual understanding; instead, people discussed the other sect in bitter secret whispers, and only among their own.'[10]

Even though talking about religion remains a sensitive issue, Syrian colloquial Arabic still contains some daily expressions referring to religion. For instance, when wishing to know the composition of a tasty dish, one may ask *shu dinu*? ('what is its religion?').

The Alawis, Druzes and Isma'ilis were all Arabic-speaking heterodox Islamic 'compact minorities' in the sense that most of them lived in a specific geographical area where they also constituted a majority of the population.[11] Regional, tribal and sectarian identities were therefore relatively stronger among the compact minorities than among groups that were spread out over the whole of Syria, like the Sunni Arabs. In the early 1960s most Alawis lived in the north-western mountain region, most Druzes in the south, and most Isma'ilis to the east and west of

Hama (particularly in Salamiyah and Masyaf). After 1963, when the Ba'th Party had taken over power, many of them migrated to the cities.

Under Ba'thist rule, the Syrian national identity was at first not promoted for Arab nationalist reasons, and it was even occasionally considered as something negative. It was only later, after Arab unity projects had failed and it had become clear that there were no prospects for Arab unity successes in the foreseeable future, that it gradually became more acceptable to be proud of one's 'Syrian identity'. There even was a popular song called *Ana Suri* ('I am a Syrian'), released in 1996 by the Syrian artist 'Abd al-Rahman Al Rashi, in which the Syrian identity was enthusiastically praised, albeit still next to the Arab identity. In earlier stages of Syrian Ba'thist history such a song might have been rejected as reflecting a kind of 'narrow-minded' regionalism as opposed to a wider Arab nationalism.

Another initial reason for the Ba'th Party in the 1950s to be strongly against the 'Syrian identity' was its ideological rivalry with the Syrian Social Nationalist Party (SSNP) of Antun Sa'adah, who promoted the idea of a 'Syrian nation' all over the Fertile Crescent area of Mesopotamia and Greater Syria together. The SSNP ideology was the antipode of that of the Ba'th Party. As the SSNP, like the Ba'th Party, was popular among minorities, it was considered to be a strong political competitor at the time, that had to be defeated.

## THE SYRIAN–EGYPTIAN UNION (1958–61)

The history of the present Syrian regime can be traced back to the summer of 1959, when a number of Ba'thist military officers were transferred – or rather exiled – from Syria to Cairo after the union between Egypt and Syria (1958–61) had been founded.

They started to meet secretly in order to discuss the future of Syria. These Ba'thist officers were not trusted by the dictatorship of Egyptian President Gamal 'Abd al-Nasir, and therefore were placed far away from their home country Syria, where it would have been easier for them to undermine Egyptian totalitarian rule over their country. The Syrian–Egyptian union (the United Arab Republic) was supposed to fulfil the wishes of many Syrians and Egyptians, who coveted Arab unity. It was the epoch of Arab nationalism and unionism and Syria was one of the most fervent Arab nationalist countries at the time. It was not without reason that President 'Abd al-Nasir called Damascus 'the beating heart of Arabism' (*Qalb al-'Urubah al-Nabid*).

One of the problems of the Syrian–Egyptian union was that it was not a union between two equals, but a union in which Egypt, led by President 'Abd al-Nasir, was by far the most dominant party. This was the price the Syrian military leadership apparently had been willing to pay, after they more or less pushed the Egyptian president into a full union between their two countries. The civilian leadership of the Arab Socialist Ba'th Party had accepted the union, as this fitted in with their unionist ideology, and they even agreed to disband their political party, as this had been one of the preconditions of President 'Abd al-Nasir. All this ended up in a kind of power monopoly by the Egyptian president, with the Syrian politicians and military playing a junior role, if any substantial part at all. The disbandment of the Ba'th Party by their civilian leadership of Michel 'Aflaq (its Christian founder and ideologist) and Salah al-Din al-Bitar (the Sunni co-founder) was strongly criticised by the Syrian military Ba'thists, among whom were those who had been transferred to Cairo. They bore a grudge against the traditional civilian Ba'th Party leadership. These leaders had, in their eyes, made a serious mistake by giving priority to the Egyptian–Syrian union – with all its deficiencies – over their ideal of Ba'thist Arab nationalism, in which the Arab nation was supposed to constitute a cultural unity in which all Arabs were to be equal, with existing differences between them 'accidental and unimportant' and which would 'disappear with the awakening of the Arab consciousness'. This was the official message in the Constitution of the Ba'th Party, the ideas of which had in fact been ignored by its leadership (because Egypt and Syria were not treated as equals), although they could not really have foreseen at the time how disadvantageous the Syrian–Egyptian union was going to be for Syria and the Syrians in general (except for the rural people who profited from 'Abd al-Nasir's land reform measures).

The 'exiled' Ba'thist military in Cairo were Arab nationalists who, just like the civilian party leadership, wanted their ideal of Arab unity to be fulfilled, but not in a way in which they and the Ba'thists in general were to play a junior role, or no role at all.

This became a more general phenomenon: many Arab nationalists wanted the Arabs to be united in the form of an Arab union, but only if they themselves were to play the dominant and leading role in it, not a subservient one. Later, various Arab unification efforts were undertaken, but they all failed, because effectively the sharing or delegating of powers was a point that in practice did not work, and was not accepted.

The system of collective leadership within the various Arab countries that for some time had such a system did not succeed either. All efforts in this sense culminated in the totalitarian leadership of one single Arab leader in Egypt, Iraq, Syria, Libya, Yemen, Algeria and other Arab countries. Arab unionist efforts between Egypt and Syria; between Syria and Iraq; between Egypt, Syria and Iraq; between Syria, Libya and Sudan; and other efforts, all failed. Only the union between north and south Yemen succeeded for some time, and they even had two co-presidents in the beginning, but in the end their rivalry led to war, because the north wanted to dominate the south.

In the heyday of Arab nationalism, various Arab leaders (like the Libyan leader Mu'ammar al-Qadhafi where the Arab Maghrib countries were concerned) generally wanted either everything or nothing where it concerned forms of Arab unification, and therefore more often than not these leaders ended up with nothing because they did not accept compromises and lacked enough pragmatism. Their ideologies prevailed over pragmatic realism, but without any success.

During the union with Egypt, the small group of 'exiled' Syrian Ba'thist officers, being far away from their country, started in 1959 to discuss in secret in Cairo what they might do to realise their Ba'thist Arab nationalist ideals in future. They had to evade all attention and distrust, which their secret meetings might have caused, from the Egyptian security authorities who closely surveyed their activities. After all, these officers were placed in Egypt not to fulfil an important military mission, but rather because they were mistrusted by the Egyptian authorities. This added to their frustration. Their internal discussions led to the formation of a secret Ba'thist Military Committee, which was to decide on further steps needed to take over power within the Syrian organisation of the Ba'th Party itself by influencing it from behind the scenes. Second, they considered steps to take over power in Syria with the Ba'th as the leading party, and its military to be in control from behind the scenes. The civilian leadership was not at all aware of this new Ba'thist military organisation at the time, and it was only to discover its existence several years later, once the secret military organisation of the Ba'th Party had succeeded in taking over power in Syria with their military coup of 8 March 1963.

During the Syrian–Egyptian union, the civilian party leadership was officially no longer active inside Syria, because they had dissolved the party organisation there with the formation of the United Arab Republic. The Ba'th Party organisation, however, was not only restricted to Syrian territory, but also had a pan-Arab structure with an organisational network in various other Arab countries, like Iraq, Lebanon, Jordan, Palestine, Sudan, Yemen and Mauritania. The traditional civilian leadership, therefore, was still active outside Syria, but officially not inside Syria itself, which actually had been the most important base of the Ba'th Party, next to Iraq. This was an anomaly caused by its civilian leadership. It did not mean, however, that there was no longer any Ba'thist activity inside Syria itself. There was a group of civilians who had rejected the disbandment of their party organisation by the party leadership, and secretly continued their activities inside Syria. Later, they were to be called the Qutriyin, or 'Regionalists', because they did not follow the pan-Arab Ba'th organisation any longer, but were mainly oriented towards Syria. In the 'orthodox' Ba'thist view this was contradictory with the pan-Arab ideology of the Ba'th Party. But dissolving the party organisation in Syria by the traditional civilian Ba'th leadership had also been contradictory with their pan-Arab ideals.

The Ba'thist Military Committee established secret contacts with the Qutriyin. After the military had taken over power in Syria in 1963, they helped bring the Qutriyin to prominence, with the aim of pushing the traditional civilian leadership aside.

## THE SECRET BA'THIST MILITARY COMMITTEE AND SYRIAN MINORITIES

With hindsight, it can be said that the members of the secret Ba'thist Military Committee were of essential importance for further developments in Syria during the next half a century.

Their social and sectarian backgrounds were to become of crucial importance as well.

The highest leadership of the Military Committee consisted of five officers, three of whom were Alawis, notably Muhammad 'Umran, Salah Jadid and Hafiz al-Asad, in order of seniority. The two others were Isma'ilis, notably 'Abd al-Karim al-Jundi and Ahmad al-Mir. Later, the leadership was extended to 15 members, five of whom were Alawis, two Isma'ilis, two Druzes and six Sunnis. Most of them had rural backgrounds and came from poor families, with two exceptions: Salah Jadid and 'Abd al-Karim al-Jundi who came from prominent local middle-class families. It should be noted that all core-members of the Military Committee had a sectarian minority background, whereas the majority of the extended Military Committee had a minoritarian background as well.[12]

In itself, it was not surprising that by far the majority of members of the Military Committee had a rural and sectarian minority background. This was because the Ba'th Party with its secular Arab nationalist ideology was particularly attractive to members of Arabic-speaking religious minorities, like the Alawis, Druzes, Isma'ilis and Christians; and these minorities were to a great extent living in the Syrian countryside. The Alawis constitute roughly 11 per cent of the Syrian population (and thereby are Syria's biggest minority), the Druzes 3 per cent and the Isma'ilis 1.5 per cent. In the 1940s, Christians still constituted more than 14 per cent of the Syrian population, of whom the Greek Orthodox accounted for approximately 5 per cent. Their numbers have strongly decreased from 14 to as little as 5 per cent, or perhaps even less, as many Christians have migrated or fled abroad for what they considered security reasons.[13]

According to its secular ideology, the Ba'th Party did not discriminate between these minorities and the Sunni majority. Other Arab nationalist parties, dominated by Sunnis, had generally given priority to Sunni Islam, as a result of which their Arabism was a kind of Sunni-coloured Arabism that might tolerate Arab-speaking religious minorities, but not as full equals. These minorities, however, not only want to be *tolerated* but they also wanted to be *respected*. Ba'thist Arabism implied the ideal of an equalitarian Arab nationalism that provided minorities with the possibility of getting rid of their minority status.

In the view of the founder and ideologist of the Ba'th Party, Michel 'Aflaq, Islam was part of the national history and cultural heritage of all Arabs, irrespective of their religion. In the view of 'Aflaq, the Prophet Muhammad symbolised 'the ideal picture of the Arabs and the Arab nation'. It was not without reason that the Arabs had been chosen to convey the message of Islam, according to 'Aflaq, and Islam, therefore, was to be considered an 'Arab movement, aimed at the renewal and perfectioning of Arabism'.[14]

Syrians occasionally like to refer to the picture of Syrian society as a peaceful mosaic with equal chances for all population groups. By way of an example, Faris al-Khuri, a Christian, has been Syria's Prime Minister, the highest position ever reached by a Christian in Syria; and it was even proposed that he would assume the office for (Muslim) Religious Endowments (Awqaf), but he declined. Al-Khuri's political success is occasionally hailed by Sunni Muslims as proof of their willingness to accept members of religious minorities as equal citizens. Presidents Husni al-Za'im (1949) and Adib al-Shishakli (1953–54) are hailed as other examples of this so-called tolerance, because they both had Kurdish ancestry. But these examples do not say much for the position of Christians in the past in general, let alone of the position of the Kurds, many of whom were stripped of their nationality in 1962. Nevertheless, the 'Syrian mosaic' compared favourably with the situation in various other Middle Eastern countries and had more often than not a peaceful character.

Another element that made the Ba'th Party relatively popular in the poor countryside was the socialist component in its Arab nationalist ideology.

The party organisation's growth depended to a large extent on personal initiatives undertaken by its original members in their native regions, and therefore developed there more strongly than elsewhere, at first.

Very few indigenous inhabitants of the Syrian capital Damascus were initially attracted by the Ba'th Party. Its founding members (including 'Aflaq and al-Bitar, who themselves were Damascene school teachers) made no serious effort to win sympathy for their ideals from the Damascene population as they were content, for the time being, with their success in recruiting rural students. The social conditions in rural areas were more favourable to the growth and spread of the Ba'th Party, which as a result 'became a big body with a small head'.[15] The fact that relatively large numbers of the original Ba'thists came from rural and minoritarian backgrounds later formed a social impediment to the membership of urban people and Sunnis, due to the traditional contrasts between urban and rural communities and between Sunnis and religious minorities. Such traditional social barriers impeded a normal country-wide expansion of the Ba'th organisation, which was still clearly manifest when the Ba'th Party had come into power in 1963.

Alongside ideological reasons, there were other factors that contributed to the high representation of officers of Arabic-speaking sectarian minorities in the Syrian army, as well as of people from the countryside in general. Many people from the poor rural areas (where most minoritarians live) saw a military career as a welcome opportunity to climb the social ladder and to lead a life that would be more comfortable than that within the agrarian sector. Under the French Mandate (1923–46) a kind of divide-and-rule policy was followed by favouring the military recruitment of special detachments among Alawis, Druzes, Kurds, Circassians and other minorities, who then formed part of the Troupes Spéciales du Levant, which were used to maintain order and suppress local rebellions. Discord between religious and ethnic communities was also provoked by the fact that the French played tribal leaders off against one another. Munir Mushabik Musa has noted that already in the 1930s the Troupes Spéciales du Levant provided their Alawi soldiers with power, changing their own positions from being 'persecuted' to 'persecuting', in particular Sunnis who had mistreated them.[16]

During the first half of the twentieth century, a 'closed community' system was still prevalent. Jacques Weulersse observed it in the 1940s and defined it as a *minority complex* which he described as

a collective and pathological susceptibility which makes each gesture by the neighbouring community appear as a menace or challenge to one's own [community], and which unifies each collectivity in its entirety at the least outrage committed against any one of its members.[17]

This phenomenon, described in the mid-1940s, would have been expected to be outdated some 70 years later, but during the war in Syria, which began in 2011, it started to come up again, albeit in a less absolute form than was described by Weulersse.

In the early 1950s, when the Ba'th Party started to rise, it was only natural that this phenomenon at least partially played a role in contact among Ba'thist officers and civilians, even though they would on ideological grounds have strongly rejected the existence of such a minority complex. Ba'thists vehemently disapproved of the phenomenon of sectarianism, but would nevertheless make use of traditional social channels within their own communities, on practical grounds. Thus, the party organisation spread through traditional social channels, alongside its attraction on ideological grounds.

As far as the secret organisation of the Ba'thist Military Committee was concerned, it was only natural that its members started to recruit members among their own communities, both regional, tribal and sectarian, on whom they expected to be able to sufficiently rely, even more than on members of other communities. This did not necessarily mean, however, that they were not serious about their ideological ideas. The fact that they recruited members in that period from their own communities should therefore not be considered as a kind of sectarianism; it simply worked better.

## SECTARIAN, REGIONAL, TRIBAL AND SOCIO-ECONOMIC OVERLAP

There is a strong overlap between sectarian, regional and tribal identities where the compact minorities are concerned, and these can have a mutually strengthening effect. Such an overlap can make it difficult to determine which categories play a role in a particular situation, and there is a risk therefore of interpreting tribal, or extended family loyalties as sectarian loyalties, for instance. Overlap may be due to the regional concentration of particular religious communities, tribes and extended families; to the fact that tribal and extended family groups as a whole usually belong to the same religious community; and to the fact that tribal, extended family and sectarian elements are sometimes inseparably linked to one another. In this respect, the compact religious communities, and the tribes and extended families belonging to these minorities, serve as clear examples. But it should be added that when it comes to loyalties or allegiances, quite different factors can play an equally or sometimes more important role, such as ideology, social class, inter-generational conflict, personal ambitions and opportunism. Alawi members of the Ba'th regime have often been suspected or accused of sectarianism, whereas their motives were quite different, such as favouritism towards relatives and acquaintances from their own region of origin. Here the intention may have been quite different from the way in which such favouritism was interpreted or perceived by opponents. But perception was not less important than intention, as it could create a sectarian dynamic that could not easily be undone.

The urban–rural dichotomy in Syria had a strong sectarian dimension, due to the fact that the compact religious minorities were mainly concentrated in the poverty-stricken countryside, whereas the richer and larger cities were predominantly Sunni. If these urban–rural contrasts are considered together with the minority complex mentioned earlier, it is easy to understand that the contrast between Sunnis in the larger cities and members of religious minorities in the rural areas must have been even greater than that between co-religionists in city and countryside. This changed gradually after 1963, when people from the countryside started to migrate in great numbers to the cities. The influx of rural people into the greater cities did not necessarily only mean that the new immigrant people were urbanised, but also that the cities, or certain quarters of it, were to a certain extent ruralised.[18]

## HAVE THE ALAWIS BEEN A PERSECUTED MINORITY WHO TOOK REFUGE IN THE MOUNTAINS?

From the Ba'thist point of view, religion as such did not play as important a role as sectarianism in the sense of social community loyalties.

Efforts of Sunni religious opponents to mobilise opposition against the Alawi-dominated Ba'th regime through religious channels and theological arguments stimulated Alawi communal solidarity much more than they caused purely religious debate and controversy. Nevertheless, they also caused Alawis to openly and officially defend their position from a theological point of view, albeit in a relatively late stage in the 1980s and 1990s. Over the centuries, Alawi religious leaders had traditionally preferred to keep silent about the details of their religion to outsiders, although *Taqiyah* (dissimulation) was, historically speaking, apparently never a factor in their interaction with the state or with members of other communities.[19] Under the newly created political circumstances, some of their leaders opened up, stressing, somewhat apologetically, that the Alawi (Ja'fari) religion was in fact similar to Twelver Shi'ism.[20] But not all Alawi leaders agreed to this.

In March 2016, for instance, several Syrian Alawi Shaykhs visited Europe on a secret mission in order to provide their views to European officials on the supposedly controversial Alawi religious identity, the position of the Alawi community within Syrian society and its relationship with the Alawi-dominated regime. The interpretation of the media at the time was that the Shaykhs had wanted to distance themselves from the al-Asad regime, but this turned out to be wishful thinking.[21] They mainly wanted to convey a message about their identity, both religious and social. They wanted an 'identity reform'. An important element in their message was that, in their words, the Alawis had always been given an identity defined by outsiders, rather than by themselves. This had to change. The Lebanese Shi'i Imam Musa al-Sadr, for instance, had officially declared in 1970 that the Alawis had a doctrinal unity with Twelver Shi'ism. Al-Sadr, as an outsider to the Alawi community, had thereby defined what the Alawis were, rather than the Alawis doing so themselves. The Alawi Shaykhs stressed that there were substantial differences between Shi'ism and Alawism, and that the Alawis were not a branch of Shi'ism. The fact that Alawism and Shi'ism shared some official religious sources did not make Alawism a branch of Shi'ism, according to them.

It was clear that there still are various opinions within the Alawi community about their religious identity. Stefan Winter has noted in this respect that 'there is little point in trying to determine, solely on the basis of religious texts, what constitutes "true" Alawism or which subcurrent of thought is closest to "original" Shi'ism'.[22]

The Alawi Shaykhs did not want the Alawis to be described as a 'minority' in Syria. They rejected as a myth the widespread narrative that, over the centuries, Alawis had solely been persecuted and discriminated against.[23]

The Alawi Shaykhs also stressed that secularism was the only political system that could guarantee equality between all communities, and were therefore against prescribing that the President of the Republic should be a Muslim.

The Shaykhs stressed that the Alawi community should not be identified with the regime, because they were not the same. Nevertheless, they did not distantiate themselves from the regime, as they needed its protection against anti-Alawi forces.

Stefan Winter has argued that Alawism

> was not an 'offshoot' of 'mainstream' Iraqi Twelver Shi'ism but rather constituted one of its central tendencies and was only retrospectively cast as a 'heterodox' variant or heresy with the institutionalisation of a literary Twelver Shi'ism in the eleventh century.

Alawism might also be seen historically as the local variant of the 'mainstream' Shi'ism rather than as a schismatic departure from it. Alawism spread out over Mesopotamia and into northern Syria, Aleppo, Hama, and finally the coastal highlands from Acre to Latakia (in that order). This was not the result of some imagined flight from oppression, but rather of a sustained missionary effort (*da'wah*). Its later concentration in the Syrian coastal mountains was above all the product of the Crusades, which spelled the effective end of the *da'wah* and increasingly forced the Alawis to organise themselves along tribal lines. The Alawis emerged from the twelfth century as something they had not been before, but which would define them for the rest of history: as a 'minority'. And whereas Alawism originally had been a religious ideal or calling, open to anyone, by the early thirteenth century it was becoming the 'outward secular identity of an increasingly circumscribed, self-conscious political community'.[24]

The idea of the 'mountain refuge', alleging that the inaccessible coastal highlands of Syria and Lebanon have, since the dawn of time, served as a haven for minority sects fleeing religious oppression in cities and plains from the interior, was first coined by the Flemish Jesuit priest Henri Lammens in his book *La Syrie: Précis Historique* (1921).[25] Lammens' ideas were adopted by many academics and others thereafter, if only because they seemed so logical and, therefore, convincing.[26] But they turned out to be a myth, which developed into a cliché. The Lebanese historian Kamal Salibi has demonstrated that the idea of the 'mountain refuge' is not borne out by any available evidence. The Alawi, Druze, Isma'ili, Shi'i or Christian populations did not come to these mountain regions in order to escape persecution elsewhere, nor were the central Sunni Islamic authorities really that unable to establish their dominance over the mountains.[27]

The Alawis of today, in the words of Patrick Seale, are like the Druzes and Isma'ilis, 'a remnant of the Shi'i upsurge, which had swept Islam a thousand years before: they were islands left by a tide that receded'.[28]

Other areas of Syria, where minorities are concentrated, like the Jabal al-Duruz and the Isma'ili centre of Salamiyah, are not located in inaccessible highlands (where they would have lived according to the theory of the 'mountain refuge'), but in relatively easily accessible lowlands.

# 1

# A SYNOPSIS OF BA'THIST HISTORY BEFORE THE SYRIAN REVOLUTION (2011)

## INTRODUCTION

This chapter is intended to help explain how it was possible for Syria to end up in the bloody sectarian-tinted Syrian War that started in 2011 after almost half a century of Ba'thist dictatorship. As will be seen, there are many similarities between the Syrian War that started in 2011, and earlier periods in which the Ba'th regime heavily repressed any opposition, particularly the Sunni Muslim opposition movements, such as the Syrian Muslim Brotherhood, and the Islamist *Mujahidin* that split off from the Muslim Brotherhood. The scale of violence before and after the Syrian Revolution was very different, however. Whereas before the Syrian Revolution opposition movements and insurgencies were bloodily suppressed locally in cities like Hama, Homs, Aleppo and Damascus, after the revolution a greater part of the country was involved in the confrontation with the regime. Moreover, different from the pre-revolution period, after March 2011 the opposition movements started to receive political, financial and military aid from abroad, from countries that started to interfere in Syria's internal affairs, giving the intra-Syrian war also the dimension of a violent war by proxy.

As far as the origins of the Syrian Revolution are concerned, much can be traced back to the power structure and composition of the regime, its dictatorship, its strong domination by people from the Alawi minority and their corruption, all combined with its incapability to introduce any substantial reforms. In order to better understand the Syrian Revolution, and the Syrian regime's reaction to it, it is important to be aware of the history and background of the Syrian Ba'thist regime since its takeover of power in 1963.

## THE BA'THIST REVOLUTION OF 8 MARCH 1963

On 8 March 1963, the Ba'thist military, under the leadership of the secret Military Committee, succeeded in taking over power by a military coup, along with the military of other groups, including Nasserists and Independent Unionists. Together they deposed the so-called 'separatist regime' that had ended the Syrian–Egyptian union on 28 September 1961, and had been dominated by a group of Sunni Damascene officers, who were now purged from the army.

It was an essential moment in Syrian Ba'thist history, decisive for the further power structure of the Ba'th regime for decades to come. After the coup, the number of minority officers greatly increased in strength at the expense of Sunnis.

A principal reason was that the Ba'thist military leaders involved in the coup had called up numerous officers and non-commissioned officers with whom they were related through family, tribal, extended family or regional ties, to swiftly consolidate their newly achieved power positions.[1]

Most of the military called up in this way had a minoritarian background, which is not surprising since most members of the secret Military Committee, who supervised the activities of the Ba'thist military organisation themselves, had a minority background, as has been noted above. This form of recruitment was later explained in a confidential internal document of the Ba'th Party's Syrian Regional Command as follows:

> The initial circumstances following the Revolution and its attendant difficulties urged the calling-up of a large number of reserve military (officers and non-commissioned officers), party members and supporters, to fill the gaps resulting from purges of the opponents and to consolidate and defend the Party's position. This urgency made it impossible at the time to apply objective standards in the calling-up operation. Rather, friendship, family relationship and sometimes mere personal acquaintance were the basis [of admission], which led to the infiltration of a certain number of elements who were alien to the Party's logic and points of departure. Once the difficult phase had been overcome, this issue was exploited as a weapon for slandering the intentions of some comrades and for casting doubts on them.[2]

The latter part of this quotation obviously referred to the accusations that some members of the Ba'thist Military Committee had, on sectarian grounds, packed the army with members of their own communities. According to the Syrian author Mahmud Sadiq (pseudonym) the representation of Alawis among the newly appointed officers was as high as 90 per cent. How extremely important the purges of 1963 turned out to be in the longer term can be concluded from the fact that the origins of a significant number of officers holding senior positions in the Syrian armed forces in the 1990s could still be traced to this batch.[3]

It is hardly surprising that Alawi officers played such an important role thereafter, because the highest positions in the Ba'thist Military Committee were occupied by Alawis, notably Muhammad 'Umran, Salah Jadid and Hafiz al-Asad. Salah Jadid first became head of personnel in the army. From this position, he could build up a network of loyalists within the army. Afterwards, he was chief-of-staff of the Syrian army between August 1963 and September 1965, also a central position in this respect. Hafiz al-Asad became commander of the Syrian airforce. Muhammad 'Umran, the eldest of the three, commanded the 70th Armoured Brigade, stationed south of Damascus, which was to be the backbone of the Ba'thist military organisation for some years to come.

The three Alawi leaders of the Military Committee played a paramount role in the Ba'thist transformation of the Syrian armed forces. They swiftly consolidated their newly achieved positions of power, thanks to their efficient organisation and planning and to all the military supporters who had been mobilised. Within a few months they succeeded in purging their most important Nasserist and Independent Unionist military opponents, who, once again, happened to be mainly Sunnis, whether coincidentally or not.

The climax of the Ba'thist power monopolisation came on 18 July 1963, when a group of predominantly Sunni Nasserist officers, led by Colonel Jasim 'Alwan, staged an abortive coup. Most of the officers who bloodily suppressed this coup were of minoritarian backgrounds, and among them Alawis played the most prominent role. This had nothing to do with sectarianism, but was later exploited as such by Sunni political opponents of the Ba'th regime, who resented that there were so many minority members among the new rulers and therefore tried to give the impression that the purges of Sunni officers were primarily based on sectarian motives. In this way, they also tried to discredit and undermine the position of the Ba'th regime in the eyes of the Sunni majority of the population.

This was a pattern that was to repeat itself every time Sunni or non-Alawi officers were deposed and purged from the army by Alawi officers. Time and again, non-Alawi officers resented the prominent position of Alawi officers in the Syrian armed forces. They suspected and accused them of sectarianism, which it was not really at first, but was nevertheless perceived as such. The Ba'thist Alawi military leaders were fervent secularists, and therefore should not be expected to be sectarian motivated. But in order to achieve power, they had allowed many loyalists to enter the army 'who were alien to the Party's logic and points of departure'. These 'loyalist' people may, from their side, have been sectarian motivated, but to get rid of them was easier said than done, because the regime depended on them. Purges of Alawi officers came only later.

And, if the Ba'thist Alawi leaders might have been sectarian motivated, it was not in the sense of religion, but rather in the sense of 'belonging to the Alawi community'.

From the Nasserist coup in July 1963 onwards, anti-Ba'thist publications started to appear, stressing the so-called sectarian character of the regime. Muta' Safadi's book *Hizb al-Ba'th: Ma'sat al-Mawlid Ma'sat al-Nihayah* ('The Ba'th Party: The Tragedy of its Beginning and the Tragedy of its End'), published in 1965, was one of the first examples in this respect.[4] As it turned out, the title was premature, because more than half a century later, the Ba'th regime was still in power. Nevertheless, Safadi's book includes many interesting observations from the point of view of Sunnis who felt discriminated against by Alawis and other minority people, who apparently had brought the centuries-old dominance of Sunni Arabs to an end. Safadi saw this as a kind of 'plot and conspiracy'. In a polemic way Safadi argued that the Ba'th Party was actually a 'sectarian movement which had designs on supplanting the traditional order in which Sunnis were dominant'. About the religious minorities, with the Alawis placed first, followed by Druzes, Isma'ilis and Christians, Safadi wrote that they 'were most ambitious to overthrow the order of traditional society in which Sunni–urban Muslims dominated'.[5] This was indeed what later took shape. The Ba'th was not a sectarian movement, however, as alleged by Safadi (who had earlier also been a Ba'thist), but rather the opposite with its secular ideology; and the takeover of the Ba'th in 1963 was not a 'sectarian plot'. More important, however, is that some Sunni observers nevertheless perceived it as such, thereby making it an inseparable part of political dynamics, whether justified or not.

Safadi, who himself was imprisoned after the abortive Nasserist coup of July 1963, wrote about his experiences in the al-Mazzah prison in Damascus in a way that reminds us of the situation more than half a century later, as it exists today:

All those who have been interrogated and submitted to torture, will remember the names of their *Zabaniyah* ('angels who thrust the damned into hell'). They will also remember that the most violent torturers among them belonged to specific religious communities, and more than that: they carried out their torture and their shouting matches with sectarian methods. The hundreds of prisoners who were brought to the al-Mazzah prison after the 18th of July 1963, and I was one of them, are not able to forget the director of the prison; neither can they forget the tortures and interrogations to which they were subjected ... and the cursing against their [Sunni] articles of faith with the most degrading words.

The prisoners who were aware of it understood the complotting measures [of creating discord between Sunnis and members of minorities]. They tried to withhold themselves from hating *all* Alawis, just because the director of the prison, or the leader of the torture department, or all his assistants were Alawis, who showed their being Alawis by insulting the beliefs of the punished [Sunni] prisoners.

Likewise, the prisoners tried to prevent themselves from hating Christians, because the most ferocious 'executor of the law' who was known in the al-Mazzah prison belonged to the Christian community. Likewise, two or three supervisors who tortured day and night were from the Druze community.[6]

Safadi's description reflects a phenomenon that might be interpreted as a kind of revanchism of sectarian minorities against Sunnis, some of whom in the past had so often had a denigrating attitude towards those minorities. In the past, many minority members had often been in a subservient position vis-a-vis Sunnis who generally had had a superior position, although some individual people from minorities, like Christians, or people of Kurdish origin, had had a prominent political role in Syria as well; but before the Ba'th came to power they were not that many.

Although Safadi's description dates from more than half a century ago, it still appears to be very similar to that of Syria's prisons of today, albeit that the situation has drastically deteriorated during the period of the Syrian Revolution that started in 2011. The number of Alawi torturers must now be even higher, whereas the importance of other sectarian minorities has declined.

Leaving polemics aside, many of Safadi's observations have turned out to be correct.[7]

## MULUK AL-TAWA'IF ('PETTY KINGS')

After the Ba'thist military had purged the army of their most important non-Ba'thist rivals, they were left among one another and started an intra-Ba'thist struggle for power. Most of the leading Ba'thist rulers had formed their own groups of loyalist supporters, who to a great extent originated from their own sectarian communities and home regions. The army and intelligence (Mukhabarat) officers gradually started to form a new kind of class, enjoying all kinds of privileges, some even controlling parts of provinces or cities, or governmental institutions, in which nothing could be undertaken, except with their approval. In the words of Munif al-Razzaz, former Secretary General of the National Command of the Ba'th Party, it appeared as if the new regime adopted characteristics similar to those of the Andalusian 'petty kings' (*muluk al-tawa'if*), with each 'king possessing a piece of the state apparatus which he arbitrarily handled as he liked'.[8]

As the military Ba'thist organisation was still full of members who had been recruited on an opportunist basis, as described above, their military leaders were obliged to rely on these same people to a large extent, in order to maintain a strong position vis-a-vis Ba'thist rivals. It turned out that selective criteria had been used when dismissing a great number of Sunni officers after the coup of 1963, and that Sunnis were being discriminated against when applying for the Military Academy and other military training centres. Members of sectarian minorities were advantaged at various levels.

Some military units started to be composed of mainly one sectarian group, like the 70th Armoured Brigade, that almost exclusively consisted of Alawi military and was led by Alawi General Muhammad 'Umran.

This phenomenon exists until the present day, and has even become stronger than it was half a century ago, due to continuous practices of co-optation and favouritism, also in the military academies.

There were also Sunni commanders, but they could do very little independently when they had to rely on crews that were mainly Alawi. The authority of these Sunni commanders over their Alawi crews could easily be brought to naught if Alawi officers serving in other armed units instructed their co-religionists not to carry out the orders of their Sunni superiors. Some Alawi officers exercised active control in this way over a far larger part of the Syrian armed forces than they were formally entitled to under the official military command structure.

Already as early as 1955 the chief of Syria's Intelligence Bureau, Colonel 'Abd al-Hamid Sarraj, 'discovered to his surprise that no fewer than 55 per cent or so of the non-commissioned officers belonged to the "Alawi sect"'.[9]

## THE POWER STRUGGLE AMONG THE ORIGINAL MEMBERS OF THE MILITARY COMMITTEE

The leading officers of the Ba'thist Military Committee started a struggle for power in which one after the other was expelled or eliminated, until only one leader was left, notably Alawi General Hafiz al-Asad, who after his coup of 16 November 1970 was to become Syria's leader for the next 30 years.[10]

### The Purge of Sunni Officers

The first member of the Military Committee to be expelled in 1965–6 was Alawi General Muhammad 'Umran, who had been the eldest founding member. It had little to do with principles or ideology, but rather with power. 'Umran was accused by the other members of the Military Committee of spreading the phenomenon of sectarianism in the armed forces. Not only Sunni officers accused him of this, but also his Alawi colleagues, Salah Jadid and Hafiz al-Asad. They, just like 'Umran, depended largely on personal Alawi military supporters in order to be able to maintain their positions of power and they profited from sectarian, regional and tribal loyalties to strengthen their positions equally as well, but they were wise enough not to speak about this openly.

'Umran, however, had openly declared that 'the *Fatimiyah* should play their role' (*Inn al-Fatimiyah yajib an ta'kudh Dawraha*), meaning that the Alawis, Druzes and Isma'ilis (being the so-called Fatimiyah) should play a key role against his most prominent rival at that time, the Sunni president and commander-in-chief of the armed forces, General Amin al-Hafiz and his Sunni supporters. 'Umran's open use of sectarianism as a weapon was to utterly fail, however, as a tactic.

Most Ba'thist officers did not want to tolerate the use of such overt sectarian-tinged declarations since, according to the secular Arab nationalist Ba'th ideology, Ba'thists should strive to banish sectarian, regional and tribal group feelings. In later periods of the power struggle among Ba'thist officers it was repeatedly proven that, in the final analysis, those who spoke openly in favour of strengthening the position of officers from their own religious community, as a result weakened their own positions rather than those of their opponents, who also reinforced their positions on a sectarian basis but did not openly speak about it. It was a clear case of 'the pot calling the kettle black'.

It was taboo to speak about sectarianism, even though the Ba'thist military were fully aware that it was extensively exploited for practical reasons. Strong fiction was upheld side by side with a reality that was completely different, and officially denied.

Personal ambitions were among the most important reasons for the power struggle between 'Umran and the other members of the Military Committee, headed now by Sunni President Amin al-Hafiz. 'Umran's overt exploitation of sectarian ties was not the main cause for his banishment by the other members, but was gratefully seized upon as an argument that could be used against him.

Munif al-Razzaz noted in this respect:

> Having consolidated his bases within the army, [Alawi] Major-General Salah [Jadid] was wise enough not to bring up the weapon of sectarianism. He preferred to profit when his [Sunni] opponents brought it up, thus proving that from the point of view of the Party and of the nationalists, he was more sincere than those who raised the sectarian banner. Notwithstanding all this, I do not know which of the two is the more serious crime: causing sectarianism or exposing it.[11]

At the same time, a power struggle was going on between Salah Jadid and President Amin al-Hafiz. During this struggle the manipulations with sectarian, regional and tribal loyalties caused the tension in the Syrian armed forces to increase to such an extent that a far-reaching polarisation between Sunnis and members of religious minorities was the result. Sectarian contradistinctions among the military consequently began to overshadow almost all other differences. This sectarian polarisation was based not so much on sectarian unanimity among military men from the same religious community, as on a common opposition and sectarian distrust.

At this stage, there was still such a delicate balance of power between the various army factions that the transfer of one single

Alawi tank battalion commander in the 70th Armoured Brigade could have caused the balance of power to shift in favour of Sunni President Amin al-Hafiz. But al-Hafiz refused the transfer of this Alawi officer ('Ali Mustafa), even though this would have been in his favour, because he had developed an anti-Alawi complex and had started to consider virtually all Alawis as personal enemies.

As a result, President Amin al-Hafiz, together with General 'Umran and many others, could be deposed by a military coup on 23 February 1966, later called Harakat 23 Shubat ('The 23 February Movement'). This coup led to the purge of some of the most prominent Sunni officers' factions, which, in turn, once again, resulted in an increase in the representation in the armed forces of members of religious minorities, especially the heterodox Islamic, to the disadvantage of Sunnis. This was a trend that was to continue for several years.

The armed units stationed around Damascus, which were mostly dominated by Alawi and Druze officers in this period, had immediately rallied behind the coup. This was a result of the strategy of minoritarian members of the Syrian military command: officers who were 'trusted' on sectarian grounds, because they came from the same religious minority communities or were from the same region or extended families or tribes, were placed close to Damascus, whereas those who, for similar reasons, were 'not trusted' – because they were mainly Sunnis – were stationed near the Israeli front, or far away from the Syrian capital more to the north of the country. This was a pattern that was to repeat itself for the next half a century: Alawi-dominated elite military units were stationed close to Damascus to help protect the regime, whereas other units were stationed further away, to help protect the country.

Such a delicate equilibrium as existed just before the coup of 23 February 1966 did not occur again. The subsequent regimes had learned how to better defend their positions from opponents.

## The Purge of Druze Officers

Shortly after the 23 February 1966 coup, the new Syrian rulers held an Extraordinary Congress of the Ba'th Party in Damascus to discuss the reasons that had led to the coup. It was decided that all those who had taken standpoints based on sectarian, regional or tribal loyalties should be severely punished, particularly if they were party members. This resolution did not have any implications for the leaders of the military coup, however, even though most of them had been guilty of such practices to some extent.

This became a phenomenon of Ba'th Party congresses: to adopt resolutions that were fully justified, but subsequently not implemented, because implementation could hurt the positions of those who had adopted them.

After the 23 February coup, the seats of government and power were redistributed, with General Hafiz al-Asad being appointed as Minister of Defence, even before the new cabinet was announced. The main Druze Ba'thist officers were disappointed that they were not rewarded with the positions they had hoped to obtain, because they had played such an important role during the coup. Moreover, they were not re-elected in their positions in the Ba'th Party leadership. As a result, Salim Hatum and Hamad 'Ubayd, the two Druze members of the original Military Committee, started to plot against the new regime. 'Ubayd had wanted to become Minister of Defence, but lacked the necessary qualifications, whereas Hatum – who had taken the lion's share during the coup – wanted the command of an armoured brigade, combined with responsibility for the army's security affairs.

All this was refused; in the case of Hatum because he was not trusted.

Together with the deposed civilian party leadership, Hatum and other Druze officers secretly started to make plans to depose the new regime. For security reasons, Hatum refused to take in any Alawi officers into his secret military organisation for fear of prematurely being discovered. When part of the plot was nevertheless discovered by accident in August 1966, various Druze officers were arrested. Salim Hatum, whose involvement had not yet been discovered, subsequently started to create the impression that all this had caused an Alawi-Druze sectarian polarisation within the army, of which the Druzes became the victims. These allegations subsequently became a self-fulfilling prophecy, and led to a situation of alarm among the Druze military and the party organisation in the Jabal al-Duruz.

In order to help solve the situation among the involved Druzes, a high-level party delegation, including President Nur al-Din al-Atasi, Salah Jadid and Jamil Shayya (the only Druze member of the Ba'th Party Regional Command), was sent to the Jabal al-Duruz. By way of a trap, Hatum had invited them to a banquet (*walimah*), but instead of giving them hospitality he arrested them with the aim of putting the regime under pressure to such an extent that his demands would yet be met.

Those arrested could have known better, because Hatum already twice earlier had made a similar attempt, but had failed.[12] The party leaders who had stayed behind in Damascus refused to negotiate, however, and Hafiz al-Asad, Minister of Defence and Air Force commander threatened to bomb Hatum's units in the Jabal al-Duruz. As a result of such heavy countermeasures, Salim Hatum's coup failed and he fled with his men to Jordan, where he received political asylum.

During a press conference Hatum later declared that 'the situation in Syria was being threatened by a civil war as a result of the growth of the sectarian and tribal spirit, on the basis of which Salah Jadid and Hafiz al-Asad, as well as the groups surrounding them, ruled'. Hatum added that the filling of

> powerful places in the state and its institutions is limited to a specific class of the Syrian people [i.e. the Alawis]. Thus, the Alawis in the army have attained a ratio of five to one of all other religious communities.[13]

Hatum reproached the regime for having only non-Alawi officers arrested, but this was also as a result of the fact that he himself had specifically excluded Alawi officers from his secret organisation on grounds of security. Hatum continued his accusations against the regime by declaring, for instance, that

> whenever a Syrian military man is questioned about his free officers, his answer will be that they have been dismissed and driven away, and that only Alawi officers have remained. The Alawi officers adhere to their tribe and not to their militarism. Their concern is the protection of Salah Jadid and Hafiz al-Asad.[14]

Hatum continued for some time with what could clearly be labelled as anti-Alawi propaganda. It would not be easy for the regime in Damascus to pacify the Druze community, after its trust in the central authorities had been severely shaken.

During the Syrian Revolution that started in 2011, the Druze community in general preferred to take a relatively neutral position, as it feared that its position could be threatened if the regime were to be overthrown by radical Islamist forces that generally hold heterodox Islamic communities, like the Druzes, in very low esteem or consider them as heretics.

After the start of the June 1967 War, Hatum returned to Damascus with the alleged intention of helping the regime, but he was accused of another plot to overthrow the regime, and executed.

By plotting against the Alawi-dominated Ba'th regime with his predominantly Druze supporters, Hatum in fact had indirectly contributed to a further strengthening of the position of Alawi officers. These, for various historical reasons, had already been the biggest officer group and their numerical presence was now even stronger.

Hatum's statement that the situation in Syria 'was being threatened by a civil war as a result of the growth of the sectarian and tribal spirit' appeared to be an exaggeration, because the power struggle that took place was to a great extent confined to the Ba'th Party military organisation and parts of the civilian party apparatus. It did not include larger parts of the Syrian population and society, as happened after the Syrian Revolution in 2011, when the whole country became involved in a civil war, that later escalated into a full-scale war involving other countries as well.

### The Purge of Officers from Hawran

It was not only Druze officers who had been purged following Hatum's abortive coup, but also some Ba'thist officers and civilians from Hawran, the neighbouring province of the Jabal al-Duruz. They also had openly expressed their concern about the Alawi predominance in the army and party, and early in 1967 some leaders of party branches in Hawran refused to join further party meetings in expression of their concern about the inter-communal sectarian and regional tensions in the party apparatus and armed forces, and also to demonstrate their concern about the predominance of 'specific' (obviously meaning Alawi) sectarian, regional or tribal factions.[15]

Externally, these tensions could be noticed when all three ministers from the Hawran region threatened to resign. Shortly after the Arab–Israeli June 1967 War, some of the most prominent civilian Ba'thists from Hawran lost their positions in the party commands and the government. On 15 February 1968, the Hawrani chief-of-staff of the Syrian army, General Ahmad Suwaydani, who once had been a prominent supporter of Salah Jadid, was relieved of his army functions.

Musa al-Zu'bi and Mustafa al-Hajj 'Ali, the two remaining Sunni Hawrani members of the original Ba'thist Military Committee, were dismissed from the army in 1967 and 1968 respectively. This implied that the most prominent civilian and military Ba'thists from Hawran had been neutralised or eliminated from the party apparatus and the army as separate power blocs.

It turned out to be, time and again, that those who openly criticised the powerful positions of the Alawi officers, already the biggest group in any case, in the end duped themselves, and indirectly contributed to making the Alawi share of the officers even bigger.

Of the 15 members of the original Military Committee, only seven members remained, of whom six were from minorities: four Alawis, two Isma'ilis and one Sunni from the (mainly Alawi) Latakia region. Of the seven Sunnis all but one had been expelled, and both Druze members had been removed as well.

This was not the end of the power struggle, however, because there still was more than one 'petty king'.

### The Struggle Within the Alawi Community and the Supremacy of Hafiz al-Asad

The two main remaining rivals who competed for power were Salah Jadid and Hafiz al-Asad. Whereas al-Asad had maintained all his military functions and extended his powers, Jadid in August 1965 had – it can be concluded with some hindsight – made the fatal mistake of giving up his military function as chief-of-staff of the army, in exchange for the key civilian position of Assistant Secretary General of the Syrian Regional Command of the Ba'th Party. For some time, he still managed to keep his grip on the military party organisation, but gradually lost control, whereas al-Asad in turn could extend his control over it.

Jadid and al-Asad had serious differences of opinion concerning the military, foreign and socio-economic policies that were to be pursued. As the main contestors for power were now only Alawis, there was also more room for expressing ideological differences. Jadid was a fervent socialist who had the strong support of the civilian party apparatus. It was a heyday for Marxists and socialists, not only in Syria, but in Europe and elsewhere in the world as well. Jadid wanted to give priority to the 'socialist transformation' (*tahwil ishtiraki*) of Syrian society. His group rejected any cooperation with 'reactionary, rightist or pro-Western' regimes, such as Jordan, Iraq and Saudi Arabia, even if this would be at the expense of 'the struggle against Israel'. They favoured cooperation with the Soviet Union and other communist countries.

Al-Asad, on the other hand, gave priority to what he saw as Arab national interests, and demanded top priority for 'the armed struggle against Israel', even if this would have a negative effect on Syria's 'socialist transformation'.

During a Ba'th Party conference in Damascus in 1968, these differences of opinion led to a confrontation. As Jadid had a great majority of supporters in the congress, his ideas were fully accepted. Al-Asad, however, rejected the results and refused to further attend the Regional Command's meetings. On paper, Jadid's faction was fully in power and issued various orders so as to bring the military organisation further under its control, but in practice al-Asad kept the upper hand, by simply ignoring the instructions of the civilian party leadership and strengthening his grip over the military. He forbade any contact between the military and civilian organisations that was not explicitly approved by him. There was a situation of 'duality of power' (*izdiwajiyat al-sultah*), with al-Asad having the de facto supremacy. Supporters of Jadid who, for instance in the Latakia Branch, wanted to purge al-Asad's followers, were simply imprisoned or transferred and replaced by sympathisers of al-Asad. The Secretary General of the Latakia Branch, 'Adil Na'isah (Alawi and supporter of Jadid), was imprisoned and only released 22 years later. This was a foreshadowing of things to come for al-Asad's party opponents, but these kept thinking along the lines of the official party rules and regulations, which had little value when they were not backed up with military power.

Al-Asad kept on purging Jadid supporters from the army. Colonel 'Abd al-Karim al-Jundi, head of National Security, committed suicide in March 1969, after his closest supportive security staff had been arrested by al-Asad's forces. Al-Jundi's arrest would have been next, and he probably feared that he would face the same fate as many of those who had been tortured or killed because of him.[16]

In 1967, Ahmad al-Mir was relieved of his military functions shortly after the June 1967 War, in which he – as a commander at the Israeli–Syrian Golan front – had played a dishonourable role, reportedly by fleeing the front by donkey.[17]

Herewith the two remaining Isma'ili officers (and original members of the Ba'thist Military Committee) were removed, making Hafiz al-Asad the only remaining military 'king' of the original 'petty kings' (*muluk al-tawa'if*), with the difference that he was now all-powerful, and the opposite of 'petty'.

The fate of Salah Jadid and his civilian supporters was sealed when they, during the Tenth Extraordinary National Congress of the Ba'th Party in November 1970, decided to pass an unrealistic resolution demanding that Minister of Defence Hafiz al-Asad and army chief-of-staff General Mustafa Talas were to be relieved of their military functions. The two were able to take countermeasures easily and swiftly. The most important opponents of al-Asad, including Salah Jadid and President Nur al-Din al-Atasi, were arrested and imprisoned for the rest of their lives. Jadid died 23 years later in prison, and al-Atasi died 22 years later, shortly after being released. Other Jadid supporters also served very long prison sentences.

Exiled opponents of the regime were hunted down and ruthlessly assassinated, like General Muhammad 'Umran, who lived in Tripoli, Lebanon, from where he maintained contact with his followers in Syria. He was shot dead in his home in Tripoli in March 1972.

Salah al-Din al-Bitar, one of the founding members of the Ba'th Party and former Prime Minister of Syria, living in exile in Paris, where he had started an opposition journal called *al-Ihya' al-'Arabi* ('the Arab Revival'), the original name of the Ba'th Party before it was officially founded in 1947, was assassinated on 21 July 1980. In his last editorial, al-Bitar accused the regime of terrorism against the Syrian people, of the ugliest crimes of suppression with a sectarian spirit, of sectarian persecution against the Muslim Brotherhood, and of massacres (including of more than 600 prisoners in Palmyra prison 'who [according to al-Bitar] had been arrested without any reason and had not had any legal proceedings and consisted of the elite of the educated youth'). He noted that the prisoners in Palmyra had been told that they were going to be released, but when they were supposedly on their way out to the exit gate, they were gunned down from above by helicopters of the regime. The situation he described was very similar to the situation that arose after the start of the Syrian Revolution more than 30 years later. In the analysis of al-Bitar, the regime had wanted to sow the seeds of sectarian fear, so as to force the Alawi community into loyalty towards it, although the majority of it did not really support the regime.[18] Al-Bitar had tried to convince President Hafiz al-Asad, in a personal conversation in Damascus in May 1978, that Syria found itself in a deep internal crisis (Syria was, in al-Bitar's words, 'very very ill'). Al-Bitar told al-Asad that the only way to help solve the crisis was to achieve Syrian national unity by opening up the one-party dictatorial system and to allow for diversity of opinion, independent political organisations and a free press. But President al-Asad could not be convinced at all, and replied that 'national unity had already been achieved', and that 'there was a democracy in Syria with the Ba'th Party having 550,000 members'.[19] More than three decades later, after the start of the Syrian Revolution in 2011, President Bashar al-Asad could not be convinced of the necessity of similar reforms either, with the well-known disastrous consequences.

Other former Syrian Ba'thists were kidnapped, and never heard of again, like Shibli al-'Aysami, one of the founding members of the Ba'th Party and former vice-president of Syria, who had retired from political life in 1992, and was kidnapped in Lebanon in 2011.

Yet there were occasions when others, who were still part of the regime, but whose loyalty was doubted, were also assassinated, more often than not under dubious circumstances.

In general, the regime of Hafiz al-Asad, and later of Bashar al-Asad, did not tolerate any opposition that could be considered a threat to their position. Opposition was dealt with ruthlessly and possibilities for sharing real power between the regime and others appeared to be nil.

From November 1970 onwards, political power was completely monopolised by Hafiz al-Asad and his officers' faction. The era of competing 'power centres' (*marakiz qiwa*) was over. The civilian section of the Ba'th Party never again regained the powerful position it had had for some time in the preceding period, particularly under Salah Jadid. The Ba'th as a party also declined in importance. Its numbers increased enormously, but its political significance declined, as it was Hafiz al-Asad who was to decide on all essential issues.[20]

On 22 February 1971, Hafiz al-Asad became Syria's first Alawi president. This ended Syria's tradition of having Sunni Muslims as president. It also symbolically represented the political evolution of the Alawis from being a discriminated against, socially and economically backward religious community to a nationally emancipated group in a position of dominance. The Sunni population generally rejected the idea that they should be ruled by an Alawi president, particularly because many of them considered Alawis to be heretics and non-Muslims.

When, in 1973, a new constitution was drafted, it did not yet contain a paragraph on the religion of the president, and neither was Islam given a special place in it. After violent riots in predominantly Sunni cities like Hama and Homs, demanding a more prominent place to be given to Islamic law, the draft constitution was adapted, and finally stipulated that the religion of the President of the Republic had to be Islam, and that Islamic jurisprudence was to be a main source of legislation. This, to a certain extent, accommodated the wishes of the Sunni Muslims – albeit not fully, because they wanted a Sunni Muslim as president, not a president who called himself Muslim – but was not acknowledged as such by part of the Sunni population.

Since challenges to al-Asad's regime came mainly from within the Alawi community itself, it was not surprising that he placed increasing reliance on persons with whom he had a close relationship, such as members of his own extended family, or village (al-Qardahah) and its surroundings, in order to secure his position even against people from his own religious community. His five brothers were all active party members and occupied prominent positions in the army, the party organisations or government institutions. Rif'at was foremost.

After the November 1970 coup, Rif'at was in command of the Defence Companies (Saraya al-Difa'), elite army units of political and strategic importance, which were stationed around Damascus and with which he was able to protect his brother's regime.

Corruption had for a long time been an issue that undermined the regime. Al-Asad, therefore, announced the formation of a Committee for the Investigation of Illegal Profits in 1977, 'to investigate crimes of bribery, imposition of influence, embezzlement, exploitation of office and illegal profits'. The campaign was apparently intended to dispel popular discontent with the government's handling of these issues, but was doomed to failure, since high-placed military officers in the direct entourage of President Hafiz al-Asad, who constituted an indispensable part of the hard core of his (Alawi-dominated) regime, could also have been found guilty of involvement in corrupt practices. To purge such officers from the army, or to take severe disciplinary action against them, could have directly undermined the power position of al-Asad, and consequently of the whole regime, as a result of which nothing was seriously undertaken against them.

The failure of the anti-corruption campaign was yet another example of the paradigmatic situation in which the Syrian Ba'th regime had repeatedly found itself since its seizure of power in 1963. This was due to the composition of the hard core of the political power elite. It was a political party, or a faction of that party, which, although pursuing an ideology that wanted to do away with sectarian, regional and tribal loyalties, found itself more or less forced to revert to those same traditional loyalties when it took over power in order not to lose the strength that was needed to realise that ideology.

This problem became a vicious circle: maintenance of that power entailed entire dependence on those loyalties, thus hindering their suppression.

## The Syrian Ba'th Regime as Antithesis of Its Own Ideals

In practice the Syrian Ba'th regime became the antithesis of its own ideals. The Ba'thists wanted to do away with primordial loyalties like sectarianism, regionalism and tribalism, which were considered to be despicable residues or illnesses of traditional society (*rawasib/amrad taqlidiyah*). But in fact, they achieved the opposite, because their behaviour strengthened in particular the factors that they claimed to abhor.

Their ideals in the sphere of socialism and social equality could not be fulfilled either, because of the fact that their regime was infested with corruption, clientelism and favouritism.

The fact that their ideals of Arab unity could not be fulfilled could not be blamed on them alone, because inter-Arab cooperation was impeded by the fact that there was not one Arab leader who would accept the relinquishing of his power, or sharing it with others.

During the last half a century, the Syrian regime has never been able to escape this vicious circle for fear of undermining its own position. Corruption even increased, and under President Bashar al-Asad the circle of those who profited from it became smaller, as a result of which his power base was also concentrated in the hands of a smaller number of people.

### SUNNI GRUDGES AGAINST THE ALAWI-DOMINATED REGIME

There must have been strong feelings of hate among Sunni Arab Muslims against the Alawi-dominated Ba'th regime. In the first place, this was caused by the dictatorial system itself, which applied to all population groups and regions of Syria. But dictatorship in itself had not been anything new; it had always been present in Syria, with the exception of a few years in the 1950s. What was new, however, was that the dictators who ruled after

March 1963 happened to be mainly Alawis and people from religious minorities. They packed the army and security services, and government institutions with their people. Therefore, the Ba'thist dictatorship was perceived by religious conservative Sunni Muslims as a – mainly Alawi – sectarian dictatorship, or a dictatorship dominated by 'heretics' or 'infidels'. Ba'thist secularism, intended as a neutral form of rule in which all people, irrespective of their religious backgrounds, were supposed to be equal, was seen by religious conservative Sunnis as a cover-up for Alawi anti-Sunni sectarian suppression, or as a system that was 'anti-Islamic' and 'infidel' Alawi. Secularism is not always seen as something neutral, and for many people in different population groups or countries, can have different connotations.

Various violent demonstrations and uprisings had taken place in 1964 and 1965 against the regime in mainly Sunni cities, like Homs and Hama, and they were all suppressed with military force.

In 1967, demonstrations took place because a Ba'thist officer, Ibrahim Khalas, had published an article in the army magazine *Jaysh al-Sha'b* ('The People's Army'), saying that religion was something of the past and was nothing more than 'a mummified statue [that belonged] in the museum of history'.[21]

Secular Ba'thist rule was experienced by parts of the Sunni population as something provocative. Within the Muslim Brotherhood this led to extremism among some of its members. These formed a separate group, calling themselves the Mujahidin ('Strugglers') and later al-Tala'i' al-Muqatilah ('The Fighting Vanguards'). In February 1976, they started to carry out assassinations against Alawis, not necessarily Ba'thists, with the aim of provoking a sectarian polarisation that would destabilise the Alawi-dominated Ba'th regime. They spoke of the 'infidel Nusayris who were their enemies and were outside Islam'.[22] In their newsletter, *al-Nadhir*, they explained their motives:

Three years ago, to be exact on 8 February 1976, the first
bullet was fired for the sake of Allah, thereby opening the
gate for the organised *Jihad* [Holy War], which has now
started to produce positive results. This first bullet, however, was the result of long and persistent suffering from
oppression and terror. The prisons of Syria were packed
with [Sunni] Muslims ... The *Zabaniyah* ['angels who
thrust the damned into hell'] of suppression and tyranny
attacked and wandered in people's quarters, schools
and universities; general liberties and civil rights were
trampled underfoot ...

The ordeal reached its climax, however, when oppression became concentrated against [Sunni] Muslims and
against the religion of Islam in particular: mosques were
destroyed; religious scholars were arrested; educational
programmes were banned; Islamic law schools were closed; atheist and disintegrative information and instruc-
tion were published; sectarian party domination increased steadily; the psychological and military destruction
of the armed forces were planned; ... [Alawi] sectarian
party militia were allowed to take the place of the regular
armed forces; the riches of the nation were plundered by
way of corruption, embezzlement, illegal trade, doubtful
transactions, and the unlawful enrichment of a handful of
people at the cost of the overwhelming majority.[23]

In the words of a member of the Fighting Vanguards,
who was brought before trial in Damascus in September 1979:
'Assassination is the only language with which it is possible to
communicate with the state.'[24]

From assassinating Alawi personalites, the 'Fighting Vanguards' transformed into an overtly sectarian terrorist organisation willing to go as far as resorting to indiscriminate mass

killings.[25] One of their most extreme acts occurred on 16 June 1979 at the Aleppo Artillery Academy in al-Ramusah. A Sunni officer called Captain Ibrahim al-Yusuf, who was affiliated with the 'Fighting Vanguards', had called the cadets of the Academy to attend a so-called urgent meeting in the mess hall. There he, together with his accomplices, separated the Sunni cadets from the others – who were mainly Alawi – and killed 35 of the latter with automatic weapons, hand grenades and his own pistol.[26] He had prepared a list beforehand, which he read out to the victims before they were killed.[27]

The anti-Alawi Aleppo Artillery Academy massacre can be seen as an important landmark in Syrian history, as far as the issue of sectarianism is concerned.[28] Together with the earlier assassinations of Alawis, it left an ineffaceable mark on the relations between Alawis and Islamist Sunnis, the influence of which was still clearly present more than three decades later during the Syrian Revolution and civil war.

Immediately after the Aleppo Artillery Academy massacre of 1979, a country-wide campaign was started to uproot the Muslim Brotherhood organisation.

The regime's subsequent propaganda and its campaign to root out the Muslim Brotherhood was seen as so crude and strident that it antagonised rather than won over a larger part of the devout Muslim population.

Notwithstanding the dangerous and bloody prospects, the Sunni Muslim extremists seemed ready to lead the country into a Lebanese-style civil war if this was the only way to bring down the al-Asad regime.[29]

Following the Aleppo Artillery Academy massacre, state repression had become such that the Muslim Brotherhood leadership decided that it was time to respond to what they saw as Ba'thist provocations, by raising the banner of Jihad themselves. The subsequent alliance, which the Muslim Brotherhood made with the Jihadist forces of the Fighting Vanguards in late 1980, provided the regime with an additional argument to brutally crush the Islamic movement.[30]

From the sidelines, Egypt's President Anwar al-Sadat, who had been criticised by the Syrian regime for his peace initiatives with Israel, fuelled the conflict by referring to the regime as the 'Alawi Ba'th' and the 'dirty Alawis'.

In 1980 there were again violent and bloody country-wide civil disturbances, mostly triggered by economic difficulties, repressive methods of the regime, and anti-Alawi feelings.

Regime military elite units, some of them led by President al-Asad's brother Rif'at, on various occasions undertook revanchist actions against the inhabitants of Hama and Aleppo. Many were killed and wounded during these operations.

When, on 26 June 1980, President Hafiz al-Asad narrowly escaped an assassination attempt in Damascus, a wave of rage swept through the Alawi community, and al-Asad's brother Rif'at took 'revenge' by killing all Muslim Brotherhood members and others in Palmyra's infamous prison. However, according to then Minister of State for Foreign Affairs Faruq al-Shar', who was a personal witness to the attempt, it was not clear who had carried it out. It appeared to have been rather amateurish, and the offenders were not caught.[31]

The repressive measures of the Syrian regime did not prevent the Muslim Brotherhood Mujahidin from continuing their opposition. On the contrary, by the end of 1980 various Sunni religious opposition groups formed an alliance under the name of 'The Islamic Front in Syria'.

The climax came in February 1982 in Hama with the bloodiest showdown in twentieth-century modern Syrian history (to be surpassed during the Syrian War after 2011).

Earlier, the regime had already combed out cities like Aleppo, Homs and Hama, cordoning off whole areas, carrying out mass arrests and allegedly killing numerous people in the process. Hafiz al-Asad's military right hand at the time, Alawi General Shafiq Fayyad, supervised such an extremely repressive operation in Aleppo, and is reported to have said to the local people: 'If a thousand of you will be killed every day, I shall not care.'[32] According to Muslim Brotherhood sources several bloody confrontations with the regime already took place prior to the battle for Hama in February 1982, including what they described as 'the massacre of Jisr al-Shughur' (10 March 1980), 'the first massacre of Hama' (5–12 April 1980), and 'the second massacre of Hama' (21 May 1980).[33]

The battles in Hama raged for almost a whole month (2–28 February 1982). Estimates of the number of killed vary between 5,000 and 25,000, mainly victims from the population of Hama itself. The battle began when, on 2 February, a group of Muslim Brotherhood Mujahidin was completely surrounded by the regime's Alawi-dominated elite forces, during their combing-out operations in the city, and decided to launch a full-scale counter-attack.

While the Muslim Brothers thereafter claimed that they had been provoked into the large-scale confrontation, and that they finally came out in self-defence, they had earlier announced that they would continue their armed struggle until the regime was deposed.

When starting their counter-offensive, the Muslim Brotherhood Mujahidin proclaimed a wide-scale Islamic revolt against the Ba'th regime, calling through loudspeakers of the mosques of Hama for a Jihad. They stormed into homes, killing some 70 officials and party leaders, they overran police posts and ransacked armouries in a bid to seize power in the city, which the next day they declared 'liberated'. Although the Ba'th regime had been confronted with previous revolts in Damascus, Aleppo, Homs and Hama itself, a full-scale urban insurrection of such dimensions had never been witnessed before.

As on earlier occasions, the Muslim Brotherhood Mujahidin had tried to provoke a sectarian polarisation between Alawis and Sunnis in the armed forces, hoping to win to their side the Sunnis who constituted a majority in the regular (conscript) army. The regime's elite troops involved in the confrontation were, however, essentially Alawi in composition, and with some exceptions they held firm, and were generally able to maintain control and discipline in the regular armed forces. According to the Muslim Brotherhood, all military men originating from Hama were expelled from key units, however, just prior to the regime's assault on the city.

The regime's forces committed wide-scale atrocities during their recapture of the city, in which tanks, heavy artillery, rocket launchers and helicopters were used. And on various occasions soldiers refused to carry out orders.

After the eradication of the Muslim Brotherhood it never truly got back on its feet inside Syria in the period before 2011. Their weakening did not mean, however, that inter-communal relations in Syria had now become peaceful. Whereas the Islamic fundamentalist opposition had been severely hit, Alawi–Sunni sectarian tensions were as severe as ever, if not stronger. The massive repression in Hama and elsewhere had sown the seeds of future strife and revenge, and it took almost 30 years for this conflict to fully come out in the open again with the start of the Syrian Revolution in 2011.

Thomas Friedman argued in 1989 that

if someone had been able to take an objective poll in Syria after the Hama massacre, Assad's treatment of the rebellion probably would have won substantial approval, even among many Sunni Muslims. They might have said, 'Better one month of Hama than fourteen years of civil war like Lebanon'.[34]

Decades later, during the Syrian War that started in 2011, Friedman's statement would have been strongly criticised, although there were probably many Syrians who thought that they would not have supported the insurrection against the regime, had they been aware in advance that the war would cost hundreds of thousands of lives, millions of refugees and immense destruction. The Syrian War that started in 2011 became much more bloody than the Hama massacre of 1982, and its number of deadly victims became multiple.

It might be asked whether it would have been possible to foresee in 2011 that the regime was going to act in the way it did. If the Hama massacre of 1982 can be used as a point of reference, it could have been expected. Nevertheless, for many observers what was going to happen went far beyond their imagination.

## THE POWER ELITE UNDER HAFIZ AL-ASAD

During the three decades that Hafiz al-Asad had the monopoly of power in Syria (1970–2000), very little changed in the power structure of the Syrian regime. Most of the prominent Alawi officers who commanded key positions in the armed forces and security and intelligence services in the early and mid-1970s were after 25 years still in the same, or similar, positions. This meant that they remained loyal, and that the regime during this period could be characterised by a great degree of continuity. Al-Asad's reported obsession with loyalty paid off in both the short and long term, as, apparently, no substantial purges were considered to be necessary, the only exception being the purge of his younger brother Rif'at.

In November 1983 President Hafiz al-Asad fell seriously ill, as a result of which the succession question became acute. The power structure which President al-Asad had built wholly depended on himself and now appeared to break down without him. From his sickbed al-Asad appointed a six-man committee to which he entrusted the day-to-day running of affairs. His brother Rif'at was not among them, however, even though he had a formidable base in the armed forces with his 55,000-strong heavily armed Defence Companies (Saraya al-Difa'). In theory, these were subservient to the army chief-of-staff and the Minister of Defence, but in practice they were not and they behaved as independent formations. Hafiz al-Asad apparently did not trust his younger brother, and did not want Rif'at to succeed him, also because of his sometimes reckless, less sophisticated and notorious corrupt behaviour.

Rif'at seized the opportunity to try to take over power from his elder brother. At the end of February 1984, his heavily armed units made an effort to enter Damascus, but it came to a stand-off with loyalist military supporters of the president, and Damascus was on the verge of a bloodbath.

Rif'at al-Asad's Defence Companies depended to such an extent on members of the Alawi sect of the Murshidiyin that they could be considered the military backbone of his power. The Murshidiyin were a sect separate from the Alawis in general. They had been discriminated against since the hanging of their leader Salman al-Murshid in 1946, in the era of President Shukri al-Quwwatli. Under the Ba'th regime, measures against the Murshidiyin were lifted. After the 8 March 1963 Revolution, various Ba'th leaders had asked the leader of the Murshidiyin, Saji al-Murshid (the elder son of Salman al-Murshid), to request his followers to join the Ba'th Party. Saji al-Murshid had answered that it was up to the Ba'th Party itself to recruit new members among the Murshidiyin. After all, if they would be instructed by the Murshidiyin leadership to join the party, their membership would not be based on conviction. Their leader Saji al-Murshid had added at the time: 'If you believe that the Murshidiyin will join the Ba'th Party on my orders, don't you believe that I can also order them to leave the party just like they entered it?'[35] Nevertheless, the Murshidiyin were encouraged by their leadership to join the Ba'th Party at the time, and many did so.

Rif'at's heavy reliance on the Murshidiyin also turned out to be his weakness. When President Hafiz al-Asad requested the 3,000 Murshidiyin military in Rif'at's Defence Companies to withdraw from their units, they responded positively, as a result of which Rif'at's revolt was made toothless. Without these men, Rif'at's tanks and armoured vehicles could not come into action, because the Murshidiyin occupied key positions in the Defence Companies.[36]

The crisis was finally solved by appointing Rif'at al-Asad as second vice-president and relieving him of his command over the Defence Companies. Although officially it was a promotion, in practice it was a demotion.

After acting as a rather invisible vice-president for some time, Rif'at went into exile.

One of the lessons learned from this crisis was that the regime could maintain its power by relying heavily on various Alawi officers' factions, but not on factions that consisted of only one element that could be considered as a separate Alawi group, like the Murshidiyin. A policy of 'putting all eggs in one basket' was risky and not to be practised again.

The crisis of 1984 with Rif'at had made Hafiz al-Asad more aware of the succession question. Apparently, he had his eldest son Basil in mind as his successor, though he was never officially mentioned as such. Within the Ba'th Party, Hafiz al-Asad had always been referred to as Abu Sulayman ('the father of

Sulayman'), which was his nom de guerre, but he never had a son by that name. It was only in 1990 that he was for the first time publicly referred to as Abu Basil ('the father of Basil'). Basil had apparently become the president's right-hand man, and appeared to be groomed for the presidency. As staff member of the Presidential Guard and chief of presidential security, Basil al-Asad was entrusted with the command of an elite armoured brigade. On 21 January 1994, then aged nearly 32, Basil died in a car accident.

From this time onwards, his younger brother Bashar came into the picture to be groomed as the new president, but again, never officially, because the Ba'th Party could not accept the idea of a hereditary presidency. It was another clear example of living in an 'as if' culture[37] and keeping up a fiction while denying reality.

After the death of Basil, Bashar returned from London where he had been studying ophthalmology. Bashar followed in the footsteps of Basil, also went to the Military Academy in Homs, and graduated as a tank commander, together with his cousin, the son of Presidential Guard Commander 'Adnan Makhluf.

It appeared as if a younger Alawi generation, consisting partly of sons and other younger relatives of the senior Alawi generals, was being prepared to eventually succeed the older one. Nevertheless, it should be noted that relatives of other prominent Alawi figures including, for instance, the sons of Rif'at al-Asad and 'Ali Duba (Chief of Military Intelligence) preferred to go into business, commerce or construction, instead of pursuing military careers similar to those of their fathers. Many sons of the Alawi elite established cross-links with other communities through intermarriage or other social relationships, and thus contributed to some change in the originally closed character of the Alawi community.

Generally, the younger Alawi generation no longer had the socio-economic motives to join the army, as much as their forefathers had. Nevertheless, the relatively high percentage of Alawis in the officers' corps kept increasing to extraordinary proportions.

Within a month of the death of Hafiz al-Asad on 10 June 2000, Bashar al-Asad was inaugurated as president, after being promoted by the Syrian Regional Command of the Ba'th Party to Lieutenant General (skipping a number of military ranks), and elected as Secretary General of the Ba'th Party Regional Command. The required age for the presidency of 40 years was decreased to 34, so as to exactly accommodate that of Bashar.

Hafiz al-Asad's high-ranking military supporters (some of whom were twice as old as Bashar) and their respective dependants accepted President Hafiz al-Asad's son Bashar as a unifying figure, symbolising their wish to continue the former president's legacy and avoid premature dissension in Alawi ranks.

## CONCLUDING REMARKS

The fact that sectarianism, regionalism and tribalism were major factors in the struggle for power in Syria does not imply that other elements, such as socio-economic and ideological factors, were not important as well, or could be ignored. On the contrary: socio-economic factors were important, and in the case of the compact sectarian minorities such as the Alawis, Druzes and Isma'ilis, they coincided to a great extent with sectarian, regional and tribal factors. The overlap of sectarian, regional and socio-economic contrasts could have a mutually strengthening effect. Popular discontent and socio-economic tensions could sometimes be directed and even stimulated through sectarian channels.

Ideological differences were also important, even though during several crises sectarian, regional and tribal ties became the dominant means of self-preservation and the retention of power. Once a political group had monopolised power and had provided itself with a solid base, it could give more priority to political and ideological ideas than to pure power politics. Those who were excluded from power, for instance because they had, on idealistic grounds, refused to apply sectarian power tactics, were consequently not in a position to put their ideals into practice. Others who had used sectarianism, regionalism or tribalism as a means to seize or maintain power, or were more or less forced by opponents to make use of them in order to maintain themselves, could later concentrate on their respective political programmes and ideas.

Because of the fact that under Hafiz and Bashar al-Asad, Syria was dominated by only one all-powerful extended military faction with a highly reliable and effective security apparatus (also effective in the sense of severe repression), the country experienced more internal political stability and continuity than ever before since independence. The fact, however, that this continuity was linked to the absence of any political reform or substantial changes in the composition of the ruling political and military elite for a period of several decades also implied the serious future possibility of strong discontinuity and disruption of the regime, once its long-serving political and military leadership disappeared. As will be described in the following chapters, this so-called stability came to an abrupt end with the start of the Syrian Revolution in March 2011.

In the era of Hafiz al-Asad, Syria was able to develop into a major regional power in its own right,[38] no longer subservient to the traditional power rivalries between other Arab countries in the region such as Iraq and Egypt, as had been the case in the past.[39] Consequently, Syria was bound to play a key role in any overall Arab–Israeli peace settlement. In the period after the start of the Syrian Revolution in 2011, Syria again lost much of its position as a regional power, because of its full preoccupation with the Syrian War, and the interference of many foreign countries in its internal affairs.

However idealistic some Ba'thist leaders may originally have been (and many Syrians may not have shared their ideals), they could not evade the socio-political reality that without making use of primordial ties they could not monopolise power in Syria, let alone maintain themselves. Irrespective of the political line taken by the Syrian Ba'thist leadership after 1963, it should be noted that sectarian, regional and tribal ties have been so important that for about half a century they have constituted an inseparable and integral part of the power structure of the Syrian regime. Without their well-organised sectarian, regional, tribal and extended family-based networks within the Syrian armed forces, the security services and other power institutions, the Ba'thists who ruled Syria since 1963 would not have been able to survive for so long. Exploiting sectarian, regional and tribal ties was simply a matter of pure and elementary power politics.

Nevertheless, both Salah Jadid and Hafiz al-Asad could also be seen as a kind of Ba'thist idealist, who from their early youth, when they joined the Ba'th Party, had wanted to achieve their secular Arab nationalist and socio-economic ideals. In power, however, both developed opposing policies and ideas, al-Asad being more pragmatic than the radical Jadid. The outcome was that former party comrades and friends turned into serious rivals and lifelong enemies once it came to carrying the heavy burden of political responsibilities and of putting into practice under extremely difficult circumstances political ideas which earlier had just been theoretical ideals and ideology.

But even after fully monopolising power, Hafiz al-Asad turned out not to be able to implement some of his most important political ideas.

The takeover by lower-middle-class and poorer rural minoritarian Ba'thists in 1963 led to a social revolution: rural minorities which earlier had been discriminated against, and traditionally had belonged to the more if not most backward segments of Syrian society, went through an abrupt process of national emancipation. Traditional relationships were more or less completely turned upside down: people of rural origin and members of religious minorities started to dominate the predominantly Sunni people of the major cities, and relatively swiftly climbed the social and political ladders of society. Once in power, traditionally discriminated against Alawis, Druzes or other rural minoritarians started to favour members of their own communities and began to discriminate against those whom they perceived as their former oppressors. This led to a certain levelling of society between poorer and richer classes, between rural and urban populations, and for that matter between religious minorities and Sunnis. Urban Sunnis particularly resented being dominated by people of peasant origin from the countryside, irrespective of whether these rural rulers were from religious minorities or Sunnis like themselves. The combination of rural and minoritarian domination only strengthened urban Sunni resentment even further.

Raymond Hinnebusch (in 1991) commented on the issue of sectarianism and social change as follows:

> in explaining political *change*, sectarianism per se gives little clue. Indeed, the importance of minority groups, notably the Alawis, has been their role as advance guard of an elite or as class coalitions rather than as sects per se. They played the role of class vanguard, then shield

of state formation; they now appear as both spearheads of *embourgeoisement* and restratification, and as the target against which anti-regime class coalitions have coalesced. It is this class/state linked role of sect, rather than sectarian rivalries per se, which is by far of greater consequence for Syria's political development.[40]

Originally, the Alawi elite had constituted one of the strongest forces in the regime favouring radical change. After having enriched themselves, however, and having obtained all kinds of privileges to defend, the same elite turned into a major obstacle to the reform of abuses enveloping the state. As a privileged recruitment pool, parts of the Alawi community, in fact, have gone from the most downtrodden to the most well-situated social segment. In the al-Asad era, the enriched Alawi officers and their families built up a kind of coalition with the rich urban bourgeoisie, the Sunni Damascene in particular, but others as well, including Christians. The latter gradually obtained a direct interest in helping maintain the Alawi-dominated Ba'th regime, at least as long as their businesses continued to prosper.

President Hafiz al-Asad (like later Bashar) on numerous occasions made an effort to build up an orthodox religious image for the secular Ba'th regime, for instance by publicly performing prayers in, mostly Sunni, mosques (including the famous Umayyad Mosque in Damascus), or by appearing in public with high Sunni religious officials, or by quoting from the Qur'an in speeches. Hafiz al-Asad also had mosques built, including in his hometown, al-Qardahah. It remains doubtful, however, whether such actions generally had a convincing effect on the greater part of the Sunni population, however sincere the intentions of both Alawi Syrian presidents may have been.

The fact that sectarian favouritism and solidarity were in the first place socially, communally and politically motivated could not prevent many of the traditional Sunni population, as well as other non-Alawis, from experiencing Alawi-dominated Ba'thist rule as a kind of semi-religious repression – which it was not, as far as the dominant Ba'thists were concerned. For the traditional Sunni population, the element of religion was much more important than it was for the secular Alawi Ba'thists.

Prospects and possibilities for broadening the real power base of the Alawi-dominated Ba'th regime in Syria were limited, at least if the regime was not to bring itself into danger by sharing powers with others.

Feelings of revanchism among people who suffered from the severe repression of the Alawi-dominated Ba'th regime clearly remained under the surface for decades, and burst out into the open almost 30 years after the Hama massacre with the start of the Syrian Revolution in March 2011.

# 2

# COULD THE WAR IN SYRIA HAVE BEEN AVOIDED?

## INTRODUCTION

It has been argued that the Syrian Civil War could have been avoided if the regime of President Bashar al-Asad had implemented substantial reforms at an early stage of the Syrian Revolution that broke out in mid-March 2011. This revolution started with small-scale and peaceful demonstrations in Deraa in the south, and later spread out massively all over Syria.[1] The question is whether or not the ensuing Syrian War was really inevitable. When taking into account the earlier history of the regime and its behaviour (and misbehaviour) during half a century in power in Syria, I come to the conclusion that the Syrian War could hardly have been avoided. Another decisive factor in Syria in 2011 and after was that, in contrast to earlier periods, opposition groups gradually started to receive support, both political as well as military, from foreign countries that thereby began to intervene in Syria's internal affairs.

As a result of this foreign support, the war in Syria developed into a war by proxy, as well as being an internal intra-Syrian war. Therefore, the terminology of 'civil war' was no longer fully appropriate after its initial stages, because it became a war with the Syrian regime and its regular army, militias and security institutions, supported by Russia, Iran and the Lebanese militia Hizballah on the one hand, and on the other side deserted Syrian military, who were later joined by many others, including thousands of fighters from other countries.

If the opposition forces had not been supported in the way they were, the revolution might possibly have been suppressed earlier with fewer victims, and the regime might have continued its repressive rule for another indefinite period. But some day in the future, there was bound to be a renewed effort by those people who had suffered from the atrocities of the al-Asad regime to have a violent reckoning.

The devastating consequences of the Syrian War were enormous. By the end of 2016, the number of dead was estimated at well over 400,000.[2] By the same year, an estimated 11 million Syrians had fled their homes since the outbreak of the Syrian Revolution in March 2011. In the sixth year of the war, 13.5 million people were in need of humanitarian assistance within the country. Among those escaping the conflict, the majority sought refuge in neighbouring countries or within Syria itself. According to the United Nations High Commissioner for Refugees (UNHCR), 4.8 million fled to Turkey, Lebanon, Jordan, Egypt and Iraq, and 6.6 million were internally displaced within Syria.[3]

In *The Struggle for Power in Syria* I came to the conclusion that it was very difficult to imagine a scenario in which the narrowly based, totalitarian regime, dominated by members of the Alawi minority – who traditionally had been discriminated against by the Sunni majority, and who themselves had on various occasions severely repressed part of the Sunni population – could be peacefully transformed into a more widely based democracy, involving a greater part of the Sunni majority.[4] A transformation from Alawi-dominated dictatorship to democracy in Syria would imply that the existing repressive institutions were to be dismantled, and that the regime would have to give up its privileged positions. A scenario in which the Alawi-dominated power elite were to be overthrown or removed was bound to be extremely violent. Therefore, it should have been clear from the beginning of the Syrian Revolution that the regime, seen from this perspective, did not really want to implement any substantial reforms, if only because these, in the end, could lead to its downfall; and this perspective had never been otherwise. Calls for freedom in Syria were understandable and justified, but expecting a transformation of the Syrian political system into a democracy to be possible without severe bloodshed was therefore wishful thinking. Regime change through peaceful negotiations did not work, as could have been expected.

Modern Syria has known various dictatorships before the Ba'th regime came into power, and periods of democracy or relative freedom have been very scarce.[5] In the period before Syria became independent in 1946 with the end of the French Mandate, there never was a democracy: not under the French Mandate, not under the Ottoman Turks, neither under the Omayyad or Abbasid Caliphs or other Islamic rulers, nor under the Byzantines, Romans or Egyptians, or before. The great majority of Syrians alive today have known nothing other than dictatorship in their country, like most of their ancestors. Their lack of democratic experience in Syria did not mean, however, that they would not have the capacity to build up a new democratic society. On the other hand, during the Syrian Revolution there were various forces present in the country that had their own political agendas and could be expected not to show any respect for democracy, once in power. This applied to the more radical Islamists in general. It tended to be, to a great extent, a matter of who was militarily the strongest and best organised. The only way to topple the Syrian regime appeared to be by counterforce. This counterforce was inspired and triggered to a great extent by the bloody suppression of the – initially – peaceful demonstrations. The Syrian regime's excessively repressive behaviour reflected the motto of '*it is either al-Asad, or we will burn the country*' (*al-Asad aw nahriq al-balad*), as wall slogans and the graffiti of regime loyalists portrayed it at the time.

If President Bashar al-Asad were to have implemented clearly visible reforms in 2011, would the opposition have been satisfied? It might have been in the shorter term, but in the longer term the opposition, both moderate and less moderate, would almost certainly have demanded further reforms that should have led to less dictatorship and more freedom, implying that at least a real kind of power-sharing could be achieved.[6] Furthermore, it could have been expected that the opposition would have demanded justice for many of those from the regime who had committed crimes against humanity, both before and after the start of the Syrian Revolution in 2011, and had blood on their hands. In the Syrian context, the regime's power elite, in the case of being brought before justice, could hardly expect otherwise than to be court martialled with a high probability of being executed. Within such circumstances it would have been unrealistic to expect that the president and those around him would voluntarily step down. A reconciliation scenario, South African style, did not seem to be possible.

In an effort to protect and save itself and to survive, the regime therefore did not want to go any further than implementing some cosmetic changes that were far from enough to appease the opposition in the longer term.[7] Drastic reforms, however, would have been an introduction to the regime's later fall.

## THE DANGEROUS TRAP OF SECTARIANISM

The fact that the issue of sectarianism during the beginning of the Syrian Revolution did not figure prominently, did not mean that it was not an important undercurrent which could fundamentally undermine the possibility of achieving freedom and democracy as demanded by Syrian opposition groups. Syrians were very much aware of it but tended, generally, to avoid talking about sectarianism openly, because it could have such a destructive effect. For almost 30 years since the Hama massacre (1982), the situation in Syria was relatively quiet on the sectarian front, in public at least. This did not mean, however, that the issue of sectarianism could not become acute again.[8]

Whereas the common sectarian, regional and family or tribal backgrounds of the main Ba'thist rulers had been key to the durability and strength of the regime, their Alawi sectarian background was also inherently one of its main weaknesses. The 'Alawi factor' seemed to be hindering a peaceful transformation from Syrian dictatorship towards a more widely representative regime. The Syrian demonstrators' main demands at the beginning were simply to get more political freedom and to bring an end to the corrupt one-party dictatorial system. The sectarianism issue was generally avoided. After all, the last thing the opposition seemed to want was another sectarian war or confrontation which would not only lead to more violence and suppression, but might also not result in meeting any of their demands. The opposition instead preferred to portray the Syrian people as one and the same, irrespective of them being Arab, Kurd, Sunni, Alawi, Christian, Druze, Isma'ili or whatever. They wanted justice, dignity and freedom. Their demands at the beginning were generally rather modest, democratically oriented and peaceful.

It is good to take into consideration that at the beginning of the Syrian Revolution there was no clear sectarian dichotomy in Syrian society, dividing the country into Alawis and non-Alawis. Syria had never been ruled by 'the Alawi community', although it was nevertheless perceived as such by a considerable number of non-Alawis, Sunnis in particular.

It was only natural that there were also numerous Alawi opponents to the regime. Many Alawis had themselves been suffering from Alawi-dominated Ba'thist dictatorship, often just as much as, or occasionally even more than, non-Alawis. According to one Alawi opposition leader Alawis were equally severely tortured in prisons, but fewer of them were killed than was the case with members of other communities. A great number of Alawi villages had people imprisoned for political or security reasons. The Syrian dictatorship was applied without exception to all Syrian regions, sectors and population groups, including those with an Alawi majority. Many Alawis were just as eager for political change in Syria, as were other Syrians.

Shortly before the Syrian Revolution broke out, a wave of demonstrations and revolts swept over the Arab world, starting in Tunisia in December 2010, and spreading out over other Arab countries like Egypt, Libya and Yemen in early 2011. Many of the demonstrators in these countries were motivated by their miserable economic situations and lack of future prospects, and they wanted to get rid of corruption and dictatorship, hoping to achieve more prosperity and freedom. The demonstrations were received enthusiastically in the Western world, where it was hoped that the authoritarian regimes would be replaced by democracies, preferably Western style. The revolutions were initially given the positive name of the 'Arab Spring', but in the end they resulted in a serious deterioration of the situations in all the Arab countries involved. In some cases they even gave rise to devastating civil wars, such as those experienced in Libya, Yemen and Syria.

The revolutions caused the fall of various authoritarian rulers: in Tunisia, Egypt and Yemen, where the presidents themselves decided to step down; and in Libya where its leader al-Qadhafi was killed after foreign military intervention came to the aid of the Libyan opposition groups.

The revolutions that took place in other Arab countries initially gave rise to hope among Syrians that the situation in their country could also be changed for the better, and that demonstrations could finally lead to the fall of the al-Asad dictatorship. When the Syrian demonstrations started in March 2011, Egyptian President Mubarak had already ceded all his powers, whereas the Libyan regime was being attacked by foreign military forces.

All this created hope among Syrians that change would come within a shorter reach.

Syrians from all social and ethnic segments initially tended to be carried away by the so-called 'successes' of demonstrators elsewhere in the Arab world and they were prepared to take great risks to help in achieving something 'similar'. They were not aware yet of the disaster-in-waiting.

It should be noted that in the other Arab countries that had been swept by demonstrations and revolts, the social composition of the regimes was completely different from that of the regime in Syria, certainly as far as the dangerous issue of sectarianism was concerned. Sectarianism made Syria into a special case, as has been described in the preceding chapters, and came to be an important factor during the Syrian War.

Whereas the high proportion of Alawis in key positions in the Syrian armed forces apparently did not constitute an obstacle to sustaining an inter-state war, with for instance Israel, it has proven to be an inherently damaging structural disadvantage in fighting an internal civil war.[9] The sectarian provocation and confrontation that the Muslim Brotherhood and its Mujahidin had unsuccessfully initiated at the end of the

1970s and in the early 1980s, and which ended with the blood-bath of Hama in 1982, triggered a kind of self-fulfilling prophecy after the beginning of the Syrian Revolution, in the sense that something similar was bound to happen again, albeit in a some-what different context.

Various observers have claimed that the Syrian regime wanted to encourage a sectarian-tinted civil war on purpose, and part of the Sunni majority of the population may indeed have perceived it as such. However, since the regime already fully dominated all power institutions that were heavily controlled by Alawis, there was no real advantage in having any further sectarian polarisation with the Sunni majority, but rather the contrary. The only shorter-term 'advantage' for the regime could have been that it might induce a greater part of the Alawi community into an unconditional and arti-ficial solidarity with the regime. But this had already been triggered to a great extent by the attitudes of the radical Islamist organisations, both present and past. Irrespective of who was the main instigator, to get out of such a polarisation would, in any case, be extremely difficult in the longer run, and could only add to further disaster in Syria.

Nevertheless, such a sectarian polarisation – whether the regime wanted it or not – was hardly avoidable because of the sectarian composition of the Syrian armed forces elite troops, its security institutions, its armed gangs like the Shabbihah, and other repressive institutions. Since these were so identifiably Alawi-dominated, those who were suppressed and were non-Alawis, Sunnis in particular, could under such extreme circum-stances hardly see their oppressors other than as Alawis. Many of the Alawi regime loyalists were considered to be easily rec-ognisable by their Arabic accents, with the heavy guttural *Qaf*, even though non-Alawis, from the same mainly Alawi areas in the countryside, have similar accents. Many people incorrectly associate the use of the phoneme *Qaf* with the Alawis alone, but it should be noted that the *Qaf* is not so much a 'sectarian' characteristic of Alawi dialects, but rather a rural feature, also present in the speech of Sunnis, Druzes, Isma'ilis and Christians or anyone else living in certain rural areas.[10]

Whereas the peaceful civilian opposition was strongly against any sectarian element in their demonstrations, the Islamist and Jihadist military opposition groups were clearly sectarian motivated in their actions against the Alawi-dominated regime, and also strongly contributed to sectarian polarisation.

According to a survey carried out by The Day After Association on the issue of sectarianism in Syria, published in 2016, there appeared to be strong differences between various sectarian communities as far as their support for the demonstrations in 2011 was concerned. The answers provided by Sunni respondents demonstrated a near-consensus on supporting the 2011 demonstrations of the opposition, whereas the answers of Alawis and Shi'is demonstrated a position against them. More than half of the Christian respondents supported them, whereas a very considerable proportion of Druze and Isma'ili respondents opposed them.[11] It should be added that the opinions given with some hindsight, after five years of the start of the Syrian Revolution, may not necessarily have been the same as they were in 2011.

The Alawi-dominated army and security forces, as well as Alawi-dominated gangs (like the Shabbihah) in fact provoked a sectarian confrontation – if only because of their sectarian composition and misbehaviour – and were responsible for provoking acts of ethnic cleansing, but, by way of intimidation, warned others against doing what the regime was doing itself. Reports about ethnic cleansing operations have not always been consistent, and were occasionally contradictory and highly controversial. The regime and the opposition accused one another of being responsible.[12]

As part of the fighting and intimidation between regime and opposition forces, ethnic cleansing operations took place in particular between Alawis and Sunnis, in city quarters, in the countryside and in and around villages. Radical Islamists also expelled Christians from their living quarters. All this had a deep impact on Syrian society and its social fabric.[13]

During negotiations between the regime and the military opposition, the idea of reshuffling parts of the population was occasionally brought up. Such reshuffles or population exchanges could have a sectarian dimension, and were, therefore, very sensitive.[14]

One example of this was the 'Four Towns Agreement' negotiated in September 2015 by the Syrian regime (represented by Iran) and opposition groups including Jabhat al-Nusrah (represented by Qatar and Ahrar al-Sham). According to this agreement, the beleaguered towns of (predominantly Sunni) Zabadani and Madaya north-west of Damascus were to be evacuated by military opposition forces, in exchange for the evacuation of fighters from the two Shi'i towns Kafarya and al-Fu'ah in the northern province of Idlib. There was also to be a population exchange, which meant a sectarian reshuffle between Sunnis and Shi'is. It took until 2017 for the agreement to be implemented.[15] Jabhat al-Nusrah wanted to expel the Shi'i population of al-Fu'ah and Kafarya also on religious grounds, considering them to be apostates (*rawafid*) who should be removed from the area. Jabhat al-Nusrah described the towns as Shi'i 'outposts' in Sunni territory, whereas the respective villages were in reality remnants of earlier times when this territory was still mainly under Shi'i domination.

During the recapture by the Syrian regime of eastern Aleppo in December 2016, opposition fighters of Jabhat Fath al-Sham (ex-Jabhat al-Nusrah), the Free Syrian Army and others, who had been cornered there, were allowed to leave for areas under control of the opposition (mainly Idlib province), on the condition that besieged pro-regime people could leave Kafarya and al-Fu'ah.[16]

Whereas some may have considered the Alawi-dominated regime of Bashar al-Asad as a protective shield for the Alawi community in general, the war that was started after the beginning of the Syrian Revolution in 2011 achieved the opposite. Instead of being a protector of the Alawi community, Bashar al-Asad's regime also caused it to become severely threatened. All the Alawi-tinted violence and suppression made any existing grudges against Alawis in general bigger, whether justified or not.

The regime, at the beginning of the Syrian Revolution, could have adequately responded to the reasonable demands of the peacefully oriented opposition by way of introducing essential reform measures. But most measures were too little too late. With his totalitarian regime, President Bashar al-Asad should, at least theoretically, have been able to control all the army and security institutions, as well as the armed irregular Alawi gangs like the Shabbihah, to guide Syria out of this crisis in a more peaceful manner. But he, together with his loyalists, did not do so. The chosen path of repressive violence finally led to a destructive war in Syria, which was to last for many years.

Later, President al-Asad was even criticised in an interview by the chief of the Airforce Intelligence Directorate, General Jamil Hasan, for having shown 'too much restraint in the early days of the Syrian uprising in 2011'. Had al-Asad, according to Hasan, 'not tried to appease his domestic and foreign detractors in 2011, an early all-out crackdown could have nipped the uprising in the bud … It would still have been better than what actually followed.'[17]

## FROM PEACEFUL DEMONSTRATIONS TO WAR

During the earlier stages of the Syrian Revolution, when the bloodshed had not yet taken its extremely heavy toll, it still looked as if there might have been a chance to solve the crisis through a kind of national dialogue with the aim of reconciliation. Some internal opposition meetings took place in Damascus in June 2011 with the aim of discussing how the crisis could be solved. Various well-known opposition members attended, including Michel Kilo, Lu'ayy Husayn, Anwar al-Bunni, Mundhir Khaddam, Fayiz Sara and others, many of whom had earlier spent years in the regime's prisons. They wanted a 'peaceful transition to a democratic, civil and pluralistic state', and called for an immediate end to the security crackdown and the withdrawal of the army to its bases. They stressed that there could be no national dialogue with a 'security solution' taking place. Confidence-building measures were urgently needed. The opposition conference called for an independent committee to investigate the killings of Syrian citizens and soldiers, the release of all political prisoners, the right to peaceful protests without the government's prior approval, and an end to the power monopoly of the Ba'th Party. These opposition meetings in Damascus were unique in the sense that they were condoned at all, but they did not result in a dialogue with the regime.

In July 2011, the regime organised an alternative meeting, led by Vice-President Faruq al-Shar' and attended mainly by regime supporters and a few opposition representatives who were closer to the regime. These meetings did not result in dialogue between regime and opposition either.

There were no signs that suggested that the opposition wanted to talk with the regime, unless important preconditions were being met. Real reconciliation would only have been possible if enough trust could have been created among the various parties. This was something that turned out to be unfeasible, however, because the regime and the opposition had one thing in common: they fully mistrusted one another.

Later, even a new Ministry of Reconciliation was created, but President Bashar al-Asad internally reportedly called the respective government a 'war cabinet', which better reflected the president's real intentions.[18]

In 2011 the regime apparently imagined that the whole crisis could be solved by brute force, just like it had managed to do in Hama in 1982 and on various other occasions. This, however, turned out to be a disastrous mistake. The situation in 2011 was completely different: the wall of fear and silence had been broken among a substantial part of the Syrian population, and they received political, financial and military support from abroad.

## AN INTRA-SYRIAN WAR AND A WAR BY PROXY

Countries like Turkey and Saudi Arabia, and organisations like the Arab League, at first undertook serious efforts to help bring the violence to an end, to help establish an intra-Syrian national dialogue, and to mediate the start of reform measures, but it all turned out to be of no avail. Once it became clear that these mediators could not achieve any positive results, and the disproportionate violence of the regime continued, these countries finally chose the side of the opposition and started to actively work against the regime by supporting its adversaries with funds, weapons and other aid. Turkey allowed weapons and other aid for the opposition to pass across its borders into Syria, which was made even easier after opposition forces occupied some of the most important border crossings, like Bab al-Hawa, Bab al-Salamah and Jarabulus. Most countries that aided the opposition claimed to support the idea of a 'political solution' to the conflict. Turkey, by way of an exception, while calling for a political solution, also openly called for toppling the regime, which would in that case be a 'military solution'. Most other countries maintained that they wanted a political solution, but in fact they wanted a regime change, albeit preferably peacefully, although this turned out to be impossible. All this gradually contributed to giving the ongoing intra-Syrian conflict the additional dimension of a war by proxy.

The Arab League froze the membership of the Syrian Arab Republic, but this turned out to be rather counterproductive because it further polarised relations between Syria and other Arab states. The Syrian National Council of the opposition in exile was allowed to participate in ministerial meetings on an 'exceptional basis', but the Arab League did not grant it the official recognition it sought to be Syria's sole legitimate representative.

Being isolated by its Arab brothers and sisters appeared to be more sensitive for an Arab nationalist country like Syria than being sanctioned by the European Union or the United States, if only because relations with the latter were already rather cool, if not hostile. Self-preservation of the regime was, however, more important for Damascus than anything else.

Relations between Damascus and Washington had already been at a low ebb before 2011 because of Syrian support to opponents of the US–British invasion in Iraq from 2003 onwards. Jihadists from Syria were allowed to go to Iraq to fight the US–British occupation. Many joined al-Qa'idah in Iraq, and came back to Syria later, well-trained to join the Syrian Revolution after 2011.[19] It was one of the examples where interfering in the internal affairs of other countries may in the end backfire.[20]

It appeared to be an omission of the Western countries not to even have tried any kind of serious political dialogue with Damascus, even though there would not have been any guarantee of success, particularly when taking into account the efforts already made by other intermediaries. Once these Western countries had declared the Syrian president and his regime to be illegitimate, possibilities for dialogue were also blocked, and it became more and more difficult, if not impossible, to find a way back towards a more neutral position from which mediation between the regime and the opposition groups might have been possible.

Most Western countries withdrew their ambassadors from Damascus in 2012, and thereby not only cut off all direct communications with the regime, but also lost their 'ears and eyes' inside Syria. As a result, it became more difficult for them to correctly monitor and evaluate developments inside the country. The continuous propaganda war between the regime and the opposition through the media made the possibility of neutral evaluation of developments even more difficult. Had they remained in Damascus, the ambassadors might have been a kind of last contact through whom attempts might have been made to influence the regime.[21]

The United States, the European Union and other countries started to impose various sanctions against the regime. These, however, did not achieve the desired results. Regime violence, intimidation and suppression only increased. Whereas these sanctions in themselves did not lead to the fall of the regime, as could have been expected, they indirectly encouraged others to help bring its downfall nearer, and made the economic situation for the population that was dependent on the regime more difficult.[22]

Imposing sanctions with the aim of hitting the hard core of the regime, while simultaneously wanting to spare the population from its negative effects, turned out to be illusionary, as could have been predicted on the basis of earlier experiences with boycotts and sanctions elsewhere (for instance in Iraq in the 1990s where the sanctions contributed to hundreds of thousands of dead). Historically, sanctions have only rarely been effective. They, more often than not, have caused a lot of damage without ever achieving the results for which they were intended.

Wishful thinkers hoped that al-Asad would step down or that he might even leave the country in order to help solve the crisis, once enough pressure had been exercised by the countries condemning him, but the contrary happened – as could have been predicted as well, if only because dictators generally do not follow the rules of democratic accountability.

## CONTRADICTORY MEASURES OF THE REGIME

The regime reacted to the initially peaceful demonstrations by using disproportionate heavy force, trying to bloodily suppress any opposition, but this only resulted in the protests becoming more hostile. Nevertheless, on 26 March 2011, within two weeks of the beginning of what later turned out to be the Syrian Revolution, a presidential amnesty was issued for the release of approximately 260 prisoners from Saydnaya. It appeared that the large majority of those released were Islamists of one kind or another, while others were members of political opposition bodies and of Syria's Kurdish minority, although claims differ over the precise breakdown. According to Charles Lister

> this may have been an attempt to appease the growing anti-government sentiments across the country; but it is more likely that it was yet another devious attempt by the Assad regime to manipulate its adversary, this time by unleashing those it could safely label 'Jihadists' or 'extremist' among its ranks.

It is not clear why the regime at such a sensitive stage 'wanted to play the cards of terrorism and military gangs to scare Syrians and the international community at the same time', nor why it would thereby have had the 'aim of distorting the Syrian

Revolution', as was argued by different Islamists of the opposition with some hindsight four years later in 2015.[23]

Indeed, some of the released Islamist leaders later played a prominent role in the Syrian War, like Hasan 'Abbud of Ahrar al-Sham and Zahran 'Allush of Liwa' al-Islam (later Jaysh al-Islam). But would the Islamists have played a much less prominent role in the Syrian Revolution, had these particular leaders not been released from prison? After all, the Islamist current had already been on the rise for a long time in Syria.[24] And there were enough Islamists who wanted to take revenge against the regime.

It did not really fit into the behavioural pattern of the Syrian regime to release prisoners – who in fact were its enemies – if they would thereby run even the minor risk of these people actively turning against the regime. Therefore, it appears more likely that these men were released to 'appease the growing anti-government sentiments'. Nevertheless, it looked quite contradictory that the regime would release some of its well-known enemies. Yet, developments had not gone out of control that much at that stage, and under previous circumstances the released prisoners could have been re-imprisoned relatively easy. From this point on developments progressed quite differently, however, from what the regime might have imagined.

The Syrian writer Ehsani (pseudonym) later, also with some hindsight, gave a view that could be considered closer to reflecting the perception from Damascus:

> As the crisis first unfolded in Daraa, Sheikh Sayasneh was invited to Damascus in an attempt by the authorities to de-escalate the situation. One of the key demands of the cleric was the release of prisoners, the majority of whom were Islamists. This pattern was often repeated throughout the early phase of the crisis. The UN mediator took up

this demand. He too requested the release of prisoners as a trust-building measure. While many in the opposition are convinced that the release of people like Zahran Alloush was engineered by Damascus to help radicalise the opposition, the truth is probably more nuanced. The Syrian State was desperately trying to stop the uprising through both using a stick (swift response against protestors) and a carrot (release of prisoners when urged). While one may still debate this argument and claim that the government's secret intent was to turn the uprising into a Jihad, the fact is that what Damascus sees today are insurgents and Islamist armed groups who want nothing less than to destroy the Syrian State and replace it with a state designed to conform to Sharia. They call it 'more Islamist in identity'.[25]

If Ehsani's comments are correct, the regime at the time did not yet fully understand that its disproportional force was completely out of balance if it had wanted to apply a successful carrot and stick policy.

Reinoud Leenders has argued that the regime might have reasoned that with a militarisation of its confrontation with the opposition, it would stand a much better chance of surviving, given its superior military capabilities. For the regime 'the military stand-off that ensued, and which lasts until today, contained a far slimmer chance of delivering regime change than the peaceful and popularly driven protests that challenged the regime in the first few months of the uprising'.[26] If this was indeed the regime's reasoning, it did not take into account the possibility that the opposition was going to receive substantial military and other aid from abroad.

In another regime gesture of appeasement, 220,000 Kurds in the north-east were given Syrian citizenship by presidential decree on 7 April 2011, after many Kurds had been rendered stateless since the early 1960s.

In April 2011, the regime started to label the uprising in explicit Islamist or extremist terms. According to the Syrian Ministry of Interior

> some of these groups have called for armed insurrection under the motto of Jihad to set up a Salafist state ... What they did is an ugly crime severely punished by law. Their objective is to spread terror across Syria.[27]

Painting some of the opposition as Sunni Salafist extremists, whether justified or not, could have helped secure the continued support of sectarian communities that were of primary importance to the Syrian regime, like the Alawis and Christians.[28] The number of Christians in Syria decreased drastically during the Syrian War and even before.[29]

On 21 April 2011, the state of emergency, in force since 1963, was abolished by President Bashar al-Asad at the demand of the demonstrators, after having been in force for 48 years. In practice, however, it made no difference because the regime simply continued with its severe repression of the population and ignored the laws that did not suit it. And some of the laws permitted the regime to do whatever it wanted, without any repercussions.

Syrian opposition leader Haytham Al Maleh has noted in this respect that according to legislative decree no. 14 of 1968:

> It is not permitted to bring criminal proceedings against anyone who worked within this administration for crimes committed while carrying out their defined objectives or where the execution is by mandate of the leader ... This text assured immunity from persecution

for the authors of crimes of torture and murder by torture. Since the publication of this decree to this day, no
one responsible for security has ever been held up before
a court of crime.[30]

In May 2011, the president's spokeswoman Buthayna Sha'ban
stated that al-Asad had ordered that there should be no more
shooting, but it simply went on. This did not necessarily mean
that al-Asad did not have his own army and security people
under control, but rather that the regime had opted for the
violent way to 'solve' the crisis, and that the spokeswoman's
statements simply did not reflect the realities on the ground.[31]

But was Bashar al-Asad really fully in control? Bashar al-Asad
was parachuted on to the top of the regime in 2000 to prevent
disunity among the officers and supporters of the late President
Hafiz al-Asad. Faruq al-Shar', Syrian Minister of Foreign Affairs
in 2000, has recounted in his memoirs that Minister of Defence
Mustafa Talas, on the day of the death of President Hafiz al-Asad,
proposed that al-Shar' should be given the task to directly prepare for a change in the constitution that would enable Bashar
al-Asad to become the new president at the age of 34 instead of 40,
as was laid down in the constitution. Al-Shar' notes that he was
originally against the principle of an hereditary presidency (just
as he was strongly against the takeover of power by Rif'at, Hafiz
al-Asad's brother, in 1984). This time the situation was different,
however, according to al-Shar': 'If Bashar al-Asad would take
over the presidency, this would be a secure way out, as well as a
peaceful alternative to a bloody struggle that might break out.'[32]
Bashar's appointment as president was to ensure continuity, in
taking over from his father, but that did not mean that he from
the very beginning had just as much power. In the early stages
of the Syrian Revolution Bashar al-Asad may not have been the
one who directly issued the orders to shoot and kill; it was more

probably those who for decades had got used to acting independently where violence and intimidation were concerned.

David Lesch has noted that the Mukhabarat's accumulation of power over the years led to systematic recklessness, which backfired against the regime. 'The right hand did not know what the left hand was doing, and nor did it seem to care – a disconnect that is both dangerous and an abdication of authority.'[33] But as President and Supreme Commander of the Armed Forces, Bashar al-Asad was fully responsible for everything his men did, irrespective of whether or not he issued the direct orders. And in March 2011, at the beginning of the revolution, he had already been in power for almost 11 years, long enough to establish a powerful position and have a lot of experience. Later, during the Syrian Revolution, repression and attacks against the opposition became more planned, rather than being improvised, as might have been the case in the very beginning. The regime created a special 'crisis cell' to deal with it.

## BASHAR HAFIZ AL-ASAD: A SON OF SYRIA, NOT OF THE WEST

In the early stages of the Syrian Revolution it was suggested quite often that Bashar al-Asad was a moderate personality, open to ideas of democracy. Many imagined that these supposed attitudes, if correct, could be ascribed to his stay in Great Britain where he studied ophthalmology for a year and a half. At first, after taking over as president in 2000, Bashar al-Asad was in the diplomatic community in Damascus even characterised as a kind of 'Snow White': a rather innocent personality who was open to reform and democracy. In practice, it turned out that he was not able, or indeed willing, to implement any drastic reforms at all. Many Syrians in the beginning had high hopes that the internal political situation in Syria might essentially change under Bashar al-Asad's rule, but this turned out to be a misconception. The so-called Damascus Spring that began in 2000, with intensive public political debates among Syrian intellectuals about future reform in Syria, died an early death in 2001, because the activities of most of those who were involved were supressed. Many who still believed in Bashar al-Asad's openness to reform ascribed the failure of the Damascus Spring to the thesis that it was the old guard, the remnant prominent personalities of the rule of his father Hafiz al-Asad, who had prevented any drastic change. Even if this contained some truth, in 2011 it was mainly the new guard, led by President Bashar al-Asad, who decided things, albeit still in the presence of some prominent people from the old guard. By 2005, most officers of the old guard, whom Bashar al-Asad had known as a child, had been replaced. Thereafter, his regime became more stable.[34]

The influence of Bashar al-Asad's exposure to the West and its ideas have generally been highly exaggerated. It was more based on wishful thinking than on realities. Bashar may have been influenced by his exposure to Western values of democracy and reform during his stay in Great Britain, but never to such an extent that he would really think that these concepts could be brought into practice in the same way in Syria. In his view it would take a long time before any kind of democracy could be practised in his country, if at all.[35] David Lesch has noted that Bashar al-Asad 'learned soon enough that to succeed in the Syrian system one had to conform to it'.[36]

Instead of being a child of the West, Bashar was an authentic child of Syria and his Syrian parents. He was born in Damascus, making him a Damascene rather than someone who was from the Alawi Mountains. He was raised in the Arab nationalist Syrian environment of his father who was president, and of his Syrian family and Syrian friends. He was thereby intensively exposed to the problems Syria went through, like the Arab–Israeli conflict, the Syrian intervention in Lebanon, the killing of Alawis in the late 1970s to the early 1980s, the assassination attempt against his father, the confrontation of the regime with the Syrian Muslim Brotherhood in Hama in 1982 and many other developments. He was a member of the Ba'th Party, received an education in the Syrian army, and was groomed to become Syrian president by his father and his entourage during a period of six and a half years, between 1994, when his brother Basil died in a car accident, and 2000 when his father died. His formative years were therefore in Syria and Syrian. His mere 18 months in London were of secondary importance.[37]


## OPPOSITION COUNTERVIOLENCE


Demonstrations against the Syrian regime continued for many months, and it was a miracle that they generally remained so peaceful for a relatively long time, taking into account the severe repression and atrocities committed by the regime against the peaceful demonstrators, their families and regions. In the past, such atrocities were not that visible, although they were well known from publications.[38] After 2011, however, they could be witnessed throughout the world via social media like Facebook, YouTube and various Arab television channels such as Al Jazeera.[39] These media showed graphic films and pictures that further contributed to great indignation and helped trigger serious counterviolence that, in the end, resulted in a disastrous war.

Next to the peaceful demonstrations, there also was armed anti-regime violence during the early stages of this revolution, probably committed from the 'side lines' by radical Islamists and others, branded by the regime as 'armed gangs'.[40] It takes only one or more armed men in a large peaceful crowd to cause a serious escalation of violence. In general, however, the anti-regime demonstrations in the beginning clearly had a non-violent character even though the reaction of the regime to them was disproportionate in every sense. It has been argued that there were some armed pro-regime *agents provocateurs* among the demonstrating crowds, but the regime did not really need such people as an excuse, because it could do whatever it wanted.

The regime reported that between 4 and 6 June 2011 nearly 120 of its soldiers and security people were killed and their bodies mutilated and thrown in a river around the town of Jisr-al-Shugur. Opposition activists claimed at the time that the dead soldiers were shot by their own superiors as they tried to defect. According to the Syrian writer Ehsani, who was close to the regime, this was incorrect. Ehsani reports that 'according to informed Western sources, electronic interception of opposition communication from that day clearly revealed that opposition fighters took responsibility for the murder of the soldiers'.[41]

Whatever the truth, it is clear that by June 2011 violence and counterviolence had increased to such an extent that any return to peaceful discussions and dialogue between regime and opposition had become extremely difficult.

No less important was the fact that the Syrian Revolution had already, to some extent, been kidnapped by radical Islamists. They saw the so-called Arab Spring developments in the region as an excellent opportunity to present themselves as viable alternatives in their efforts to spread the rule of Islam.[42]

At the beginning, the demonstrators just asked for freedom and peacefulness. It was only after being confronted with additional bloody suppression by the regime's military and security forces that protestors gradually started calling for the toppling of the regime, the departure of the president and even for his execution.

Were the demonstrators so naive as to expect the regime to really make any drastic political reforms leading to a more democratic political system and to freedom of expression? Did they really believe that the regime would peacefully give in to their demands, or even that peaceful demonstrations could cause its downfall? It would be unjust to label these courageous demonstrators as naive. They were rather overtaken by their enthusiasm after being inspired by 'Arab Spring' developments elsewhere, and they imagined that they were going to be supported by Western countries in achieving their aims for freedom and reform. After all, the ambassadors from the United States, France and elsewhere had shown solidarity with the demonstrators by personally going to Hama in July 2011, thereby openly taking sides in the conflict under strong criticism of the regime in Damascus. Whereas France had had close and friendly relations with the Syrian regime previous to the Syrian Revolution, the US–Syrian relationship had since Syrian independence always been more hostile than friendly.[43]

Also, other Western governments at first reacted positively and optimistically about the possibilities for democratic change in Syria, and thereby encouraged the Syrian Revolution. Given the circumstances, the demonstrators at the beginning did not have much of an alternative to demonstrating peacefully. Most of them did not have any arms. This changed drastically, however, once they were supplied with arms from abroad, via Turkey and Jordan.

The demonstrators may not have had any well-contemplated plan or strategy at the beginning. It was rather a spontaneous reaction to the violence and repressive actions of the regime, first in Deraa province, and later elsewhere, all over Syria. They apparently simply wanted to get rid of the Ba'thist dictatorship that had already existed for almost half a century. The youth – and older people as well – were fed up with always living under dictatorship, having no freedom of expression, and, more important perhaps, not having any prospects for positive change in their often miserable lives. In the years preceding the Syrian Revolution the agricultural economy had been severely affected by drought, reportedly the worst for at least 500 years, causing more than a million rural people to migrate to the cities.[44] This added up to the situation being explosive.

Those who had only read or heard about the regime's violence and its repression, but had not experienced it themselves first hand, were, under the perceived new circumstances, prepared to take immense risks, without having the slightest guarantee of success. But those who themselves in the past had already directly experienced the regime's extremely bad treatment in prisons and its torture chambers were equally willing to take those risks.

Robin Yassin-Kassab has observed that Syrians stopped acting 'as if', and shocked themselves in the process. 'Participants often describe[d] their first protest as an almost mystical experience of liberation through honest self-expression, of breaching the limits imposed by fear, and of finding true solidarity with the community.'[45]

After earlier mediation efforts had failed, Syrian opposition forces started to be militarily supported to a great extent by the United States, Turkey, Saudi Arabia, Qatar and other Arab Gulf states, France and Great Britain, whereas the regime was supported in particular by Russia, Iran and Hizballah. For some of these countries and parties, intervention in Syria was part of their strategic ambitions or perceived interests. For instance, the regional rivalry between Saudi Arabia and Iran played a role. Iran had its regional ambitions in Iraq, Syria and Lebanon, in which Syria constituted a bridgehead across which Hizballah could be supported in Lebanon. Saudi Arabia wanted to counter this, and was active in extending the influence of its Wahhabism.[46] The Syrian–Iranian axis had little or nothing to do with religion, but mainly with strategic interests. It was an alliance between a theocratic and a secular regime. It was not a Shi'i alliance, as has sometimes been suggested. And many Iranian Shi'is may not even consider Syrian Alawis as Twelver Shi'is like themselves. As was mentioned above, this also applies to some of the Syrian Alawi Shaykhs, who consider Alawis to be different in religion from the Iranian Shi'is. The link between Syria and Hizballah was strategic as well, and had little to do with religion. Each party had its own motives.

Russia wanted to prevent the emergence of an Islamist state on its southern flank.

## WHO WANTS AN ALAWI STATE?

During the Syrian War, various kinds of speculations have come up suggesting that the Alawis would like to have their own state or autonomous region, once the Alawi-dominated Ba'thist regime falls, and revenge killings against Alawis would take place on a large scale, within the context of a sectarian war, with Alawis and Sunnis as the main opponents.

There have been suggestions from the anti-regime side that Alawis should be given certain assurances for their future so as to prevent a further sectarian polarisation, and to induce them to distantiate themselves from the regime. But the big question remained whether or not such assurances could be trusted, and by whom such so-called guarantees could be made, particularly as long as the sectarian-tinted Syrian War was going on.

Peter Harling and Robert Malley have argued in July 2011 that

> [t]he Assad regime is counting on a sectarian survival instinct, confident that Alawite troops – however under-paid and overworked – will fight to the bitter end. The

majority will find it hard to do so. After enough mindless violence, the instincts on which the regime has banked could push its forces the other way. Having endured centuries of discrimination and persecution [47] from the Sunni majority, Alawites see their villages, within relatively inaccessible mountainous areas, as the only genuine sanctuary. That is where security officers already have sent their families. They are unlikely to believe that they will be safe in the capital (where they feel like transient guests), protected by the Assad regime (which they view as a historical anomaly) or state institutions (which they do not trust). When they feel the end is near, Alawites won't fight to the last man in the capital. They will go home.[48]

It should be added that it may indeed be true that many original Damascenes do (or want to) consider Alawi people as 'transient guests'. But I do not think that Alawis who were born in Damascus, and spent their whole lives there, share those feelings. On the contrary, many Alawis are already there as part of a second, or even third, generation. To them, Damascus has become their 'home'. For them, therefore, they would not go 'home' or 'return' to the mountains, because they never lived there. This does not mean that they might, during a certain stage, not feel safer in 'the mountains'. What complicates things is that very many rural people have become urbanised, or even Damascenes, for instance, as has happened on so many earlier occasions in history, be they Sunnis, Alawis, Druzes, Christians, Isma'ilis or others. How many inhabitants of Damascus are really Damascenes when taking their ancestors into account?

President Bashar al-Asad was born in Damascus, and spent most of his life there. But he may be buried one day in al-Qardahah (the birthplace of his late father Hafiz al-Asad) out of tradition. Bashar al-Asad's perception of himself will most probably differ from what original Damascene people think about him.[49] All these factors have severely complicated the sectarian-tinted war, because various ethnic and sectarian groups have geographically strongly intermingled, all over Syria. There are even some strategically located, predominantly Alawi military-dominated quarters in and around Damascus that could serve to protect the regime, including Dahiyat al-Asad (the 'al-Asad Suburb').[50] Alawi majority quarters have also come up around other Syrian cities, like Homs or Hama.

In the theoretical case that the Alawis were to flee in great numbers to the 'Alawi Mountains', this would be as part of large-scale ethnic cleansing operations and migration movements, not just of Alawis, but of other communities as well, drastically changing the distribution of the Syrian population. In my view the internal migration of people from all over Syria has taken place on such a large scale and over such a long period of time that it cannot be fully undone, and therefore has reached a point of no return.[51] Moreover, large-scale ethnic cleansing operations and forced migration movements would bring a solution to the conflict further from reach than ever. Nevertheless, terrible developments such as these cannot be fully excluded.

Many would expect the Alawi region to have economically profited because of the fact that so many Alawis occupy important positions in Syria. The reality is different, however, because the Alawi mountain regions have in general been quite neglected and remain relatively poor. This is not in line with the idea that the Alawis would one day like to have a state in their regions of origin.

Fabrice Balanche has argued that the *potential* for a separation of the Alawi region from Syria is well founded. Balanche sees evidence of such a potential development in both the transport infrastructure and the presence of certain military bases in the Alawi region. He interprets these as having strategic importance for the defence of the Alawi territories within the Syrian internal context.[52]

It should also be concluded that there is no serious danger of territorial fragmentation of Syria, at least if it were really up to its inhabitants themselves to decide. Nobody, or hardly anyone, would want it. The Alawis do not want it, the Druzes do not want it, the Isma'ilis do not want it, the Christians do not want it, and the Sunnis do not want it. It is more that some communities suspect other communities of wanting it. Among the Syrian Kurds there are those who would like to have a kind of regional *administrative* autonomy, albeit for the time being within the framework of a unitarian Syrian state. The Kurdish Democratic Union Party (PYD – Partiya Yekîtiya Demokrat) is an exception, wanting a kind of *political*, not only an administrative, autonomy.

And Israel may want it, as it would fit better in its vision of a Middle East divided into entities based on ethnic and/or sectarian identities, in which Israel as a Jewish state might, in the opinion of various Israelis, be better accommodated.[53]

The Syrian identity has become well embedded today, irrespective of half a century of Arab nationalist Ba'thist indoctrination claiming that the Arab national identity should be considered as an identity of supreme importance, being of a higher order than the Syrian identity.

John McHugo has observed that few Western commentators want to sound as if they are advocating the redrawing of the map of the region,

> yet just raising the possibility can almost make it sound like something inevitable … This is an outbreak of the old Western disease of drawing pretty lines on maps and then expecting the people of Greater Syria to step neatly into the zones marked with the

particular colour chosen for them. Things do not work like that.[54]

There were some Alawi leaders who in 1936 reportedly signed a petition addressed to the French, stating that they wanted to continue the separate entity of the predominantly Alawi region under the French Mandate: L'État des Alaouites ('The State of the Alawis'), later called Gouvernement de Lattaquié, that had already existed for 14 years since 1922. The petition, supposedly signed by only six persons, including the grandfather of Hafiz al-Asad (Sulayman Asad), has often been (mis)used by opponents of the Syrian regime to discredit the present-day al-Asad family, even though it was more than 80 years ago, and Hafiz al-Asad himself was a fervent Arab nationalist, whereas his father was explicitly against a separate Alawi state.

Even the French invoked this 'separatist' petition when Syrian Permanent Representative Bashar al-Ja'fari in 2012 gave a negative portrayal of French Mandatory rule before the United Nations. His French counterpart, on behalf of Foreign Minister Laurent Fabius, used the petition as an argument to say that President Bashar al-Asad's [great-]grandfather had had a pro-French position.

Another document, which is generally ignored, is a 'unionist' petition that was signed by some 86 Alawi notables, including 'Ali Sulayman al-Asad, the father of later President Hafiz al-Asad, who wanted the Alawi region to be incorporated in a greater Syrian state. These Alawi notables were strongly against any separate region for the Alawis. Opponents of the regime obviously do not refer to this document, because it would confirm the 'unionist' credentials of the al-Asad family for at least three generations.

And when scrutinising the first mentioned 'separatist' document, it turns out that it is most likely a falsification.[55] But even if the 'fake petition' turned out to be genuine, one might pose the question: 'so what?' One's present-day political views are not determined or (de)legitimised by what one's father, grandfather or great-grandfather (or for that matter whatever family member or relative) may or may not have said on a certain day.

According to a poll conducted by The Day After Association in 2016 about the opinion of Syrians on decentralisation, Alawis turned out to be among the strongest opponents of this idea, implying that they were against the formation of an Alawi state or a separate predominantly Alawi region. Respondents from all religious minorities overwhelmingly opposed the Democratic Self-Administration except for Isma'ilis. Alawis constituted the group of respondents who opposed it the most (70.5%).

The most cited reason for rejecting self-administration in regime and opposition-controlled areas was the 'fear of partition'.[56] In 2016, the circumstances and context were completely different from those in 1936, if only because of the Syrian War. Whether justified or not, this time the idea of partition could be associated with the dark picture of ethnic cleansing, and was, therefore, seen as something very negative by Alawis and others (even though the half a million Alawi residents of Damascus could have profited from 'Democratic Self-Administration').

But decentralisation would also imply the Alawi-dominated regime losing control over the whole of the country. Alawis in general may have perceived this as a danger to their community – something that could also lead to the loss of the privileged positions of many Alawis.

**3**

# CONFRONTATION BETWEEN THE MILITARY OF THE REGIME AND THE OPPOSITION

## THE MILITARY OPPOSITION

Within two months of the start of the peaceful demonstrations in 2011, the Syrian army and security forces started to suffer from defections.[1] Some military and security forces reportedly fled after refusing to shoot at demonstrators. Some of those who refused orders were shot.[2] Some defectors fled abroad, the most prominent among them being General Manaf Talas of the Republican Guard, in 2012. He played no further role thereafter, but his departure was taken very seriously by the regime, because he had been so close to Bashar al-Asad. There were very few Alawi military who defected for fear of severe repercussions for their families. One of the exceptions was female Alawi Colonel Zubaydah al-Maqiti from the Golan, who defected in October 2012.[3] There was a very little-known small Alawi military opposition group called Harakat Ahrar al-ʿAlawiyin ('Movement of the Free Alawis'), reportedly active in the regions of Latakia and Tartus for some time, but they apparently decreased or stopped their activities.[4]

In general, not much Alawi dissension was visible, however, although several prominent opposition personalities were

Alawis, and were clearly visible in the civilian opposition both outside the country (like Mundhir Makhus, and others), and inside Syria (like Lu'ayy Husayn, 'Arif Dalilah and others).

Most military defectors stayed inside Syria and at first started to regroup under a loose umbrella organisation called the Free Officers' Movement. In July 2011, they officially announced the formation of the Free Syrian Army (FSA). The FSA developed into one of the most well-known military opposition organisations, but did not become the most powerful nor the most effective one. Western countries recognised the FSA as a moderate – and initially also secular – organisation with which they were prepared to cooperate against the regime, and at a later stage against the Islamic State. The FSA leadership resided in southern Turkey, not inside Syria itself, which turned out to be a weak point, as far as both efficiency and legitimacy were concerned. The FSA depended to a great extent on the help of various supporting countries that themselves did not, however, effectively coordinate their military support, and did not always provide the FSA with the military supplies necessary to be able to capably defend themselves, let alone to defeat the regime. FSA lack of unity or fragmentation had therefore to a certain extent its origins in the lack of coordination and cooperation between the supporting countries themselves.

Had the United States and other Western countries given more support to the FSA in the earlier stages of its existence, the chances might have been better for it to develop into a more important military actor.[5]

Various donor countries gave priority to what they considered to be their regional interests and policies over ending the conflict. Numerous military groups were operating under the umbrella of the FSA, but its organisational structure and capabilities remained relatively weak. Attempts to establish and operationalise a Supreme Military Council, provincial military councils and a ministry of defence within the Syrian Interim Government in exile in Gaziantep did not really contribute to success on the ground inside Syria.[6] The Syrian Interim Government wanted all funds and aid to be channelled through its own institutions, but donors were generally hesitant, and preferred to provide aid directly to the groups involved. This in turn undermined the legitimacy of the Syrian Interim Government.

Military command centres were established in both southern Turkey and Jordan, to channel military support to armed opposition groups in northern and southern Syria respectively. In Turkey, it was the MOM (Müşterek Operasyon Merkezi – Turkish for Joint Operations Centre) and in Jordan (Amman) the Military Operations Center (MOC). The various members of the MOC and MOM (including Turkey and Jordan as host countries, the United States, Saudi Arabia, Qatar, the United Arab Emirates, Great Britain, France and others) channelled their respective military aid to various opposition groups, but there was no clear overall coordination among them which could have helped strengthen the involved military opposition groups as a whole. Each country acted more or less independently from the others and followed its own priorities. This lack of concerted action not only contributed to a proliferation of insurgent factions, but also to the FSA's incapacity to present a genuine threat to the Syrian regime.[7] Western criticism of the military opposition, concerning a lack of coordination, was therefore unjustified insofar as this was a result of a lack of Western military coordination.

Thomas Pierret, on the other hand, has concluded that 'whatever financial resources state sponsors pour into their insurgent partners, they cannot make a rebel faction successful when its leadership is dysfunctional, nor can they lastingly impose unity on rebel groups against their inherent centripetal dynamics.'[8]

Patrick Cockburn has noted that, according to one of his informants, meetings of the FSA Military Council were invariably attended by representatives of Saudi Arabian, UAE, Jordanian and Qatari intelligence services, as well as intelligence officers from the United States, Great Britain and France:

> At one such meeting the Saudi Deputy Defence Minister, Prince Salman bin Sultan addressed them all and asked Syrian leaders of the armed opposition 'who have plans to attack Assad positions to present their need for arms, ammo and money'.

According to Cockburn, one gets the impression 'of a movement wholly controlled by Arab and Western intelligence agencies'.[9]

Donor countries (like the United States and Turkey) sometimes simultaneously gave contradictory instructions to Syrian military commanders in battles with the Islamic State, threatening to stop their military aid if their instructions were not followed up. Syrian commanders also complained about the lack of relevant military intelligence, which could have been provided in time by their foreign supporters, and about lack of sufficient ammunition (which they occasionally described as a kind of 'drip-feeding'). Opposition commanders sometimes felt betrayed.

Also important were the salaries paid to the opposition military involved. Some FSA soldiers went over to Jabhat al-Nusrah or the Islamic State, simply because they received better pay, which they needed to maintain their families.[10]

The influence of 'state backers' in southern Syria was smaller than in the north because of the stringent border controls by the Jordanian authorities. Next to the MOM and MOC, illegal private finance channels played a role, mainly originating in Saudi Arabia, Qatar, Kuwait and other Arab Gulf states.

As well as the FSA, other insurgent movements started to emerge. Among the most important military opposition organisations next to the FSA, with more effective organisational structures, were: Islamist organisations like Ahrar al-Sham and Jaysh al-Islam; the Jihadist Jabhat al-Nusrah (linked to al-Qa'idah and al-Qa'idah Iraq); and the Kurdish YPG (Yekîneyên Parastina Gel or People's Protection Units). The Islamist organisations tended to be better organised and enjoyed more sustained and reliable sources of support from outside than did the FSA, in particular from Qatar. Turkey and Jordan influenced the way in which certain groups could obtain more support than others, because of their control over the borders.

In April 2013, another powerful group emerged in Syria under the name of the Islamic State in Iraq and the Levant (ISIS) (al-Dawlah al-Islamiyah fi al-'Iraq wa al-Sham). Since 2006, it had already been active in Iraq under the name of the Islamic State in Iraq (ISI). It attracted many foreign Jihadists. In July 2014, it gave itself the shorter name of the Islamic State (IS), implying a much wider framework, supposed to be for all Muslims without geographic limitation. Al-Raqqah was declared to be its capital. Its (Iraqi) leader Abu Bakr al-Baghdadi proclaimed himself as the new Caliph. He announced the incorporation of Jabhat al-Nusrah into IS (with which organisational links had originally existed via al-Qa'idah in Iraq), without informing it beforehand. Jabhat al-Nusrah refused, however, and in 2014 both organisations effectively declared war on one another.[11]

ISIS, and later IS, was given by outsiders the name of Da'ish, which is meant to be derogatory (and strongly disliked by IS), although it is no more than the acronym of the Arabic name for ISIS.[12] The word *Da'ish* was previously unknown in Arabic but can be associated with the verb *Da'asa*, which means 'to trample down'.

IS became infamous for its excessive use of horrifying violence and executions. Minorities, like the Alawis, Druzes and Yazidis, were considered as infidels and heretics whom it was permitted to kill on religious grounds. The fourteenth-century Hanbali jurist Ibn Taymiyah was quoted by radical Islamists as having issued a fatwa saying that it was considered legitimate to kill Alawis. The fatwa concerned had also been used before by the Muslim Brotherhood Mujahidin as a 'justification' for assassinating Alawis in the late 1970s and early 1980s. That Ibn Taymiyah's fatwas were not all that clear about the Alawis (and that he appeared to be not that well informed about Alawis, if only because he confused Alawis with Isma'ilis) was not important to those who used him as a justification.[13] Their perception of it was more important than historic reality and precision.

IS submitted Christians and others to severe rules that were supposed to be fundamentally Islamic, and Sunni Muslims were forced to follow the harsh practices as prescribed by IS. In education at schools in areas under IS control, children were exposed to intensive indoctrination according to the IS curriculum, which, in itself, could have a profound long-term effect. IS challenged the legitimacy of al-Qa'idah as the leading authority within the global Jihad by presenting itself as its rightful replacement.[14]

IS was considered a threat to Western countries because of terrorist attacks in the West. As a result, Western countries shifted their priorities and started to focus more on battles against IS than on the fight against the al-Asad regime. Several Syrian military opposition groups were requested to shift their policies accordingly, but for many the fight against the Syrian regime was at least as important, if not more, than the fight against IS.

Some argued that without al-Asad's regime there would not have been any IS in Syria, but IS emanated from Iraq and al-Qa'idah after the fall of President Saddam Hussein (following the US–British occupation of Iraq in 2003), and would probably also have tried to expand into Syria without al-Asad. The Syrian War made it easier for IS, however, to penetrate the country. Those who wanted the struggle against al-Asad to be given priority also argued that the numbers of victims caused by IS was much lower than those caused by the al-Asad regime. But the lower death toll of IS should not be confused with lower degrees of brutality, because IS committed extreme human rights violations, including mass executions, regularly filmed beheadings and public executions. According to the Syrian Network for Human Rights, the al-Asad regime was considered to be responsible for about 90 per cent of all civilian casualties in the Syrian War.[15]

Christopher Phillips has noted that IS had 'many parents', and that if the Asad regime bore responsibility for IS, so did his many international enemies. 'Through a mixture of bungling, short-termism, indirect and intentional policies, the west, Turkey, Qatar and Saudi Arabia all played a role.' IS would not have had a chance if the Iraqi regime of President Saddam Hussein had not been toppled after the US–British invasion in 2003. Because of the relatively premature US military withdrawal from Iraq in 2011 a weak and unprepared Iraqi army was left behind, that could be easily overrun by IS in Mosul in 2014, enabling them to capture huge amounts of weapons. Because of the empowerment of a Shi'i, sectarian-dominated, government in Baghdad, the Sunni population was put at a disadvantage, creating fertile ground for IS. Turkey's open border enabled foreign fighters drawn to IS to pass into Syria relatively easy. The Syrian regime initially saw advantages in the rise of IS as a counterweight to other enemies.[16] Concerning the role of Saudi Arabia, IS ideology draws heavily on Saudi Wahhabism, forming a link between decades of Saudi-funded religious propaganda and the appeal of radicalism in the Muslim world.[17]

In some cases the United States started military training programmes for the Syrian opposition that were intended exclusively to fight IS. The so-called Train & Equip Programme was an example. Syrian opposition military who took part in it were requested to commit themselves exclusively to the fight against IS.

Weapons provided to them were not allowed to be used in battles against the regime. As a result, the Train & Equip Programme utterly failed. The Syrian military opposition wanted to decide on its own priorities instead of having them prescribed by foreign powers.

In 2015, at least 150,000 insurgents with as many as 1,500 organisationally distinct armed groups were reportedly involved in different levels of fighting across Syria, some under broader umbrellas and fronts and others existing entirely independently.[18] As a result it was obvious that Syria could not be geographically divided schematically into territories with clear military frontlines.[19]

Thomas van Linge published a diagram in 2016, titled *The Syrian Rebellion*,[20] in which he schematically divides the military opposition groups into '*Rebels*', including the Free Syrian Army and many others; '*Islamist rebels*', including Ahrar al-Sham and Jaysh al-Islam; '*Jihadists*', including Jabhat al-Nusrah; and finally '*Rojava*'[21] in the mainly Kurdish region in the north, including the Kurdish YPG and other organisations fighting in this region under the umbrella of the 'Syrian Democratic Forces'.

Some of the 'rebel', 'Islamist rebel' and 'Jihadist' organisations cooperated under the umbrella of 'Jaysh al-Fath', mainly in Idlib Province; others cooperated under the umbrella of 'Fath Halab', mainly in the Aleppo region. Some of these organisations were active in both Jaysh al-Fath and Fath Halab, like Ahrar al-Sham, whereas some of the Jihadist organisations, like Jabhat al-Nusrah, were only active in Jaysh al-Fath.

The cooperation of Jihadists like Jabhat al-Nusrah with moderate forces like the Free Syrian Army under the same umbrella, was criticised by Western countries, because they considered Jabhat al-Nusrah to be a terrorist organisation because of its links with al-Qa'idah. In July 2016, Jabhat al-Nusrah's leader Abu Muhammad al-Jawlani officially declared that his organisation had no longer any 'affiliation to any external or foreign entity', and from then on continued under the name of 'Jabhat Fath al-Sham' ('The Front for Conquering al-Sham or Greater Syria – the Levant'). He kept praising the al-Qa'idah leadership, however, and did not say explicitly that his relations with al-Qa'idah had been broken off. Whatever the case, Western countries kept considering al-Jawlani's group as a terrorist organisation, as it was before, whatever its name.

The military opposition groups sometimes operated in the same region, and sometimes felt obliged to cooperate for practical reasons under the same umbrella, temporarily or in the longer term, irrespective of ideological differences. This occasionally affected the willingness of Western countries to offer military support to the relevant groups, particularly if more moderate groups fought alongside and coordinated closely with Jabhat al-Nusrah. But for the military, including the FSA, the realities on the ground were decisive. For them it could be a battle for life and death, in which they did not have the luxury to critically draw sharp lines, according to ideological and organisational criteria. From the perspective of a member of the opposition this was clearly explained as follows: 'You are left alone dying and somebody offers you a hand – would you refuse it in order to please the ones who left you alone?'[22]

Due to lack of sufficient Western aid to the more moderate military opposition, the Jihadists were indirectly given the space to emerge as the dominant players in Syria. Charles Lister has made the sombre prediction in this respect in 2015 that

> Syria will continue to represent the centre of the world for Jihadist militancy for many years to come, and the consequences for such policy shortsightedness will not only fall upon Syria and Syrians, but will affect the world at large.[23]

## THE MILITARY FORCES OF THE REGIME

Various scenarios have been suggested about what might have happened in Syria after the start of the Syrian Revolution. One of the theoretical options was a military coup from within by Alawi officers, who were very critical of the regime's behaviour, in cooperation with dissident military from other communities. It would have been extremely risky, however, because of the enormous dangers involved. Anyone even contemplating such an idea and sharing it with others would seriously run the risk of immediate execution. And the Syrian regime already had decades of experience in how to prevent a military coup. Whatever the case, the regime's hard core stayed tightly together.[24]

Hicham Bou Nassif has made a study of the discontent of defected Sunni army officers who complained about the preferential treatment received by their Alawi colleagues. They expressed their deep resentment of what they perceived to be systematic anti-Sunni discrimination in the military institutions, making a prominent military career for them very difficult, if not impossible. The interviewed officers maintained that

Sunni officers suffered from more discrimination in the military under Bashar al-Asad than under his father. The officers maintain that Hafiz al-Asad's grip over his generals was stronger than Bashar's. Whereas Hafiz al-Asad was able to rein in the military elite in order to keep at least a veneer of inclusiveness in the Syrian officer corps, Bashar was not able to do so. The regime became more decentralized under Bashar, with several powerful military barons jockeying for power and competing to place their Alawi followers throughout the different sectors of the armed forces. Consequently, Sunnis' share of prominent appointments in the military shrunk even more over the last decade.[25]

Bou Nassif provides detailed tables of military commanders by sectarian affiliation in which he demonstrates that under the rule of Bashar al-Asad until the eve of the Syrian Revolution (2000–11), by far most have been Alawis. This, in itself, is not surprising, as the Alawi officers' component had almost continuously grown for almost half a century, but the way it has been documented provides new detailed precision to this issue. All directors of Syrian intelligence agencies in charge of controlling the armed forces were Alawis, just like all the commanders of the Republican Guard, of the 4th Armoured Division, and all subcommanders of the Special Forces.[26] Statistically, 86 per cent of the involved officers were Alawi and only 14 per cent Sunni.

Since the early 1980s, Alawis have, according to Bou Nassif's study, made up 80–85 per cent of every new cohort graduating from the Military Academy.[27]

If there were ever to be a political solution to the Syria conflict, it would be inevitable to bring the over-representation of Alawis in the armed forces to some more 'normal' proportions (not necessarily an exact reflection of their numbers in Syrian society, but something closer to it).

Almost all of Bou Nassif's 24 interviewed officers agreed that the combat preparedness of the Syrian armed forces had been in steady decline, at least since the early 1990s, and that it reached abysmal lows on the eve of the 2011 uprisings. 'The neglect of the armed forces was made even more problematic in light of the preferential treatment lavished on the all-Alawi special combat units.' Other officers stressed that 'the Republican Guard and the 4th Armoured Division are in charge of the regime's security, whereas national defence per se is incumbent on the armed forces at large'. They noted that the '"All in the family" tactics did not change when Hafiz al-Asad passed away'. The non-exhaustive list of family members appointed in senior positions under Bashar al-Asad included his brother Mahir, the de facto commander of the 4th Armoured Division; his cousin, Dhu al-Himmah Shalish, in charge of units responsible for the safety of the president and his family; another cousin, Hafiz Makhluf, who headed unit 251 in the General Intelligence and was widely considered to be the real commander of that service; yet another cousin, Hilal al-Asad, who was commander of the Military Police in the 4th Armoured Division; and al-Asad's brother-in-law, Asif Shawkat, the strong man in the intelligence apparatus until his death in 2012.[28]

Any suspected dissidence from the regime was severely punished, and several prominent members of the regime died under suspicious circumstances, including General Ghazi Kan'an, Minister of Interior and former Head of Security of the Syrian troops in Lebanon (1982–2002) and Head of Political Security in Syria, who reportedly committed suicide under doubtful circumstances in October 2005.[29] General Mustafa Ghazalah [Head of Syria's Political Security Directorate (Sunni)], who died on 24 April 2015, after having been hospitalised with severe injuries, also died under suspicious circumstances.[30]

On 18 July 2012, a bomb blast at the National Security Office killed its director, Lieutenant General Hisham Ikhtiyar, in addition to Bashar al-Asad's brother-in-law, then deputy Defence Minister General Asif Shawkat, as well as the Defence Minister General Dawud Rajihah, and Rajihah's predecessor, General Hasan Turkmani. The attack was claimed by opposition forces, but this appeared to be doubtful at the time, if only because it was almost impossible for any force to penetrate so deeply into the heart of the regime. It was later reported to have been a paid inside job.[31]

As Aron Lund has described, the Syrian regime under Bashar al-Asad remained as secretive as that of his father: 'an impenetrable black box of family, clan, business, and intelligence elites', virtually impenetrable to outsiders within Syria, let alone from outside Syria.[32] Although it was a severe blow, the core of the regime was not really shaken, and the regime simply rearranged some of its most senior officers.

According to some estimates, the Syrian army had about 220,000 soldiers in 2011, of whom the regime had only been able to rely on approximately 65,000 troops.[33] In battles with the military opposition the regime preferred to use the units it considered to be the most reliable. Almost by definition these had a high proportion of Alawis, as a result of which the death rates among Alawi military were also relatively high. This was a very sensitive issue for the regime, because of the high number of funerals in the Alawi villages, which must have had profound social consequences.

On 26 July 2015 President al-Asad, in a public speech for the first time, admitted to a shortage of soldiers and military setbacks. The power balance threatened to turn to his disadvantage, and in September 2015 Russia started to intervene militarily on his behalf on a large scale, changing the situation in the regime's favour. Military forces from Iran and Hizballah had already had a lengthy and strong military presence inside Syria in support of Damascus. The repeated claim of the opposition that without all this outside help the regime would already long have collapsed before is probably an exaggeration, but the regime was clearly in a difficult position as far as manpower was concerned. Offensive operations of the Syrian army were, after the beginning of the Russian intervention of 2015, generally supported by Russian warplanes and helicopters. Troops from Iran and Hizballah also played an important supportive, and sometimes even leading, role in offensives.

Being a conscript army, the Syrian armed forces are, by composition and to a great extent, a reflection of Syrian society
where its soldiers are concerned, and therefore Sunni by majority. Many Sunni military defected, even though the regime had
made defection very dangerous, not only because defectors
were shot when discovered, but also because their relatives
came under serious threat, and had to bear the consequences.
The defection of Sunni officers reflected their alienation from
the regime, combined with their refusal to slaughter civilians –
mostly fellow Sunnis. In effect, defection remained mainly a
Sunni phenomenon.[34]

There was no strong coordination among the military
opposition forces, and numerous parallel battles were fought
simultaneously in the most diverse regions of Syria. It was not
a relatively simple and clear frontline of less than a hundred
kilometres like, for instance, in the Golan Heights – there was
a multitude of fronts all over the country, with altogether enormous distances for which the Syrian regular army was not well
prepared.

Various well-equipped Special Forces of the Syrian army
played an important supplementary role in suppressing military
opposition activities in various regions, notably the Tiger Forces
(Quwwat al-Nimr), under the command of the prominent
Alawi General Suhayl Hasan, who was popular in his own
circles.[35] They were trained to be an offensive unit, able to swiftly
intervene in battles all over Syria. Almost as important were the
Desert Hawks (Suqur al-Sahra'), led by General Muhammad
Jabir, trained in ambush tactics, and employed in special
assignments on several fronts elsewhere. Next to belonging to
the regime's most important offensive formations, the two organisations were considered to be bitter rivals, as a result of which
they did not share fronts. Moreover, they were considered to be
corrupt, defending their own interests and not always those of

the regime. The Desert Hawks were notorious for their smuggling in the oil sector.[36]

As the regime's army and security forces were not sufficiently effective to defeat the opposition forces on their own, use was being made of additional support in the form of militia-like Popular Committees and the new National Defence Forces, in 2013 believed to be 50,000–60,000 strong.[37] Irregular units like the Shabbihah were involved as well. These units and groups were active in villages, towns and cities to fight opposition forces.[38] At first they helped the regime to better survive, but later they simultaneously also undermined it because of their corrupt and independent behaviour. Many of its members in the course of time started to disregard instructions from the central military command, and operated more and more independently in their own regions of action. They started to build up their power bases like warlords, earning money from extortion and other activities like smuggling and kidnapping.

After several years of war, many sources of income had been lost and many sought a form of economic substitution and compensation to survive. With public wages barely enough to feed the conscripts themselves, al-Asad's men, according to defence policy analyst Tobias Schneider, started feeding off the land and the civilian population, as a result of which a larger part of loyalist fighting formations no longer fully relied on the regime for the majority of their income.

Sometimes there were clashes between the regime and these organisations, as well as with some of the Special Forces of the army that were supposed to be loyal, but were not always so when it came to their personal and economic interests. As an important side effect of the prolonged war and the deteriorating economic situation, corruption increased correspondingly. As a result, the central authority of the regime started to be undermined to some extent by its own original supporters.

Tobias Schneider in August 2016 gave one of the bleakest descriptions of the situation on the ground by concluding that the 'decay of the Syrian regime was much worse than generally thought':

> Over the past three years, despite foreign military aid and support, the regime under Assad has continued to atrophy at an ever increasing pace. If these trends continue, the Syrian president will soon find himself little more than a primus inter pares, a symbolic common denominator around which a loose coalition of thieves and fiefdoms can rally. Thus, with the slow decay of the once powerful state, military, and party establishment, the person of Bashar al-Assad himself has increasingly come to embody the last remaining pillar not of a state but of 'the regime' and its brutal war against its own citizens …
>
> Indeed, after five years of war, the regime's force structure today is not entirely different from that of opposition militias. While much better supplied by the Syria Arab Army's still-standing logistics skeleton, the government's fighting force today consists of a dizzying array of hyperlocal militias aligned with various factions, domestic and foreign sponsors, and local warlords …
>
> Today, where briefing maps now show solid red across Syria's western governorates, they ought to distinguish dozens and perhaps even hundreds of small fiefdoms only nominally loyal to Assad. Indeed, in much of the country, loyalist security forces function like a grand racketeering scheme: simultaneously a cause and consequence of state collapse at the local level.[39]

The extent to which the regime was still firmly in control or severely undermined as a result of the prolonged war situation was still a matter of controversy and debate at the time. Opponents of the regime were inclined to give the impression that the regime was weaker than it was in reality, whereas the regime did the opposite and wanted to give the impression that it was stronger than it really was (which is normal in military propaganda warfare).

Whatever the case, the Syrian regime, with the help of its military supporters (both foreign and domestic), turned out to be strong enough to gain the upper hand and retake the city of Aleppo in December 2016. This was an important turning point in the war in Syria, to the advantage of the regime.

According to Cody Roche, it was clear that Syrian loyalist militias were playing an increasingly large role in fighting for the al-Asad regime, and that the 'militiafication' of loyalist Syrian forces strongly increased in number, size and strength from 2015 through 2016. The main intertwined reasons for this were, according to Roche, the 'degradation and exhaustion' of the Syrian Arab Army, the financial difficulties of the regime and the dire economic situation in Syria generally. The latter factor contributed strongly to making the numerous local private militia more attractive for men who urgently needed to feed their families. Being local (and the Syrian conflict was extremely localised on all sides) meant that they could stay close to their families. Moreover, they could profit from the amnesty offered by the regime to draft dodgers.

Roche disputes the view that the Syrian Arab Army 'barely exists any longer', with the fight being in the hands of the various foreign militias and military forces that have joined the fighting on the regime's behalf. Nevertheless, the importance of these forces should, according to Roche, not be ignored: foreign forces have indeed played key roles for the regime, including taking the lead in several important offensives. The Syrian Arab Army continues to exist, however, albeit as a 'much diminished shell of itself, mustering less than half the manpower of the pre-Civil War figure'.[40]

On the side of the 1,500 or more opposition groups there was a similar phenomenon of warlords going after their own interests, which did not necessarily coincide with the interests of the Syrian Revolution against the regime.

The Syrian War was not a conventional war between two or more regular armies. In the beginning, it was a violent confrontation with the regular Syrian armed forces on the one hand, assisted by the security forces, and their adversaries on the other. These at first were mainly peaceful civilians, but they were gradually flanked more and more by armed groups who became more powerful thanks to support from abroad. Among the military opposition forces the Islamists and Jihadists gradually gained dominance, as a result of which Islamism developed into a strong dimension among the opposition. The Jihadi opposition was by definition radical Sunni sectarian and anti-Alawi.

During the battle for Aleppo in August 2016, Jabhat Fath al-Sham even named its military attack on the Aleppo Artillery Academy, close to al-Ramusah to the south of Aleppo, after Captain Ibrahim Yusuf (Ghazwat al-Shahid Ibrahim al-Yusuf), who in 1979 had been responsible for the massacre of Alawi cadets there. It was a clear message that the Jihadists intended to eliminate in particular the Alawi forces of the regime. In addition, three battalions were formed by Islamist radicals, named after the main perpetrators of the Aleppo Artillery massacre, notably the battalions of Ibrahim al-Yusuf, 'Adnan 'Uqlah and Husni 'Abu, who had all been killed within a year following the Aleppo massacre.[41]

Earlier, the leader of Jabhat al-Nusrah, al-Jawlani, had declared that he would 'protect those Alawis who would give themselves up on their own initiative, distantiated themselves from the regime, and would express their regret for their idol-atry (*shirk*) and would return to Islam'.[42] Alawis therefore had to give up their religion in order to be accepted. It was obvious that not one Alawi followed his advice, and that they would not have trusted al-Jawlani. Jabhat al-Nusrah wanted to impose the Shari'ah on all areas conquered by them.

It should be stressed that all this did not mean that other mil-itary opposition groups were also similarly sectarian inclined. Many of them were not, but they were not the dominant forces.

After the severe defeat of the military opposition groups in Aleppo, Jabhat Fath al-Sham (ex-Nusrah) initiated a new umbrella organisation in January 2017 under the name of Hay'at Tahrir al-Sham (HTS – 'Council for the Liberation of al-Sham'). The aim of HTS was to incorporate as many Jihadist and Islamist military opposition groups as possible, prefer-ably in the form of a merger, so as to regain a stronger posi-tion vis-à-vis the regime. Ahrar al-Sham refused to join HTS, and formed its own alternative umbrella organisation under its original name. A considerable number of experienced Ahrar al-Sham fighters defected to HTS, however, weakening their mother organisation. Both Ahrar al-Sham and HTS succeeded in incorporating a number of other military groups (most of them relatively small, and sometimes only parts of them), but their mutual rivalry also diminished their military potential, with HTS gaining a stronger position than Ahrar al-Sham at the time. Infighting among Jihadist, Islamist and FSA factions undermined the position of the military opposition groups as a whole. The Jihadist–Islamist mergers also negatively affected the willingness of Western and regional countries to keep sup-porting the involved groups, in particular because of their per-ceived links with al-Qa'idah via HTS, and the blurring of the lines between radical Jihadists and Islamists. Some – originally moderate – FSA factions went over to HTS and Ahrar al-Sham, reportedly just because they already received insufficient Western and regional support. Disunity among the military opposition groups worked in favour of the Syrian regime. The geographic intermingling of Jihadists, Islamists and FSA factions made it difficult to arrange local ceasefires between the regime and non-Jihadist opposition factions, because of the presence of HTS and other Jihadists amongst them.

## SHIFTING MILITARY ALLIANCES

During the Syrian War, military alliances or rather military 'marriages of convenience' shifted on various occasions, depending on what was considered to be the most advantageous or least harmful at a particular moment for the parties involved. The cooperation between the more moderate military groups and Jabhat al-Nusrah or other radical Jihadi movements has already been referred to. The groups involved had little in common ideologically speaking, but merely cooperated on certain occasions in order to survive or to be able to win. Generally, such forms of cooperation and coordination were only of a temporary nature.

The regime was on various occasions accused of cooperating with IS, or of condoning IS victories, as for instance in the historic desert city of Palmyra in May 2015.

The reality seemed to be more complicated. In the first place, Western allied airforce units might have been able to prevent the capture of Palmyra by IS, if they had attacked their highly visible military columns, exposed in the open desert on their way to the historic city. It is not really known why the Western military allies ignored such a relatively easy military target. One reason might have been that they did not want to be seen as defending the regime. Their aim was to attack and eliminate IS on their own, but not in cooperation with the regime; that was strongly rejected. After various battles, Palmyra was recaptured by the Syrian army with Russian military support.

IS was an enemy for the regime as well, but as long as IS was fighting the military opponents of the regime elsewhere in the country, it was beneficial to the regime because it could save its urgently needed military capacities for fights in other places. Once the military threat of other opposition groups was eliminated, the 'marriage of convenience' with IS would certainly have been over.

On other occasions the regime was accused of threatening not to defend certain towns against IS, like Salamiyah to the east of Hama, and instead condoning its occupation by IS, if the local population refused to provide enough new conscripts for the army. Salamiyah was inhabited by many Isma'ilis and was for some time considered an anti-regime bulwark. As Isma'ilis were considered to be heretics by IS, they ran the risk of being massacred if IS occupied Salamiyah.

The regime was also accused of tacitly cooperating with the YPG, the military arm of the Kurdish PYD, against other opposition forces. In reality the PYD was an enemy of the Syrian regime because of its aim of achieving an autonomous Kurdish status in northern Syria, which had always been anathema to the Ba'th regime, because it wanted a unitarian *Arab* state. In March 2016, the PYD declared the establishment of a federal system of government in the 'Federation of Northern Syria – Rojava'. This initiative was strongly rejected by most other Kurdish parties and, of course, by the regime. Nevertheless, in the case of the Syrian War, the PYD was used by the regime as a military counterbalance against other military opposition groups, including IS.

At first, Turkey did not mind the PYD fighting against the regime or against IS, but when developments turned in favour of the PYD, once it succeeded in conquering bigger parts of northern Syria, the PYD came to be seen in Ankara as an imminent security threat against Turkey.

This was one of the factors that induced Ankara to drastically adapt its Syria policies by the end of 2016, and to be prepared to initiate political cooperation with Russia and Iran to help find an end to the conflict. On 23–24 January 2017, Russia, Turkey and Iran initiated a series of International Meetings on Syria in Astana, Kazakhstan, in an effort to launch talks between the Syrian regime and several armed opposition groups, to try to reach a ceasefire and to contribute to reinvigorating the UN-facilitated political process.[43] Real face-to-face negotiations were not realised, however, and there could not be found any room for compromise. The United States was sidelined this time, and only attended as an observer.

Turkey could play a key role because of its control over military supplies to the armed opposition groups in Syria across the Turkish–Syrian border.

The PYD was considered by Turkey to be the same as the Turkish Kurdistan Workers' Party (Partiya Karkerên Kurdistanê, PKK), which Ankara considered a terrorist organisation. The PYD not only succeeded in controlling a bigger part of the three mainly Kurdish areas in northern Syria, of which were two adjacent areas in the east (Qamishli and Kobani) and one in the west (Afrin), but also wanted to link them up geographically by occupying the border area in between (Kobani-Afrin).[44] This was something Turkey wanted to prevent at all costs because of the negative security effects it could have in the view of Ankara on the Kurdish area inside south-eastern Turkey. At the same time the United States, contrary to the wishes of its ally Turkey, supported the PYD because it was considered an effective force in the war against IS, which was their priority. In the case of the regime succeeding in defeating the other opposition groups in the north, it would certainly no longer condone PYD's self-declared autonomous zone there and would try to eliminate it.

The Syrian regime was also supported by Iraqi Shi'i militias in its fight against the Syrian military opposition, including in the areas of Shi'i holy places.[45] It was another example of strange alliances. Western governments cooperated with the Shi'i-dominated regime in Iraq in its fight against IS, whereas they considered any cooperation with the al-Asad regime against IS a taboo. Nevertheless, the Iraqi regime in turn allowed, or at least condoned, Iraqi Shi'i fighters to fight on the side of al-Asad in his war against the Syrian military opposition groups who were supported by the same Western countries. The Iraqi Shi'i militias were supported by Iran, yet another adversary of Western countries. It was a strange and seemingly contradictory network of alliances, although all these links had their own explanation.

All such alliances were generally meant to be temporary, depending on the military and political priorities of the day, and therefore could better be considered as temporary 'marriages of convenience' that were intended to prevent developments turning from bad to worse for the parties involved.

A big question remained. Which party would take over the territories that were under control of IS, after IS had been defeated: the regime, the military opposition groups like the FSA, PYD, Islamist and Jihadist forces, or others? It all depended on the military balance of power on the ground, and the political consequences could be far-reaching.

# 4

# THE AMBIVALENT WESTERN APPROACH
# TO THE SYRIA CONFLICT

The Western approach to the Syrian uprising was from the very beginning dominated by an overdose of wishful thinking, because precedence was given to supposedly democratic and moralistic ideals over *realpolitik*. Many Western politicians apparently based their positions on their day-to-day domestic political reflexes, rather than on the long-term vision and result-oriented pragmatism that was needed to work towards genuinely helping to solve the conflict. Most Western politicians early on became fixated on the idea that the conflict could only be resolved if President al-Asad was removed from power. Many really thought that the regime would fall within a relatively short time. Some expected al-Asad to have gone by the summer of 2012. The strength of the regime was completely underestimated, partly out of ignorance and lack of knowledge of the Syrian regime, as well as because of misplaced optimism.[1] Those who predicted that there was a realistic chance for the al-Asad regime to survive for a longer time ran the risk of being accused of being pro-Asad,[2] or even of being against democracy. Ideological arguments sometimes prevailed over realistic ones.

Objective reporting about developments in the war in Syria turned out to be a sensitive affair. It became only too easy for academics, journalists or politicians to be labelled or accused of either being pro- or anti-regime. Even the United Nations and its Special Envoys for Syria were from time to time accused of being one-sided after the slightest move that could be interpreted as partial, whether correct or not.

Academics and journalists who, during an earlier stage in the Syrian Revolution, observed that during the bloody events the opposition was not only peaceful but also occasionally used violence and attacked the army and security forces with arms were strongly criticised by the opposition and others, if only because that might give some credibility to the regime's story of its being attacked by so-called 'armed terrorists' and could help shatter the image of the strictly peaceful opposition, a peacefulness which provided the opposition with a strong kind of moral legitimacy.

Another point was that many people had a tendency to mix up so-called objective thinking with wishful thinking. On top of that, at least in the case of present-day Syria, people in the West generally did not want to be seen as providing any analysis that might perhaps be interpreted as being against, or critical, of those courageous Syrians who had good and peaceful intentions and who were opposing the al-Asad dictatorship, but had not yet succeeded in achieving their aims of a more democratic Syria. Criticism of the violent Islamist radicals who started to overshadow the peaceful opponents of the regime was easily interpreted as criticism of the whole opposition, including those who were peaceful.

Western politicians generally had clear thoughts about what they did *not* want, but no realistic or clear ideas of what they wanted in al-Asad's place. They wanted a kind of democracy in Syria, but a violent ousting of al-Asad could not realistically have been expected to result in such a desired peaceful democracy.

Many of the decisions or positions taken by Western countries were too little, too late. Politicians did not always keep up with the realities on the ground and so-called 'politically correct' slogans continued to be used even though the situation on the ground no longer fully justified them. The Syrian opposition that originally had only expressed moderate and modest demands continued to be described as peaceful and democratic, even long after more radical forces, including Islamists and Jihadists, had hijacked its platform and the Syrian War was already well on its way. Subsequently, the concept of peaceful opposition became more of a myth than the reality it was in the beginning.

Sami Moubayed has noted that senior figures of the Syrian opposition were sceptical of Jabhat al-Nusrah when its creation was announced in early 2012, and at the time

> were desperately trying to prove that no Islamists existed in the Syrian rebel community – only secular soldiers who had defected from the Syrian army. If Jabhat al-Nusra was real, then it threatened to do away with all that they had been working for since March 2011.[3]

Inside Syria it was generally the military opposition forces who had taken over, whereas outside Syria various civilian opposition groups were politically active and predominant. For a long time, the civilian opposition outside the country was generally not much respected by these military opposition groups, and neither did the military recognise the opposition groups outside of Syria as representing them. It took several years of struggle before better contacts and political coordination started to emerge between the civil opposition outside Syria and the military inside the country. The Riyadh opposition conference in December 2015 led to substantially better contacts between military and civilian opposition groups.

## THE WEST CREATING FALSE EXPECTATIONS

Most Western countries closed their embassies in Damascus in 2012, intending to send a message of strongest condemnation to al-Asad from the United States, the European Union and other Western countries. The symbolism, however, was probably wasted on the Syrian president, who was unlikely to have lost any sleep over the withdrawal of the Western community. He had other priorities, notably the survival of the regime. The withdrawal of ambassadors certainly did not contribute to helping to find a solution, but rather the opposite. Finding a solution to a serious conflict appears to be more difficult without adequate channels of communication. Isolation generally does not help.

All this does not mean that if Western efforts for dialogue with the Syrian regime had been taken up much more seriously at an early stage, there would have been any guarantee of success. But in 2011, when much less blood had been shed (with first 'only' hundreds of dead, but later hundreds of thousands), a compromise would arguably have been less difficult to reach than it was later. It appears to have been a missed chance, which, given the extremely serious circumstances and therefore heavy responsibilities, should at least have been taken, as a result of which the Western countries involved might have had a 'cleaner political conscience'.

In 2011, I noted that continuing to insist on prosecuting the hard core of the al-Asad regime and having real justice done (before any political solution was achieved) was bound to only further increase its determination to survive. It would also contribute to increasing the possibility of a destructive sectarian war, which would cost many more lives without any certainty at all of achieving a better and more democratic Syria as a result. Of course, as part of day-to-day politics it was easier for

foreign politicians to increase sanctions and to ask for justice to be done. This would give them more popularity in the
short run, but they also carried the co-responsibility for further
bloodshed and all its victims, if they did not at least try to help
find a solution more constructively. The key question remained
at the time: how to end dictatorship so as to help Syria obtain
the better future it deserves, while at the same time saving as
many Syrian lives as possible.[4]

With some hindsight, it might be concluded that serious
dialogue with the al-Asad regime would probably have been to
no avail, similar to the experiences of Turkey, Saudi Arabia, the
Arab League and others. But nothing was ventured and therefore nothing gained.

When arguing that all efforts to convince the regime that a
political solution would have been preferable to a military one
would have been in vain, it might logically have been concluded
that in that case the main alternative would have been to bring
the regime to its knees by militarily defeating it. But the opposition was not supported sufficiently by its allies to help achieve
this, as a result of which the war dragged on with severe bloodshed, and direct foreign military intervention was not seriously
considered either.[5]

With this combination (no sufficient foreign military support
for the opposition, and no foreign direct military intervention)
the Syrian Revolution was doomed to failure, certainly as long as
the regime received sufficient military aid from its allies Russia,
Iran and Hizballah, combined with their direct military interventions in Syria. All this caused the military balance of power
to shift in favour of the regime. For the countries supporting the
Syrian Revolution all of this was no reason, however, to change
their principled policies towards the conflict in Syria.

Richard Haass has noted in this respect that the 'lesson of the
last five and a half years must be taken to heart: those who engage

Syria with limited will and limited means must set limited goals if they are to accomplish even a limited amount of good.'[6]

Yet, even after more than half a decade of bloody war, and well over 400,000 dead, many Western politicians still tended to be blinded by wishful thinking, as a result of which they kept approaching the conflict in Syria from the supposedly moral high ground. They did not want to accept the above-mentioned basic principle, that with a limited will and limited means only limited goals could be achieved. They either ignored these basics or pretended not to be aware of them.

By continuing to maintain so-called ethically and politically correct points of view concerning justice without, however, providing the necessary means to help realise their just aims, various Western and Arab politicians indirectly helped the war to continue with all its victims, refugees and destruction. Many maintained that they wanted to help the Syrian opposition, but in effect their so-called ethical correctness obtained an unethical dimension, by wanting to remain principled. Through not being pragmatic enough to achieve their professed principles, these actors ensured that the bloodshed and multi-dimensional destruction were bound to continue, 'against better judgement'.

A pragmatic attitude, which might have helped achieve a political solution, could have been considered of higher ethical value than political positions that theoretically might have been ethical, but in practice did not achieve much more than a continuation of the bloody war.[7]

In their seemingly unwavering conviction that the opposition would in any case be preferable to al-Asad, many Western countries overlooked the fact that the al-Asad regime was supported by a part of the Syrian population, perhaps some 30 per cent, including a substantial part of the Arabic-speaking minorities (like the Alawis, Christians and Druzes). This support should not be interpreted as the existence of real sympathy for the regime, but rather as the prevalent feeling among many that an alternative regime could be even worse. Many Syrians for the time being preferred to preserve their livelihoods under the existing dictatorship, rather than having their livelihoods, their shops and spare sources of income and belongings (if any) destroyed as a result of the internal war, let alone having themselves and their families killed, or forced to become refugees. Many were just as afraid or uncertain, if not more, of what an opposition victory might bring as they were of the regime's way of ruling in the past.

According to Dr Sami Khiyami, former Syrian ambassador to London, living in exile, the Syrian negotiators in Geneva (2016) of both the regime and the opposition together

> represent at most less than 30% of unconditional supporters among the Syrian people. The vast majority of Syrians unjustly described as grey, is certainly not silent but split into two major groups, the first (expected to be the larger) disapproves the regime but dislikes the opposition (chaos and oppression driven) even more. The second disapproves the opposition but dislikes the regime (corruption and oppression driven) even more.
>
> Needless to say that in the absence of true freedom of political activity and expression and considering the prevailing congested situation, any attempt to conduct elections will lead to a coerced (love–hate) alignment of these two major groups to the respective conventional antagonists, government and opposition. This fact is being used by the two presently negotiating parties to claim questionable popularity and representation.
>
> The obvious strategy is to allow these two major (majority) groups to lead the society to peace by

providing them with a true representation of their popular weight. The negotiating teams currently meeting in Geneva will de facto join the process at a later stage.[8]

Did the Western countries still have options to help solve the conflict?

Western military intervention with 'boots on the ground' seemed to be out of the question. There was no political appetite for it, certainly not when taking into account earlier experiences in, for instance, Afghanistan, Iraq and Libya. When the Syrian regime reportedly used chemical weapons in summer 2013, thereby crossing US President Obama's so-called 'red lines', neither the United States nor the United Kingdom reacted militarily, although it had been suggested they would. This seriously undermined Western credibility and demonstrated that their threats had no teeth. Later, when chemical weapons were reportedly being used again, nothing was done either, except for issuing statements. It was only in April 2017 that the US, under Obama's successor President Trump, reacted with a limited cruise missile attack on a Syrian airbase, shortly after the Syrian regime had reportedly used chemical weapons in an attack on Khan Shaykhun, in Idlib province.

The deal agreed upon in September 2013, to have the chemical weapons arsenal of the Syrian regime removed by mid-2014, meant that the countries that had maintained that al-Asad had lost his 'legitimacy' in fact considered him to be 'legitimate' again for at least the period concerned. At the same time, any Western military intervention seemed to be off the table. Nevertheless, it can be concluded that the deal to remove the chemical weapons arsenal was achieved because of the *threat* of military force. Military strikes themselves might not have achieved it, except perhaps if these had led to the fall of the regime.

The Western countries' declared aim of arming the opposition, thereby strengthening their chances of forcing the regime into political negotiations, or even winning the war, turned out to be rather restricted when it came to reality. When the EU arms embargo against Syria was lifted at the insistence of the United Kingdom and France in 2013, there was – contrary to expectations – no great change as far as arms deliveries to the opposition were concerned. It turned out that there was no political will to really arm any part of the opposition to such an extent that they had a real chance to win the battles against the regime, even where the predominantly secular side was concerned. Questions were raised about which of the many opposition groups should be armed and with what aim, as the Western countries obviously wanted to avoid the possible establishment of an Islamic extremist dictatorship. But was there any guarantee that arms provided to others would not end up in the hands of Islamists and Jihadists? And were the arms really intended to help topple the al-Asad regime? Or was providing arms mainly intended to help the opposition in defending itself? Or mainly to fight IS, Jabhat al-Nusrah and other Jihadist organisations? Was it a humanitarian gesture? No clear US or EU strategy was visible, except that defeating IS had priority. The more radical Islamic groups, like Ahrar al-Sham, al-Jabhat al-Islamiyah (later Jaysh al-Islam), Jabhat al-Nusrah, IS and al-Qa'idah, had in the course of time become stronger than the Free Syrian Army. Countries like Saudi Arabia and Qatar focused their support also on Islamist armed organisations like Ahrar al-Sham and Jaysh al-Islam.

What the West clearly wanted to see was a moderate democratic secular pluralist successor regime, but such a possibility was not a realistic prospect; certainly not in the foreseeable future. As far as the secular armed groups of the FSA were concerned, they gradually also became more radicalised, as a result of the prolonged bloody war. The Islamic current in Syria had become stronger during the Syrian War, and secularism had correspondingly become less popular.

It had been argued that delivering arms to the predominantly secular opposition (as far as this still existed) might provide a counterweight to the regime, to such an extent that it would be strong enough to help force a negotiated settlement.

The thesis that the regime would have been prepared to negotiate when under enough pressure seemed doubtful, however, for the war was a struggle for life and death in which the regime's main aim was to survive, not to share powers with others that could lead to its downfall. According to Patrick Seale, 'the arming of the opposition seems not to have advanced the opposition's cause but to have given the regime the justification for crushing it'.[9]

David Lesch has concluded that the Syrians (i.e. the regime) did 'not like to be told what to do – or even to have something strongly suggested', let alone by outside powers. And that

> the regimes of Hafiz and Bashar al-Assad have always refused to make concessions from a perceived position of weakness: they will only do so from a perceived position of strength. Cracking down hard on demonstrators while offering political reforms are two sides of the same coin. This is the Syrian way – under the Assads.[10]

The problem was that after 2011, Bashar al-Asad did not want to negotiate from a position of relative strength either, at least if this could lead to a sharing of real power with the opposition. Nevertheless, mutual negotiations would have been the better, or least bad option, taking into account all death and destruction. The question remained, however, whether the party that

thought it could win the battle would ever be prepared to negotiate, except perhaps for tactical reasons.

In the meantime, Western politicians continued to pay lip
service to what they considered to be the predominantly secular
opposition – but as long as they did not provide them with the
necessary means to gain the upper hand in battle, their moral
support did not have any decisive value on the battleground.
While they may have cleared their 'political conscience' by
expressing support for the opposition, they were, in reality,
unintentionally contributing to prolonging the war and helping al-Asad move towards partial (or total) victory, particularly
after Russia started to intervene militarily on the regime's behalf
in September 2015.

Western leaders on various occasions called for measures
against the Syrian regime, measures which they could have
known in advance were not going to be implemented. But to
do nothing or not to react at all was, politically speaking, not an
acceptable option for democratic governments. Nevertheless, it
can, rationally speaking, be argued that in some cases it would
have been wiser to do nothing rather than to do the wrong thing
with disastrous consequences.

Politicians were expected 'to do *something*'. Expressions like
'shouldn't we intervene there?' or 'how can you just sit by and watch
how people in Syria are being oppressed and slaughtered?' became
quite common, but not much was done in practice to drastically
help change the situation of the Syrian population on the ground.

Peter Harling has noted in this respect that 'all the policy
talk about "what can we do?" will remain empty until its meaning becomes "what can we do for millions of Syrians?" and not
"what can we do to rid ourselves of the problem?"'.[11]

Various Western countries at first were fixated on the departure of President Bashar al-Asad and started to support the
opposition; then they started to focus on the Islamic State,

which was more dangerous for them than the regime had ever been, because of the terrorist attacks of IS in the West; and finally, they started to focus on the issue of the many Syrian refugees coming to Europe. All these issues were linked, of course, but in order to be able to solve the refugee problem, for instance, the core issue of the Syrian War had to be tackled first.

On several occasions Western leaders called for the imposition of *no-fly zones* in Syria to protect the opposition and population from air-based regime attacks, but nothing came of it. This was partly due to the fact that imposing a no-fly zone implied direct military confrontation with the Syrian regime, which no Western country had the intention of doing (and after September 2015 it would also have implied military confrontation with Russia).

The creation of *safe havens* was suggested repeatedly as well. Creating a safe haven somewhere in a border area would imply occupying Syrian territory, however, and therefore military confrontation with the Syrian regime. As a result, safe havens were not imposed by foreign powers either.

Western leaders on various occasions also called for setting up *humanitarian corridors* to help the population gain access to food aid. This also turned out to be unsuccessful.

In February 2014, the UN Security Council unanimously adopted Resolution 2139, demanding that all parties allow delivery of humanitarian assistance, cease depriving civilians of food and medicine indispensable to their survival, and enable the rapid, safe and unhindered evacuation of all civilians who wished to leave. It demanded that all parties respect the principle of medical neutrality and facilitate free passage to all areas for medical personnel, equipment and transport.

UN Secretary-General Ban Ki-moon welcomed the adoption of this resolution but noted that it 'should not have been necessary', as humanitarian assistance 'is not something to be negotiated; it is something to be allowed by virtue of international law'. The relevant resolution was a success only on paper, because it was clear that humanitarian corridors could only be imposed against the will of the Syrian regime by direct military confrontation which, predictably again, no country was prepared to undertake.

In 2016, various countries even set a deadline (or a kind of ultimatum) for 1 September that year, announcing that they would start food drops from the air inside Syria, if the regime by that date had not lifted the food and humanitarian aid blockades imposed on various Syrian areas over land, particularly those under opposition control. But it was an empty threat, because foreign aeroplanes flying with this aim over Syria without permission of the central government would run the serious risk of being shot down. And if humanitarian aid was to be delivered by air, aid convoys over land would have been allowed as well, more so as it was more efficient and less costly. Earlier in 2016, food drops by air had been made by way of an exception in the region of Dayr al-Zur, but this concerned an area that was to some extent under regime control, and therefore it had, in this particular case, been in the interests of the regime to allow it.

Most actions by Western countries were reactive, with no clearly defined plan or aim for the future beyond removing President al-Asad and his regime from power. The absence of this type of analysis was surprising, particularly given the fact that a future regime could, for example, if it were to be a radical Islamist dictatorship, turn out to be just as bad as the regime in power.

Most Western policies were no more than declaratory, with few tangible positive results that could lead to a political solution for the opposition on the ground. The good intentions that were widely expressed were generally not followed up by decisive concrete actions, because the Western countries had, to a great extent, tied their hands because of domestic and international politics.

A key question that ran throughout the debates around the Syrian crisis was: is justice to be done? The answer was: yes, of course, but at which cost? It was easy to say, for instance, that President al-Asad was to be tried for crimes against humanity at the International Criminal Court (ICC) in The Hague. But this did not help in finding a solution. The idea that al-Asad would ever be able to leave Syria alive for such a court case was extremely unrealistic. Some people did even imagine that President al-Asad would start to behave and think differently once he was more aware of the future possibility of being tried at the ICC. It all appeared to be wishful thinking.

Calling for justice was good in itself, as was the documenting of all the war crimes that had been committed. This had to be done, of course, but not over and above efforts to proactively work towards finding a solution and preventing the further bloodshed that would undoubtedly continue if no serious negotiations were facilitated among Syria's various clashing factions. The call for justice needed to be part of wider efforts to create peace, rather than only focusing on who were guilty of the crimes committed against the Syrian people in the recent past. A political solution had to be found before justice could be done. It could not be the other way around.

The West in fact created false expectations, and gave the opposition hope for more Western support, which, in the end, was not provided.

By branding the rule of President al-Asad as illegitimate, Western countries may have been morally just, but they thereby prematurely blocked any opportunity they might have had to play a constructive role in finding a political solution to the crisis. The question was what should have priority: being morally correct or helping to find a solution?

Domestic political factors were apparently considered more important. US ambassador Robert Ford had reportedly opposed calling for al-Asad's departure, arguing that the United States would not be able to bring it about, but his counsel was overruled.[12] According to Christopher Phillips, 'the domestic cost of not calling for Assad's departure was perceived as getting too high' in the United States:

> The need to be on the 'right side of history' again was raised, and some feared embarrassment should Assad fall *before* Obama called for his departure …
>
> It was not unreasonable for the Syrian opposition and their regional supporters to rejoice and expect future help … Qatar, Turkey and Saudi Arabia would proceed to act in Syria on the assumption that eventually the United States would step up … Yet much was based on limited knowledge or capacity to follow through on powerful rhetoric, such as Obama's demand for Asad's departure, without the intent to enforce it. Yet such positioning served to escalate the divisions within Syria, with each side believing their external patrons were behind them. Rather than act to deter conflict, external actors helped to fan the flames of war.[13]

The solidarity visit of US ambassador Robert Ford and his French counterpart Eric Chevallier to the opposition movement in Hama in July 2011 looked sympathetic from a Western point of view, but in fact led to the end of the possibility for the United States and France or other countries to play any role as mediator in the conflict. Their visits rather created false hopes among the opposition that essential Western support was forthcoming – and in the end it was not as forthcoming as had been suggested.

In some ways, the situation looked similar to that of southern Iraq in 1991, when the United States and others encouraged the Shi'i community to rise up against the rule of President Saddam Hussein, but did nothing to help them when their uprising was bloodily suppressed.

Ford's actions were universally praised in the United States and elsewhere in the West 'as a courageous act that drew attention to the plight of the protestors, and in so doing helped prevent what some had been predicting: another massacre like the one in Hama in 1982'.[14] But it is more probable that their actions achieved the opposite.

The notion that the Syrian dictatorial regime could be pressurised into refraining from violence against its perceived internal enemies through some ambassadors' show of solidarity with the Syrian opposition also showed some naivity in Western thinking.

When more than five years later, the Syrian regime reconquered the eastern part of the city of Aleppo in December 2016 – which had been under the control of military opposition forces for more than four years (and lay in rubble as a result) – the greater part of the international community, including the Western and Arab Gulf countries that had supported most of the military opposition forces, could not do much more than stand idly by, and issue statements of the strongest condemnation and moral outrage concerning the bloodshed and atrocities that had reportedly taken place. They were powerless to intervene politically or militarily, because they had already excluded any military intervention in Syria several years before, and no longer had any real influence over the Syrian regime (with which they had broken off relations years before), nor over its allies Russia and Iran, to change their policies concerning

Syria. Moreover, they apparently had not provided the military opposition groups with enough military support to be able to win the battle for Aleppo. Various Western politicians had warned, several months before the regime's recapture of Aleppo, that another 'Rwanda' or 'Srebrenica' could occur. Dutch Minister of Foreign Affairs Bert Koenders, for instance, warned on 31 July 2016 that

> not unlike Rwanda or Srebrenica, there is a real risk that the name 'Aleppo' will become synonymous with the world's failure to act. Disaster can only be averted through international pressure. The UN, the International Syria Support Group (ISSG) and other states should be more vocal in calling for the Assad regime to lift the siege.[15]

In practice, however, nothing could be done by the international community to substantially change the situation on the ground, if only because Russia, having the co-chair in the ISSG, was fighting on the side of the regime and wanted to serve its own strategic interests. No declaration in the United Nations, or elsewhere, could help change that.

A 'politics of outrage and indignation' or 'naming and shaming' were clearly far from enough to help bring a solution to the conflict. By way of an alternative, French presidential candidate François Fillon suggested during his election campaign in mid-December 2016, after the defeat of the military opposition in Aleppo, that Europe should undertake a diplomatic initiative to bring to the negotiating table all parties to the Syrian conflict that would be able to stop it, without exception. This was contrary to the French conventional policy followed from the earlier stages of the conflict, of refusing any direct contact with the Syrian president; they only kept demanding his departure. Fillon commented that Europe had to choose and could 'not just continue to be indignant ... Europeans were not responsible for the crimes committed in Syria, but one day history will say they were guilty of not doing anything to stop them'.[16] Reactions to Fillon's statements were in the first instance generally not positive, and the moral high ground and political principles of those criticising him at first instance kept prevailing over the pragmatism that was needed to help in finding a solution to the conflict.

The regime and the main opposition groups had already been in Geneva several times with the aim of negotiating under the auspices of the United Nations, but real negotiations did not take place. If Fillon's initiative was intended to widen European contacts so as to include the al-Asad regime with the aim of influencing the policies of Damascus, it was something new.

In 2012, leading figures in the Syrian National Council (SNC), like Burhan Ghalyun and Basma Qadmani, still spoke of their preference for military intervention, as if it was a realistic possibility. Christopher Phillips has noted that as

> rebels formed militias, many based their strategy on taking sufficient territory not to fully defeat Assad, but to persuade the US to finish him off ... Yet far from dispelling this assumption, the rebels' regional allies actively encouraged the opposition to expect US military intervention.

As Basma Qadmani later recalled, 'the regional powers were absolutely confident that intervention would happen ... I recall very well, they were always reassuring the opposition, "it is coming, it is coming definitely, the intervention is coming"'.[17] All this showed the paradox of perceived US power in the region: 'regional leaders simply refused to countenance the possibility that, after decades of muscle flexing, the US would not eventually step in'.[18]

It took a long time before the opposition started to be sufficiently aware that they had become the victims of the false expectations created by their so-called friendly supporters, who did not want to openly confront them, and themselves, with the realities of the situation.

# 5

# INTRA-SYRIAN TALKS BUT NO NEGOTIATIONS

## UNITED NATIONS AND ARAB LEAGUE ACTION: KOFI ANNAN'S MISSION

In February 2012, the UN Security Council failed to adopt a resolution backing an Arab League plan to help solve the crisis in Syria, as both Russia and China vetoed it. The Arab League plan, as outlined in the draft, called for

> a Syrian-led political transition to a democratic, plural political system, in which citizens are equal regardless of their affiliations or ethnicities or beliefs, including through commencing a serious political dialogue between the Syrian Government and the whole spectrum of the Syrian opposition under the League of Arab States' auspices, in accordance with the timetable set out by the League of Arab States.[1]

Russia criticised some Council members who had, in its view, actively undermined opportunities for a settlement by pressing for regime change. The Russian veto was internationally strongly condemned, suggesting that the situation in Syria would have drastically changed for the better if its veto (and that of China) had not been imposed. Whatever the case, the bloodshed continued unabated, with or without a Security Council resolution. It would have been an illusion to expect that the internal situation in Syria would suddenly have been much different without a Russian and Chinese veto. Russia, through its political position, remained one of the very few countries that still remained on speaking terms with the regime of President Bashar al-Asad, and thereby maintained some possibilities to influence it, also because it had refused to discuss any scenario that would aim for a regime change. Later, various Western countries needed to use the Russian channel to put pressure on al-Asad, because they themselves had lost most if not all possibilities to do so. Also Syria's ally Iran might have been a possible channel for influencing Syria's behaviour and position, but was excluded mainly because of the conflict on the nuclear issue, between the West and Teheran, that was still ongoing at the time.

In March 2012, the UN Security Council in a presidency statement announced that it gave full support to efforts of the Joint Special Envoy of the United Nations and the Arab League, former UN Secretary-General Kofi Annan, to end violence in Syria. Annan's mission was at this stage apparently the only remaining realistic possibility to help solve the crisis through dialogue and by peaceful means. Although Annan's so-called Six Point Plan[2] was strongly criticised by many as being a failure right from the start, it remained at the time 'the only game in town' to help bring about a peaceful solution.

## GENEVA 1 AND THE GENEVA COMMUNIQUÉ

On 30 June 2012, UN and Arab League Special Envoy for Syria, Kofi Annan, initiated the meeting of an 'Action Group for Syria' in Geneva (later referred to as the Geneva 1 Conference on

Syria). It was attended by the Secretaries-General of the United Nations and the Arab League, and the Foreign Ministers of the five permanent member states of the UN Security Council, Turkey, Iraq, Kuwait, Qatar and the European Union.

The resulting Geneva Communiqué of 30 June 2012 was subsequently considered as a cornerstone for any further negotiations. All permanent members of the United Nations Security Council endorsed the Geneva Communiqué.

It should be noted, however, that neither the regime nor the opposition had been represented at this meeting about their country, although, according to the Geneva Communiqué, 'a wide range of Syrians' were consulted beforehand.

The Action Group for Syria agreed on a number of principles and guidelines for a Syrian-led transition. One of the most important guidelines dealt with a political transition that should be made possible through

> the establishment of a transitional governing body which can establish a neutral environment in which the transition can take place. That means that the transitional governing body would exercise full executive powers. It could include members of the present government and the opposition and other groups and shall be formed on the basis of mutual consent.

The position of President Bashar al-Asad and the main figures of his regime in the 'Transitional Governing Body with full executive powers' became a principal point of dispute. US Secretary of State Clinton suggested that President al-Asad could not take part in such a transitional governing body, whereas Russian Foreign Minister Lavrov denied this. The Syrian opposition in general strongly rejected any role for President al-Asad in the 'transitional period'. For the Syrian regime itself it was President al-Asad who was to decide on such issues, not the opposition, nor foreign countries.

After the June 2012 meeting, Lakhdar Brahimi, former Minister of Foreign Affairs of Algeria with huge international experience, was appointed as the new UN Special Envoy for Syria, successor to Kofi Annan. In close cooperation with Russia and the United States he started to prepare for a new international conference on ending the war in Syria, in which this time two Syrian delegations, both government and opposition, were to participate.

In the meantime, the bloody war in Syria went on unabated.

## GENEVA 2

It took a year and a half before the conference – 'Geneva 2' – could start on 22 January 2014 in Montreux, Switzerland. Foreign ministers from some 40 countries made statements. US Secretary of State John Kerry conveyed the US view that there was no way that President Bashar al-Asad could regain the legitimacy to rule Syria in the future, after all that had happened. Syrian National Coalition leader Ahmad Jarba, who led the opposition delegation, called on the Syrian Government to immediately transfer power to a transitional governing body with full executive powers, in line with the Geneva Communiqué.

Syrian Foreign Minister Walid al-Mu'allim stated, however, that no one in the world had the right to confer or withdraw the legitimacy of a president, a constitution or a law, except the Syrians themselves. The position of Bashar al-Asad as president was non-negotiable. For the Syrian regime, any transfer of power without its own approval was anathema.

After two rounds of talks no tangible results could be reached and there were no real negotiations. A third round of negotiations was therefore to be planned.

Lakhdar Brahimi resigned as UN Special Envoy for Syria in May 2014. His tremendous efforts to help bring peace in Syria turned out to be a *mission impossible*. He was succeeded in July 2014 by the diplomat and high UN official with wide experience, Staffan de Mistura.

## THE INTERNATIONAL SYRIA SUPPORT GROUP

Various international groups had been founded in an effort to help solve the conflict in Syria. There was the Friends of Syria group, initiated by France in 2012, first consisting of some 70 to 114 countries that participated in the first four meetings in 2012. Later, it was restricted to a core group of 11 countries, referred to as 'The London 11', after their meeting in London in 2013. They were Egypt, France, Germany, Italy, Jordan, Qatar, Saudi Arabia, Turkey, the United Arab Emirates, the United Kingdom and the United States. These groups and conferences were mainly intended to help the opposition and the Syrian population in general.[3]

After various unsuccessful international initiatives, the International Syria Support Group (ISSG) was established in Vienna in 2015 with some 20 participating countries and international organisations. The importance of the ISSG lay in the fact that this was the first time (outside of the United Nations) that both supporters and opponents of the Syrian regime participated, making the potential for a solution somewhat more realistic. The ISSG was co-chaired by Russia and the United States. It included all permanent member states of the UN Security Council, as well as most countries that were, by proxy, involved in the Syria conflict, among which were the 'London 11'. Iran also participated this time. No Syrian delegation was invited, however.

In the final ISSG communiqué of 14 November 2015, reference was made to the Geneva Communiqué and it was stated that the participants, together with the United Nations, would explore modalities for, and implementation of, a nationwide ceasefire to be initiated on a certain date in parallel with the renewed political process of Vienna. It was stressed that Syria's unity, independence, territorial integrity and secular character were fundamental, and that the political process should be Syrian-led and Syrian-owned, and that the Syrian people should decide on the future of Syria.

In fact, the principles laid out in Vienna were decided on behalf of the Syrians, who themselves were not represented. The Syrians of the opposition, who did not want secularism, rejected the Vienna outcome.

In December 2015 the UN Security Council endorsed the 'Vienna Statements' in pursuit of the full implementation of the Geneva Communiqué, as the basis for a Syrian-led and Syrian-owned political transition in order to end the conflict in Syria. It requested the UN Special Envoy for Syria to convene representatives of the Syrian Government and the opposition to engage in formal negotiations, with a target of early January 2016 for the initiation of talks. The UN Security Council acknowledged the role of the ISSG as the central platform to facilitate the United Nations' efforts to achieve a lasting political settlement in Syria.

## THE RIYADH OPPOSITION CONFERENCE

Until 2015, the Syrian opposition groups generally had not really worked together to help find a solution. They were divided over various – sometimes rival – groups. Internationally, the most widely recognised opposition organisation was the National Coalition of the Syrian Revolution and Opposition Forces (or Syrian Opposition Coalition – SOC), based in Istanbul. They initially claimed to be 'the sole legitimate representative of the Syrian people' and were recognised by over a hundred different countries, albeit with some variations, such as 'the sole legitimate representative' or 'the legitimate representative' or just 'a representative' or 'legitimate representatives of the aspirations of the Syrian people'.

The SOC emanated from a unification in November 2012 between various opposition groups and the SNC, that had been founded in exile in August 2011. Many members of the SOC were prominent Syrians, including intellectuals who were well known in the Syrian opposition inside Syria, some of them long before the Syrian Revolution started (like Haytham al-Malih, Michel Kilo, Riyad Sayf, Anwar al-Bunni and 'Arif Dalilah), others after 2011. Many of them had endured imprisonment by the regime, and therefore could not in the least be reproached for being 'salon revolutionaries', living a luxury life outside Syria. Some had played a role in the Damascus Spring, some had participated prominently in the debating societies (*Muntadayat*) that started after Bashar al-Asad took over as president (like the Jamal al-Atasi Forum of Suhayr al-Atasi), but which were suppressed after a short period, because they asked for more freedom. Some had signed the 'Manifesto of 99' in September 2000, demanding freedom of speech and the lifting of the state of emergency, to be followed by the 'Manifesto of 1000', which called for the replacement of one-party rule by a multi-party democracy.

Nevertheless, some of the civilian opposition groups inside Syria, and particularly the military opposition groups, reproached the SOC outside Syria as not representing the

Syrian Revolution inside. After all, they had formed an organisation in exile outside Syria of which the members had elected a leadership from within their own circles without, allegedly, having obtained enough legitimacy from inside Syria. Some opponents considered the SOC leadership as a self-appointed body.

From time to time, members of the SOC left the organisation, protesting about its representivity. In November 2016, a group of some 170 Syrian intellectuals issued *An Appeal for Syria*, criticising the SOC's (lack of) representivity, and demanding a full revision of its structure so as to truly represent the Syrian Revolution. According to the signatories – among whom was the prominent Michel Kilo, who until then had been a member of the Political Committee of the SOC – the National Coalition of the Syrian Revolution and Opposition Forces (SOC) made an artificial distinction between 'revolutionary' forces in the military field and 'opposition forces' abroad. Who was a 'revolutionary' and who the 'opposition'? This was a strange phenomenon and one that had to either be clarified or changed. The founding document of the SOC had, according to the declaration, not clearly defined the principles on which the coalition was based and how its members were chosen from which organisations, and how seats were being distributed. It appeared as if seats were divided on the basis of ethnicity, sectarian background, parties, regions and families, instead of 'services to the Syrian people'. The SOC founders had been appointed as being 'national personalities'. The SOC had represented itself as 'the only legitimate representative of the Syrian people', and had obtained wide international recognition. The signatories demanded re-electing a General Assembly on the basis of clear criteria that really implied representivity of the Syrian people, both civilians and military factions. They demanded the dissolution of the SOC 'Parliament' after having served for four years in November 2016, and called for the election of a new one on the basis of criteria proposed by them.[4]

The lack of possibilities for organising really free and representative elections, both inside as well as outside Syria, remained an obstacle, of course, and therefore obtaining a fully representative body remained a real problem. But there were possibilities to improve some imperfections. And, indeed, the SOC had made a serious effort to include personalities from most population groups and also the smaller communities. This was also reflected in the Opposition Conference in Riyadh of December 2015, where 'Arabs, Kurds, Turkoman, Assyrians, Syriacs, Circassians, Armenians and others' were invited. But whether all those invited could really be considered as 'representative' of the people of Syria is another question. Being a Turkoman or Assyrian representative in the Riyadh Conference, for instance, did not necessarily mean that the involved personalities would represent 'the Turkomans' or 'the Assyrians' in Syria, because comprehensive elections had been impossible under the circumstances of war, and there was no quota system for specific population groups (which was rejected by many). The SOC and the Riyadh Conference, however, had to manage with what was possible under those extremely difficult circumstances, in order to make the best of it.

SOC members, on the other hand, accused the civilian opposition groups inside the country of being little more than people who were in one way or another linked to the regime. Opposition organisations inside Syria, like the 'National Coordination Committee for Democratic Change' (NCC) and 'Building the Syrian State' (BSS), on the other hand, criticised those outside of Syria for lacking enough realism or pragmatism to be able to contribute to a political solution. One of the main differences was their position towards President Bashar al-Asad's role during the transition period and the negotiations towards it.

Opposition organisations which operated inside Syria (like NCC and BSS) considered that those who were active outside Syria and criticised them were in a relatively comfortable position, and one from where they could easily talk about those who were active inside Syria, without fully taking into account the extremely difficult circumstances under which they had to operate in the presence of the regime. Some argued that after all the bloodshed and ruination that had taken place, it had become more important to save and preserve Syria than to topple the al-Asad regime.

The NCC and BSS refuted accusations that they were close to the regime. According to Ahmad al-'Asrawi, one of the NCC leaders, the NCC had struggled against the regime from the beginning of the revolution. Sixty-four of the NCC members had together experienced more than 500 years in Syrian prisons, which, he argued, was proof enough of their attitude towards the regime (and vice versa). BSS leader Lu'ayy Husayn had also been imprisoned several times.[5] It was obviously much easier to criticise the regime from outside the country than inside it.

After the beginning of the Syrian Revolution, thousands of prisoners were killed by executions, severe torture or other means in the prisons of the Syrian security services (*Mukhabarat*), as was illustrated later by thousands of pictures that had been smuggled out of the country in 2013 by an official forensic photographer for the Military Police, code-named *Caesar*, who had defected.[6] In 2017, Amnesty International published a report, indicating that in Saydnaya Military Prison alone, the Syrian authorities methodically had organised the killing of thousands of people in their custody.[7]

The opposition organisations inside Syria resented the fact that most of the attention of the international community went to the SOC, after it had been recognised by over a hundred countries. Some Special Envoys for Syria reportedly were not even allowed by their governments to have contact with the NCC and BSS.

When most of the opposition groups, both military and civilian inside and outside Syria, came together in Riyadh with some 116 people on 9 and 10 December 2015 at the invitation of the Saudi government, they, for the first time, overcame their differences to a great extent and came to a common position for future negotiations with the regime. This in itself was a substantial achievement.

According to the final declaration of the Riyadh Conference 'the Syrian Revolution and Opposition Forces' held an expanded meeting with the participation of men and women who represented the Syrian armed factions and opposition groups both inside Syria and abroad, 'with all parts of Syrian society being represented', including Arabs, Kurds, Turkoman, Assyrians, Syriacs, Circassians, Armenians and others. The aim of the conference had been to unite ranks and reach a common vision for a negotiated political solution to the Syrian conflict in accordance with the Geneva Communiqué of 2012 and relevant international resolutions, without relinquishing, however, 'the principles and the constants of the Syrian revolution'.

The participants expressed their commitment to the territorial unity of Syria and their belief in the civil character of the Syrian state, in addition to its sovereignty over all Syrian territories based on the principle of administrative decentralisation. They also voiced their commitment to the mechanism of democracy through a pluralistic system in which all Syrian groups, including both men and women, would be represented, without discrimination or exclusion on the basis of religion, denomination or ethnicity and to be based on the principles of human rights, transparency, accountability and the rule of law as applied to all.

The participants pledged to work to preserve Syrian state institutions with the requirement that state security and military institutions should be restructured.

They demanded that the UN and the international community compel the regime to implement measures to confirm its good intentions before the beginning of negotiations. Such measures were, according to the final declaration, to include the release of prisoners and detainees, lifting the sieges on besieged areas, allowing humanitarian convoys to reach those in need, the return of refugees, an immediate cessation of forced migration, and an end to the targeting of civilian areas with barrel bombs and other means. The participants stressed their demand that Bashar al-Asad and the inner circle of his regime should leave office at the beginning of the transitional period.

At the end of the Riyadh Conference it was agreed to form a 'High Negotiations Council for the Syrian Revolution and Opposition Forces' (HNC), having its headquarters in Riyadh. The HNC was to select a team to negotiate with the representatives of the Syrian regime. The negotiation delegation was not to act independently, but should act in consultation with the HNC, which was to remain its reference point.[8]

The Riyadh Conference chose a High Negotiations Council of 34 members with Dr Riyad Hijab (ex-Prime Minister of Syria who had fled the country in August 2012 and joined the opposition) as president.[9]

The main opposition parties, from both outside and inside Syria, were represented in the HNC: the SOC, the National Coordination Committees for Democratic Change, Building the Syrian State, military organisations like the Free Syrian Army, Ahrar al-Sham (Labib Nahhas) and Jaysh al-Islam (Muhammad 'Allush), and independents. The position of Ahrar al-Sham was ambivalent, because its representative Labib Nahhas had signed the final declaration of the Riyadh Conference, but was criticised for it by the military of his group at home.

Whereas the Kurds were represented in Riyadh by Dr 'Abd al-Hakim Bashar, President of the Kurdish National Council, which was established in October 2011 and included most Kurdish parties under one umbrella,[10] the only Kurdish party with real military power, the PYD, led by Salih Muslim, was not present. Representatives of the 'Cairo Group' were present as well.

Simultaneously with the Riyadh Conference, two other opposition conferences were held, all claiming to be the representatives of the Syrian people – one in Damascus and one in the predominantly Kurdish north of Syria.[11] The meeting in Damascus was essentially set up to delegitimise the meeting in Riyadh, and had nothing to do with independent anti-government forces organising themselves. The other meeting was in Derek, in north Syria, where the PYD was heavily represented. As a regional outsider, human rights activist Haytham Manna' took part.

The High Negotiations Council appointed a delegation that was to negotiate with the regime in Geneva, and demanded that only they could negotiate and not any other group or party. Russian attempts to add other groups, among which were members of its 'Moscow group', were rejected.

The negotiations delegation was composed of General As'ad al-Zu'bi (FSA), head of delegation, George Sabra, deputy head of delegation, Muhammad 'Allush (Jaysh al-Islam), chief negotiator and 13 others, both military and civilians. Three members of the negotiating team, George Sabra, Muhammad 'Allush and Suhayr al-Atasi, were simultaneously members of the HNC and the negotiations delegation.[12]

## GENEVA 3

It took until February 2016 before the new intra-Syrian talks could start in Geneva. UN Special Envoy Staffan de Mistura not only invited the Syrian Government delegation and the HNC negotiations team, but also asked for the advice of representatives of the 'Moscow group' and the 'Cairo group', some 'independents' and later also the PYD, which had been excluded from the Riyadh Conference (2015). This was in line with the Vienna declaration 'to bring together the broadest possible spectrum of the opposition'. The consulted personalities did not belong to any of the negotiation teams, but were considered as 'platforms' that might contribute to helping find a solution.

De Mistura in February 2016 also established a Syrian Women's Advisory Board, with the aim of strengthening the role of women in the political process. This was the only advisory body that had members from both the opposition and women close to the regime and was, in that sense, unique.

HNC leader Riyad Hijab had protested against any efforts to add others to the HNC negotiations team. If, for instance, the PYD wanted to join the negotiations they should, according to the HNC, join the regime's delegation, because they were considered by the HNC as an ally of the regime. According to President Bashar al-Asad, the Syrian regime had provided the PYD with arms 'to fight IS'.[13] That made the PYD into an ally of the regime. But the PYD also militarily attacked the FSA and other units supported by the HNC, and therefore, among other reasons, was considered even more to be an adversary of the HNC.

It had been the intention of the Security Council that there should be a cessation of hostilities during the envisaged negotiations. The fighting against IS, Jabhat al-Nusrah and other al-Qa'idah-linked groups, all being officially considered as terrorist groups, was to continue in the meantime. A full cessation of hostilities between the regime and the military opposition did not materialise, however. It only slowed down for a relatively short time.

In its Resolution 2254 (18 December 2015) the Security Council had called on the parties to immediately allow humanitarian agencies rapid, safe and unhindered access throughout Syria by most direct routes; allow immediate, humanitarian assistance to reach all people in need; release any arbitrarily detained persons, particularly women and children; and demanded that all parties immediately cease any attacks against civilians and civilian objects as such, including attacks against medical facilities and personnel, and any indiscriminate use of weapons, including through shelling and aerial bombardment. They welcomed the commitment by the ISSG to press the parties in this regard, and further demanded that all parties immediately comply with their obligations under international law.

HNC President Riyad Hijab and the opposition delegation insisted that the Syrian regime first comply with UN Security Council Resolution 2254, in particular paragraphs 12 and 13, mentioning humanitarian access, the release of prisoners and attacks against civilians, including the use by the regime of barrel bombs. The opposition delegation noted that their demands in this respect were not to be seen as preconditions for starting the negotiations, because these already were obligations that the regime should comply with because of Security Council Resolution 2254. Riyad Hijab even considered the fulfilment of UNSC Resolution 2254 as a 'promise' to be fulfilled by the international community. The regime, however, continued its humanitarian blockades, did not release prisoners as requested, and continued using its barrel bombs unabated.

As a result, only talks by proxy took place with UN Special Envoy de Mistura as mediator, and real negotiations did not materialise.

The leader of the delegation of the Syrian regime, Dr Bashar al-Ja'fari, wanted his delegation to be addressed as the delegation of the 'Government of the Syrian Arab Republic', not as the delegation of the 'regime'. The opposition delegation, on the other hand, refused to be addressed as terrorists, and kept talking about 'the dictatorial regime of Bashar al-Assad and his clique who committed heinous crimes against the Syrian people'.

All delegations wanted to be addressed in their official capacities, but the adversaries on both sides did not do so, if only because this would imply some official recognition of the other party, which they refused, irrespective of the necessity to negotiate with it.

Al-Ja'fari also criticised the composition of the opposition delegation, notably the fact that Muhammad 'Allush of the Islamist Jaysh al-Islam had been appointed as chief negotiator. Ja'fari criticised 'Allush for having said that the transitional period could only start with 'the departure of Bashar al-Asad or his death', and that there could be no transition with this regime and its head in place. The Syrian regime considered Jaysh al-Islam as a terrorist organisation.[14]

Riyad Hijab took a hard line concerning the obligation of the regime to first implement UNSC Resolution 2254. Being a former Prime Minister of Syria under President Bashar al-Asad he could assess perhaps better than anyone else in the HNC what he could expect of the regime, and what he could not.

During one of the meetings in March 2016 in Geneva between the HNC and the Special Envoys for Syria, Muhammad 'Allush asked the Envoys who represented the permanent members of the UNSC what their countries were going to do to help implement UNSC Resolution 2254, particularly paragraphs 12 and 13. After all, their countries had fully subscribed to it. The reaction was that they were 'fully committed' and would 'go for it'. In reality these countries were not able, however, to impose the resolution they had adopted, because they had excluded direct military intervention.

It was only gradually that the opposition started to be fully aware that the support they had expected to receive from Western and Arab Gulf countries, the Friends of Syria in particular, was generally no more than political and moral support which, together with the (substantial) military support they received, was not enough to force the regime into the expected changes. Many opposition members had expected that they could achieve some real progress with the help of such powerful countries as the United States, Great Britain and France, but the realities turned out to be very different. The good intentions of the countries involved were just not enough. Good declarations and statements were of little real help.

The opposition started to feel betrayed and abandoned because of the false expectations that, from their perspective, had been created by their Western supporters.

Later, Muhammad 'Allush withdrew from the HNC negotiations delegation, out of protest that so little had been achieved, but he remained a member of the HNC itself, which was perhaps more important than being a member of the negotiations delegation which had to follow the negotiation policies agreed upon by the HNC.

The regime delegation presented a paper to de Mistura, called *Basic Elements of a Political Solution in the Syrian Arab Republic*. It had ten items, including:

> Respect for the sovereignty of Syria, its independence, the integrity of its territory, the unity of its land and people, the inadmissibility of giving up any piece of it, working to restore the occupied Syrian Golan up to the line of June 4, 1967, and rejecting direct or indirect foreign interference in the internal affairs of Syria in any

shape or form, while Syrians alone will decide the future of their country by democratic means, through the ballot box, and hold the exclusive right to choose the form of their political system, far from any imposed formula which the Syrian people do not accept.

The document also said that Syria was a

secular-democratic country built on political pluralism, the rule of law, the independence of the judiciary, and equality between citizens in rights and duties, defense of national unity and cultural diversity of Syrian society's communities, and protecting general freedoms.

In addition to:

Fighting terrorism and renouncing intolerance and extremism and all *takfiri* ideologies, which is considered a national duty, and supporting the army and armed forces in operations against terrorism.[15]

At first sight it sounded relatively positive on paper, but the political reality in the Syrian Arab Republic was completely different. Syria under Ba'thist rule had never been a 'secular-democratic country built on political pluralism, the rule of law, the independence of the judiciary'. Besides, many of the armed opposition groups were considered 'terrorists' by the regime.

The presence inside Syria of the military forces of Russia, Iran and Hizballah was not considered by the regime as foreign interference in the internal affairs of Syria, because they were there at the request of the government in Damascus.

The regime's proposal completely ignored the discussion of a 'political transition' or of UNSC Resolution 2254, and thereby had little practical value for the intra-Syria talks in Geneva.

With respect to 'restoring the occupied Golan', Muhammad 'Allush later declared that his fighters had

> no intention to go to war with Israel … If we compare all the killing in the history of the Arab–Israeli conflict, the Syrian regime has committed many more crimes than the whole conflict. Our aim now is to get rid of the Syrian regime.[16]

As there was not the slightest hint that the regime wanted to submit to any part of UNSC Resolution 2254, the HNC delegation threatened to leave and break off the Geneva talks, three days after they had started. Just before it could get that far, de Mistura decided on 4 February 2016 to announce a temporary pause of the intra-Syrian talks, because there was still 'a lot of work to do'.

The talks that were resumed in April 2016 did not bring any positive results either, and were therefore suspended again until further notice, without a date being set.

The ISSG initiated a Task Force that was intended to help implement a Cessation of Hostilities and a Task Force for Humanitarian Aid so that people in the besieged areas could receive the necessary supplies. Both groups were, like the ISSG itself, led by a Russian and US co-chairman, but in the end the desired results were far from being achieved, as the war in Syria continued with all its ferocity.

In February and March 2017, another two rounds of intra-Syrian talks took place in Geneva. The stated aim of UN Special Envoy de Mistura was to promote talks on substance concerning the three subjects 'governance, a new constitution and elections', as formulated in UNSC Resolution 2254. In conformity with the wishes of the Syrian regime, the subject of 'terrorism' was added as part of a fourth basket, under the heading of 'counter terrorism, security governance and CBMs'. According to de Mistura, none of the Syrian delegates could possibly be in favour of terrorism, and therefore there should be nothing against discussing it. The problem was, however, that both the opposition and the regime continued to accuse one another of being 'terrorists' and of supporting 'terrorism'. And as long as the regime and the opposition did not have the slightest intention of sharing substantial power with one another, it appeared to be premature to discuss the proposed subjects in depth, except by way of confidence-building measures. But there was no mutual trust or confidence, the more so as the bloody war in Syria continued in all its ferocity. Like before, there were no direct negotiations in Geneva between the Syrian parties, but only separate talks of each side with de Mistura as the mediator.

The opposition representatives had, according to the regime's delegation leader Bashar al-Ja'fari, 'only one delusion in their minds, which was handing over the keys to Syria and the power to them'.

Nasr al-Hariri, the chief negotiator on behalf of the HNC, reiterated that the core of the political process was the requirement of a political transition, which was the transition from the regime. According to the HNC 'it required Bashar Assad and his clique, whose hands had already been stained with the blood of the Syrian people, to step down immediately as the premise of the transition.'

The HNC opposition delegation kept repeating its earlier position that a political solution could only be found through the establishment of a transitional governing body, in which president Bashar al-Asad would not have any role, either in the transitional period, or in the future of Syria. They further-more declared that they would not rest until the perpetrators of crimes in Syria were brought to justice.

Nasr al-Hariri lamented that the opposition was dealing with a regime 'that did not want to reach a political solution'. The opposition, however, did not have the military power to impose its political will on the regime.

Actually, both sides wanted a 'political solution', but exclusively on their own terms. For the time being the positions of the regime and the opposition appeared to be fully irreconcilable, and the deadlock remained as before.

### ARABISM VERSUS PLURALISM AND KURDISH NATIONALISM

In September 2016, the HNC presented a 22-page proposal called *Executive Framework for a Political Solution Based on the Geneva Communiqué of 2012.*[17]

It was a serious effort to come to a political proposal in more detail. The regime had never made a worked-out proposal, but restricted itself more to basics and generalities, supposedly leaving everything to be negotiated after.

The chances that the regime would be prepared to negotiate on the basis of the HNC document was minimal, if only because it stated again that the 'establishment of the Transitional Governing Body shall require the departure of Bashar al-Assad and his clique who committed heinous crimes against the Syrian people'. The document further noted:

Syria is an integral part of the Arab World, and Arabic is the official language of the state. Arab Islamic culture represents a fertile source for intellectual production and social relations among all Syrians of different ethnic backgrounds and religious beliefs as the majority of Syrians are Arabs and followers of Islam and its tolerant message which is distinctly moderate ...

Their political system shall be based on democracy, plurality and citizenship which provides for equality in rights and duties for all Syrians without discrimination on the basis of color, gender, language, ethnicity, opinion, religion, or ideology ...

The Kurdish cause shall be considered a national Syrian cause and action shall be taken to ensure their ethnic, linguistic, and cultural rights in the constitution ...

The Syrian state shall adopt the principle of administrative decentralization in managing the country's affairs, giving the people of each governorate and district a role in managing their local affairs: economic, communal, and daily life affairs in ways that do not adversely affect the unity of the country ...

All forms of foreign interference should be prevented. Subordination and alignment policies by the regime are rejected. All non-Syrian fighters, sectarian militia, armed groups, mercenaries and military or paramilitary forces belonging to foreign countries should be expelled from all Syrian territories.

The HNC *Executive Framework for a Political Solution* differed somewhat from the Riyadh Declaration, adopted nine months earlier. This time the Arab character of Syria – and the Arab character of Islamic culture – were stressed and given prominence, noting however that there should not be any discrimination on the basis of ethnicity and religion. In Riyadh (2015) the Arab dimension of Syria had not even been mentioned, and neither had Islam. The Kurdish issue had not been referenced in Riyadh either, but was now explicitly mentioned as 'a national Syrian cause' for which action was to be taken to ensure their ethnic, linguistic and cultural rights in the constitution.

In Riyadh it was about a 'democracy through a pluralistic system in which all Syrian groups would be represented without any discrimination', and therefore without any group being more prominent than the other. For the Kurds this had been a better formula, because they wanted to be considered as fully equal to the other ethnic or religious groups in Syria.

During intra-Syrian Track-2 meetings[18] outside Syria it turned out that various representatives whose organisations had agreed to the Riyadh Declaration in reality did not fully subscribe to its principles and ideas on essential points. They, for instance, rejected the idea of a plural society in which all Syrians were equal, and preferred a society that was predominantly Arab and Islamic, while at the same time respecting minorities. They wanted Syria to be explicitly a part of the Arab and Islamic world. The Kurds, on the other hand, preferred the Riyadh formula of a plural society where no ethnic or religious group would be given prominence over others, and in which the Syrian identity was given priority over other identities. Besides, they argued, Islamic culture was not only Arab. Other ethnic groups had also played an important role in it.[19]

Various participants in the Track-2 meetings wanted a strict separation between religion and the state. A secular system would guarantee equality and neutrality among Syrians. Others insisted that the (Sunni) Islamic identity should have a central place in the Syrian state and its constitution. They expressed the thought that the least they could demand was an Islamic character for the 'new Syria'. Islam was an inseparable part of their identity, they argued. The Syrian War would have been futile in their view if this Islamic identity could not at least be realised in the 'new Syria'.

Kurdish participants in the same intra-Syrian Track-2 meetings noted that it had already been agreed in Riyadh that democracy should function through a pluralistic system in which all Syrian groups would be represented without any discrimination. They stressed that the Syrian identity should come first for all Syrians. Other identities were to be secondary and subordinate. They rejected the idea that Syria should be explicitly considered as part of a wider trans-national identity, like that of the Arab world. In reaction to the Arab demands for their Arab and Islamic identity to be given prominence, Syrian Kurds claimed that in that case they should also be entitled to claim to be part of a larger trans-national entity, notably of a greater Kurdish nation of more than 50 million people (spread over Iraq, Turkey, Iran and Syria).

In order to officially express the equality of all Syrians, irrespective of their ethnic background, the Kurdish participants wanted to change the name of 'The Syrian Arab Republic' to 'The Syrian Republic', analogous with Iraq which was called the 'Republic of Iraq', without referring to any ethnic or linguistic group. Most Arab opposition members strongly rejected this idea.

The new HNC document of September 2016 was a clear indication that the demands of the Arab Islamist opposition members had been accommodated.

Irrespective of the declarations and communiqués adopted by the opposition, it may be asked what would happen with such differences of opinion, if the same parties were to share power one day.

The Kurdish parties represented in Riyadh in the HNC supported the idea of *administrative* decentralisation. In contrast, the Kurdish PYD (not present in Riyadh) aimed at a kind of *political* regional autonomy, which was rejected by the others, including the regime. The type of autonomy that was demanded by the PYD was considered a threat that could undermine the unity and territorial integrity of the Syrian state, and could even lead to a form of separatism. Autonomy for specific groups of the population was moreover considered as unrealistic, since most minorities have many members spread out all over Syria. Whereas Kurds may constitute a majority in three geographical regions of northern Syria, many live also in Damascus (for instance in the Hayy al-Akrad – the Kurdish Quarter) or in Aleppo or other bigger cities, like Hama or Homs.

Alawis are not only living in the 'Alawi Mountains', or the Latakia and Tartus regions, but have migrated in big numbers to Damascus and elsewhere. In Damascus and other cities like Hama and Homs there are even neighourhoods that are Alawi by majority. In 2015 the number of Alawis in the capital was fast approaching half a million.[20] The Druzes are, obviously, not only living in the Jabal al-Duruz, and the Isma'ilis not only in Salamiyah and Masyaf.

Several decades ago, the Kurdish nationalist movements in Iraq, Turkey, Iran and Syria were mainly restricted to each country separately. There was no clear trans-national Kurdish movement, connecting the Kurds with one another across the international boundaries. They were only really interested in the Kurdish issues in their own countries.[21]

In contrast to Iraq, Iran or Turkey, the Syrian Kurds do not have one single geographically connected area that is mainly populated by Kurds. Various Syrian border areas in the north, that were formerly inhabited to a great extent by Kurds, have since the 1960s become more heavily populated by Arabs who have settled there as part of the Ba'thist policy to Arabise the northern Syrian border areas, the so-called 'Arab belt'. It goes without saying that undoing these Arabisation schemes half a century later will not be possible without serious conflict. During the Syrian War the PYD has been active in 'ethnically cleansing' part of the Arab population in the north.

The Kurds in Iraq may continue to inspire the Kurds in Turkey, Syria and Iran in their wishes for more autonomy or even independence.

## MAJORITIES AND MINORITIES

During various meetings, Islamist members of the opposition, in particular, strongly criticised the special attention the Western countries have generally given to minorities, without giving enough attention to the Sunni Arab majority as well.

There is, indeed, a tendency in Western countries to focus much more on religious and ethnic minorities than on the religious or ethnic majority in countries. The categories of ethnic and religious majorities are, however, different from what could be considered as 'political majorities'.[22]

Concerning minorities and majorities, it should be self-evident that it is not only the numbers of a religious 'community' that are decisive. If a dictatorship is dominated by people from a population group that constitutes a minority, for instance, the conclusion is easily drawn that it would then be a kind of 'minority rule'. If, on the other hand, a dictatorship is dominated by people from a population group that constitutes a numerical majority of the population, then it is often conveniently considered as a type of 'majority rule'.

The rule of President Saddam Hussein of Iraq has, for instance, been described by many as a kind of 'minority rule', because he was Sunni Arab, and the Sunni Arabs are not a majority in Iraq. But does this mean that Iraq now has a majority rule, because the rulers are now mainly from the Shi'i majority community? Both types of rule can be considered as totalitarian, and therefore are, almost by definition, not representative of the majority of the population. Being from a certain type of religious or ethnic majority does not necessarily mean that those in power also represent those majorities, certainly where totalitarian regimes are concerned.[23]

If we take the example of the Islamic State, which is fully dominated by Sunni Arabs, it would be clear immediately that they are not a 'majority regime' that represents the Sunni Arab majority of Syria in the areas under their control (or the Sunni Arab 'minority' in Iraq).

The Syrian opposition writer Yassin Al-Haj Saleh has noted that: 'The real political majority in Syria should not refer to the Arab Sunni majority, but rather to a social majority that is cross-communitarian.' He argues that a

> just solution in Syria should be based on establishing a new political majority in the country, one in which an expanding majority of Syrians become familiar with its political representation, and do away with minoritarian, oligarchical rule, in turn laying the foundation for a new Syria and an assimilative Syrian regime. This requires the end of Assadist rule, and of Daesh and any Salafist-jihadist groups, in addition to instituting political and cultural equality for the Kurds with no nationalistic hegemony. It requires laying the foundations for a democratic Syria that is based upon citizenship.[24]

Nevertheless, the tendency remains to apply those categories that are considered to be suitable to one's argument.

## OBSTACLES TO AN INTRA-SYRIAN COMPROMISE

In order to make the smallest beginning of a political solution possible, the regime should have been prepared to make a kind of compromise, but there was no positive sign, not even the smallest hint of this in Geneva. The regime had not sufficiently responded to calls from the UN Security Council to allow humanitarian assistance to reach all people in need, to release arbitrarily detained persons (of which there were many,

many thousands), to cease attacks against civilian targets, and to immediately stop the indiscriminate use of weapons. In fact, all these elements did not even need a UNSC resolution, because they were already obligatory under international law (as was the case with UNSC Resolution 2139 of February 2014). As long as the regime did not give the slightest indication that it was pre-pared to comply with such obligations, the opposition saw no reason to engage in further talks or negotiations. If the regime was not prepared to give in on these points, even if it were only a little, what could the opposition expect?

What the opposition needed was at least a clear sign that the regime was prepared to give in on some essential points.

From the point of view of justice, the opposition, operating under the umbrella of the High Negotiations Council led by for-mer Syrian Prime Minister Riyad Hijab, was generally speak-ing correctly as it was seeking a negotiated political solution in accordance with the Geneva Communiqué of 2012 and relevant international resolutions. But being right did not necessarily mean that the respective rights could also be obtained. What counted most in the end were the results; and these were to be decided to a great extent by the balance of military power on the ground. In this context, both Russia and Iran, with their heavy military presence in Syria, did not want to lose their strategic ally in Damascus, and therefore kept supporting the al-Asad regime.

Just like the regime, the opposition had a *winner takes all* attitude, based on their conviction that they had the right fully on their side. The Friends of Syria, however, were not able or willing to support the Syrian opposition to such an extent that they could obtain or realise those rights.

Various personalities and organisations prepared plans about the political future for Syria, some of them in the greatest detail. The various UN Special Envoys for Syria, Kofi Annan, Lakhdar

Brahimi and Staffan de Mistura, all made serious efforts to help bring about a political solution by formulating plans and trying to mediate between the main conflicting parties. The Action Group for Syria formulated the Geneva Communiqué (2012) that was endorsed by the permanent members of the UN Security Council; the Friends of Syria came with further ideas; the International Syria Support Group formulated proposals; Russia came with proposals; Iran came with proposals; the United States came with proposals; the various opposition platforms and groups came with ideas; the High Negotiations Council formulated an *Executive Framework for a Political Solution*; and the regime proposed some general ideas. Then there was *The Day After Project* developed by a number of well-known opposition figures; the plans of former Syrian ambassador Sami Khiyami called *Virtues of Nomination in Indoctrinated Nations*; the *We Are Syria Initiative* of former Minister of Economy and Trade Nedal Alchaar; the *My Home Syria Initiative* of former Parliamentarian and later SOC president Riyad Sayf; ideas of various opposition figures formulated during Track-2 meetings; and other initiatives.

Most of these plans were based on the presumption that there should be a political solution, based on negotiations with the regime. Here, however, much faltered because the hard core of the regime did not want to negotiate its own departure, as was demanded by most of the opposition and many others.

Most parties had a clear aim in mind, but a clear plan of how to achieve it with peaceful means was generally not there.

## LONG-TERM PROSPECTS

Negotiations appeared to be the better option, both for the regime and the opposition. But the al-Asad regime turned out not to be serious about negotiations insofar as these would imply real power-sharing.

In the view of Peter Harling:

> Syrians are devastated by their own delusions. The sublime revolutionary illusion, which still drives many of them five years on, has degenerated beyond redemption. Meanwhile, on the other side, most presumed 'loyalists' discern, deep down, that the regime has committed the irreparable and unforgivable, hurtling down a path from which there is no return. They know, although they can't admit it, that what is left of a state is a fallacy and a fraud. And still, all continue to make immense sacrifices in the name of a cause however corrupted. There is seemingly, no way back anymore.[25]

Al-Asad intended to overcome the revolution and win the battle for Syria, whatever the costs. And the higher the costs, the more there was a will to continue the struggle, if only to prevent all the victims from having died in vain. This applied to both the regime and the opposition, certainly as long as there was no war fatigue. The earlier mentioned regime slogan 'it is either al-Asad, or we will burn the country' was put into practice to the furthest limits. It remained a battle for life or death, with hardly any room for compromise.

# CONCLUSIONS
## BASIC ELEMENTS OF THE SYRIAN CONFLICT SINCE THE REVOLUTION OF 2011

The conflict in Syria may be very complex, but various basic elements remain the same, and are sometimes overlooked or ignored. It may be useful, by way of a conclusion, to review some of those basic elements.

The conflict in Syria is a struggle for life or death between the Syrian regime and various opposition groups. The regime is not prepared to negotiate its own departure, downfall or death sentence.

The main opposition groups, on the other hand, have a lot to gain from a political solution in which they would share powers with members of the regime in a transitional governing body, in conformity with the Geneva Communiqué of 30 June 2012.

The Geneva Communiqué envisages

The establishment of a transitional governing body which can establish a neutral environment in which the transition can take place. That means that the transitional governing body would exercise full executive powers. It could include members of the present government and the opposition and other groups and shall be formed on the basis of mutual consent.

'Mutual consent' implies that such a transfer can only happen when the Syrian regime also gives its consent. And it is doubtful whether this will happen. The whole concept of transfer of powers is anathema for the Syrian regime, as this could be a prelude to its own downfall. The regime refuses a kind of regime change through political negotiations.

Therefore, a compromise has to be found. Thus far, neither side has shown any willingness to make any substantial concessions.

In general, negotiations are supposed to end in a compromise, in which neither side obtains all of what it wants. If the aim of both negotiating parties is to obtain almost everything they want, leaving the other side with almost nothing, a compromise is practically impossible.

The main opposition groups have insisted time and again that it is unacceptable for them to have to share power with President Bashar al-Asad and his main supporters with blood on their hands. Therefore, a compromise in which the Syrian regime would keep the greater part of its powers seems to be unacceptable to them. For the opposition, which accepts the Geneva Communiqué, the compromise is that they accept members of the regime in the transitional governing body who do not have blood on their hands. Such a transitional governing body should in their view exclude the hard core of the Syrian regime, which therefore is rejected by the regime in Damascus. For the regime, the compromise is to include some members of the opposition in a 'government of national unity', without giving them any powers that could threaten the position of the regime. As long as President Bashar al-Asad is in power, he is the main decision-maker from the regime's side when it comes to negotiations. The opposition keeps saying that their aim is to achieve the fall of President al-Asad and his regime.[1] This explicit demand has made real negotiations with the al-Asad regime impossible.

'Normally', negotiating parties do not negotiate themselves out of existence, except if they have something to win from such an outcome; but in the Syrian case the opposition wanted the hard core of the regime leadership to have disappeared by the end of the negotiations (and the beginning of the 'transitional period'), combined with the possibility of subsequently bringing them to justice with a high probability of capital punishment. This turned out to be unrealistic.

The thesis that the Syrian regime will be prepared to seriously negotiate once it is put under sufficient pressure appears to be logical, but will probably turn out to be unfounded when it comes to reality. For the regime it is (almost) everything or nothing. It will at most accept some cosmetic changes, as far as its powers are concerned. The regime's will can only be broken by military defeat, after which negotiations (with the regime) would no longer be necessary.

Further arming the opposition will not have the desired effect if it is only meant to put the regime under pressure. Only a military defeat of the regime could bring a real 'political' transition or 'regime change'. The situation that might follow after toppling the regime could be extremely difficult to control, however, because quite different groups could assume power instead of the moderate secular groups that were initially supported by Western countries and others. A radical totalitarian Islamist alternative to the al-Asad regime would not be unlikely, taking into account the dominance of Islamist and Jihadist military opposition groups, as well as the growing Islamic trends among other opposition groups. The war has led to further radicalisation. It appears that there is no good future for Syria with President Bashar al-Asad in power, but without al-Asad future prospects for Syria do not look promising either.

Nevertheless, political decisions have to be made and steps must be taken about Syria's future.

In 2013, when the regime reportedly carried out attacks with chemical weapons against opposition areas close to Damascus, direct military attacks were expected to be carried out against it by the United States, because US President Obama had warned beforehand that the use of chemical weapons 'would be totally unacceptable', that there would be 'consequences' and that al-Asad would 'be held accountable'. Such military attacks did not take place, however. They could have shaken the regime and could have brought it out of balance. Had such attacks been intended mainly as a limited punishment, without resulting in its toppling, the regime would most probably have stood up on its feet again and would have considered its survival as a victory (just as the regime did in the wake of its military defeat by Israel in 1967).[2]

All-out military intervention in Syria would have been unwise, taking into account the possible grave consequences (as happened in Iraq after the US–British military intervention of 2003 and in Libya in 2011, as well as in Afghanistan). Threatening with military intervention, however, albeit only implicitly, and subsequently not carrying it out strongly undermined the credibility of the United States, and Western countries in general. It, moreover, gave the regime the impression that it could get away with almost anything.

Obama's successor president Donald Trump followed a different line. Shortly after the Syrian regime had reportedly used chemical weapons in an attack on Khan Shaykhun in Idlib province in April 2017, President Trump swiftly reacted with a limited cruise missile attack on the Syrian airbase of al-Shu'ayrat from where the attacks had allegedly been carried out. The stated aim was to prevent the Syrian regime from 'ever using chemical weapons again'. Both the Syrian regime and Russia denied any responsibility for the use of chemical weapons, however, and claimed that the Syrian Air Force had hit a local chemical weapons storage belonging to the opposition.

The American attack led to severe tensions between Russia and the United States.

The regime is not prepared to implement the drastic reforms demanded by the opposition, because these could lead to its downfall. This is one of the reasons why the regime has not been willing to go further than establishing a 'government of national unity', including some opposition figures acceptable to it. The main opposition groups refuse the imposition by the regime, or by the international community, of any kind of political 'solution' that they consider unjust. Continuation of the present regime with all its extreme injustices remains unacceptable to them. Therefore, it is extremely difficult, if not impossible, to find a compromise that would be acceptable to both sides.

Many Syrians living in regime-controlled areas (not necessarily regime loyalists) reject, on nationalist grounds, any 'solution' that would be imposed by foreign forces, arguing that the fate and future of Syria should be decided by Syrians alone.[3]

In order to be able to achieve a political settlement, it should be obvious that all relevant parties should be involved, particularly those that exercise power inside Syria. (The Islamic State and al-Qa'idah-related organisations, like Hay'at Tahrir al-Sham, should be excluded, but in any case, these organisations are not prepared to negotiate.) The precondition that President Bashar al-Asad should be excluded from playing any role in the future of Syria will by definition block any political settlement, if only because al-Asad should cooperate in helping find a solution as long as he is in power. If it is demanded beforehand that he should give up his position as president, he will surely not cooperate and will reject such an option.

Declaring a foreign head of state to be illegitimate (or as having lost all legitimacy) and demanding his resignation as a precondition to achieving a political solution with his regime is unique, and bound for failure from the beginning. Declaring President

Bashar al-Asad to be illegitimate, whether justified or not, has only contributed to a prolongation of the conflict. The Western position was based on wishful thinking that al-Asad would leave his position as president on his own initiative (which was an assessment not based on any sound insight into, or knowledge of, the realities in Syria). There have been no reliable reports that al-Asad has ever had any intention to step down as president and leave.

Declaring that President Bashar al-Asad had lost his legitimacy as a result of the bloody developments in Syria might have been considered by many parties as justified on moral grounds, but when taking *realpolitik* as a reference it was not realistic, if a peaceful solution was to be reached. After all, al-Asad was in power in a major part of Syria and could be expected to remain so for a long time to come, except if his regime were to be toppled or if a successor were appointed or chosen in a legal institutional way. Having a successor to al-Asad, however, would not mean that the conflict would be solved.

Declaring the president to be illegitimate also created some ambiguities or inconsistencies in the political process. It would be strange to start negotiations with a personality who has officially been declared to be illegitimate. Nevertheless, Western countries (rightly) supported the intra-Syrian talks in Geneva under the auspices of the respective United Nations Special Envoys for Syria. Western countries thereby supported the negotiations by the Syrian opposition groups with a president whom they, as well as the opposition, had declared to be illegitimate. Some of them, including HNC President Riyad Hijab and various Western political leaders, demanded officially that President al-Asad should be brought to justice in the International Criminal Court. Next to the latter prospect being highly improbable, such contradictions were not really conducive to speedily helping solve the political conflict.

Conversely, the regime considered members of the Riyadh negotiations delegation to be terrorists with whom it, therefore, did not really want to negotiate.

The fixation on the departure of al-Asad constituted a serious obstacle to helping to find a solution to the conflict. Alternative personalities who might have taken over the Syrian leadership were not dwelt upon at any great length for lack of clearly identifiable options, and those who were specifically mentioned – like at the time Generals 'Ali Habib and Dawud Rajihah – were thereby disqualified by definition by the regime, if such suggestions from outside the regime did not already constitute a 'kiss of death'.[4]

Often the fact that the departure of Bashar al-Asad and his most powerful loyalists would not in itself bring a solution to the conflict was ignored. It was demanded by the opposition that the whole regime leadership with blood on their hands should leave. This would imply hundreds, if not many thousands of people with blood on their hands, when including the lower echelons (for instance of the security services). All these people could be expected to want to fiercely defend their positions and interests. They would not be prepared to leave of their own free will if this could lead to their being severely punished or sentenced to death.

If they were to leave, it should also be decided who should preferably replace them and which institutions should be reformed or abolished altogether. The many security institutions (not less than 15) should, according to the opposition, be reduced to the bare minimum, and be fully reorganised.

The strong domination of the officers' corps by Alawis was also bound to be addressed as part of a solution.

The power of the regime has been systematically underestimated by many Western politicians and others as well. This was partly a result of wishful thinking and partly a lack of knowledge of a regime that had been able to gather experience for over half a century on how to stay in power in the most unscrupulous manner. Appointing loyal supporters at sensitive key positions, eliminating (assassinating or imprisoning) those who were even only suspected of opposing the regime, has enhanced its power position for a long time. Confidants from the same region as the regime's leaders, from the same extended families and religious communities (Alawis in particular), often got preferential treatment, although the people involved did not escape a barbaric fate if they turned out to oppose the regime, or were suspected of it.

In this respect the Syrian regime was in various ways similar to the Ba'thist regime of President Saddam Hussein of Iraq. On the other hand, it had few similarities with the regimes in countries where revolutions had taken place within the context of the so-called Arab Spring, like in Egypt, Libya or Tunisia. Expectations that the Syrian regime was bound to fall soon after the fall of the regimes of Egyptian President Mubarak and the Libyan leader al-Qadhafi were completely unfounded. This did not, however, prevent the Syrian opposition, in the earlier stages of the Syrian Revolution, from drawing inspiration from the revolutionary developments elsewhere in the region. And they were encouraged in this respect by Western countries. The Syrian regime was different in various ways and rather unique in its power structure, dominance by members of the Alawi minority, and a network of strong sectarian, regional and extended family relations.

Since the repressive power institutions, such as the elite army units, the security services, the Shabbihah and other regime organisations, were so clearly identifiable as having a strong Alawi dimension (even though these institutions also contained non-Alawis), the war in Syria was bound to get a destructive sectarian character, leading to a polarisation between Alawis and Sunnis in general (which was also encouraged by Islamist and Jihadist Sunni circles, not for the first time in Syrian history, taking into account the assassinations of Alawis in the late 1970s and early 1980s, that led to the Hama massacre in 1982).

As a result, many Alawis felt obliged to support the regime out of fear of being violently prosecuted by Sunni-dominated Islamist opposition groups on a 'day of reckoning'.

Any political solution should therefore take the sectarian problems (which are much older than the Syrian Revolution) into serious account.

The war in Syria clearly developed into a war by proxy, with various countries (particularly the United States, Turkey, Saudi Arabia, Qatar, Great Britain and France) interfering in the internal affairs of Syria by supporting different armed and other opposition groups. Russia and Iran have strategic interests in Syria and are themselves clearly present militarily. They do not want to give up the regime, because that would imply losing their strategic ally, in which they have invested so heavily. President Bashar al-Asad as a person may have been considered as less important to Russia and Iran, were it not that his departure might contribute to the collapse of the regime. This is what these countries do not want to risk and therefore Syria with al-Asad in power is for the time being preferable to both Moscow and Teheran. Moreover, the departure of al-Asad would most probably lead to immediate additional demands for the whole regime to depart.

The Western approach to Syria has on various occasions been based on wishful thinking, in which priority was given to ideological democratic and moralistic ideals over *realpolitik*. Many Western politicians did not reckon with the realistic possibility of Bashar al-Asad staying in power for a longer time, and counted on his swift disappearance as president. They apparently were convinced that al-Asad's dictatorial regime could be replaced by a democracy through peaceful negotiations because this was considered by them to be morally justified and better for Syria. But realities turned out to be completely different, and many Western politicians considered it very difficult to admit that their earlier positions had been premature and unrealistic, because it could mean loss of face.

Western and regional support for the opposition has generally been too little too late, being insufficient to give the opposition a serious chance to prevail over the regime. Western and regional countries repeatedly created false expectations among the opposition that decisive support was forthcoming, thereby helping the war to intensify, rather than helping to solve the conflict. Moral support was not followed up with sufficient material or military support, or with effective political pressure. Having broken off relations with Damascus, Western countries lacked the necessary means to influence the Syrian regime. Only Russia and Iran had the means to do so to a certain extent, though their possibilities to really influence the regime were also limited.

The opposition (like their Western supporters) apparently did not see (or want to see) why their expectations were not always realistic, taking the military balance of power on the ground into consideration, as well as the (limited) support Western countries were really prepared to give. The involved Western countries may have had good intentions in supporting the opposition, but in practice they were not always fully sincere in clarifying to the opposition that their ability to influence the situation on the ground was more limited than was suggested by their statements. In fact, the Western countries were engaged in Syria with a limited will and with limited means, but they were not prepared to adapt their goals accordingly, as a result of which they were not in a position to achieve what they claimed they wanted.

The opposition felt abandoned and betrayed by Western countries, but was left with few if no alternatives.

With Western countries providing the opposition with insufficient support, the chances for Russia and Iran to get the upper hand were increased. The Russian military intervention that started in September 2015 made the prospects for the opposition even worse.

Providing more intensive support to the military opposition forces was bound to lead to an intensification and prolongation of the war, but would not necessarily lead to a defeat of the regime.

Much depended on the extent to which the foreign countries involved in the war by proxy were prepared to go to bring Syria even deeper into the war in which it had already found itself.

The concept of 'realistic' turned out to be controversial and sensitive. The various sides to the conflict tended to perceive their own positions and points of view as 'realistic', but did not always take enough into account whether or not their views could also be brought into practice, either through negotiations or military struggle. Much depended, in this respect, on the military balance of power, and which side was more powerful than the other to impose its will, with the help of its foreign supporters.

Being 'right' and 'just', as far as principles were concerned, was generally considered as being 'realistic' by the side that subscribed to them, even though on the ground these principles turned out to be unachievable, taking into account the all-decisive balance of military power.

On the other hand, it should be taken into consideration that opening positions during negotiations are not necessarily the same as those at the outcome of these negotiations, at least if a compromise is to be reached. The regime wanted the opposition 'to scale down its expectations' to some marginality, whereas the opposition wanted the regime to accept its own disappearance.

On various occasions, Western political leaders called for measures which they could have known in advance were not going to be implemented or carried out, because it would have implied a military confrontation with the regime, and its military supporters. This applied to Western calls for no-fly zones, safe zones and the imposition of humanitarian corridors. Such calls led to an undermining of the credibility in Western vigour. The same applied to various United Nations Security Council resolutions that were unanimously adopted, but could nevertheless not be implemented, because they turned out to be unenforceable, for lack of military will, because of the growing awareness that large-scale military intervention might make the situation even worse. Lack of such a military will seemed to be justified because of the probable disastrous consequences.

The adoption of UNSC resolutions that subsequently were not implemented led to a further lack of trust in the 'international community' among the Syrian opposition.

'Exerting pressure' was a concept that was used in a gratuitous manner in the Syria conflict. When questioning which concrete means really existed to put the other party under pressure, it turned out that these were rather limited. Western countries no longer had contact with the regime in Damascus, and therefore had no ability to put it under pressure by means of convincing or persuasion. For lack of such direct contact, third parties had to be asked to mediate, for instance Russia or Iran. The relations with these countries, however, were overshadowed by other issues, for instance by the issue of Ukraine, or the nuclear capabilities and regional ambitions of Iran. And since both

Russia and Iran had their own interests and aims in Syria, they were not found ready to follow the very different agendas of Western countries. The influence of the United States on Russia and Iran was for similar reasons rather limited.

Whereas there was no Western country that was prepared to directly intervene militarily in Syria against the regime (with boots on the ground), there was a lot of indirect military intervention by countries that supplied weapons to the armed opposition groups and were funding them: the United States, Saudi Arabia, Qatar, the United Arab Emirates, Turkey, Great Britain, France and others. On the regime's side there was the military presence of Russia and Iran, and its Lebanese ally Hizballah. After the Russian military intervention that started in September 2015, Western military intervention inside Syria became even more complicated because it could lead to a direct military confrontation with Russia.

When taking the threat of the population as a criterion for intervention on the basis of the principle of Responsibility to Protect, which was adopted by the member states of the United Nations in 2005, Syria would certainly have been eligible, even more so than at the time when part of the Libyan population was threatened by al-Qadhafi. The latter intervention turned out to be a disaster, however, partly because there was no serious aftercare once the Libyan regime had been toppled. In Syria such aftercare might oblige the intervening powers to stay on for perhaps a decade or more, without any guarantees that the situation would improve after their withdrawal from the country. Therefore, there was no political will, let alone the military capacity, to apply the principle of the Responsibility to Protect where Syria was concerned.

In general, military interventions have more often than not created additional problems that turned out to be extremely difficult to solve, and have caused enormous loss of human life.

Even in a case where al-Asad were to fully win the present war in Syria, this would not mean the end of the story. Because it seems to be inevitable that one day there will be a reckoning from the side of opposition forces, or the enemies of the regime, because of the many atrocities committed by the regime and its supporters. Therefore, serious negotiations between the regime and the opposition seemed to be by far the best option for both. Every possibility in this respect should have been seized upon, but was not.

There should be a political solution, not a military one. As long as the involved parties are not prepared, however, to negotiate on the basis of mutually acceptable conditions, it seems obvious that they will try to militarily impose their own conditions and ideas. This has been the case in almost all countries in the region, both in the past and in modern times. Bearing that in mind, developments in Syria could be expected to go further in the direction of a military 'solution'.

The options are not that many: 1. The war continues for an indefinite period, bringing further death and destruction. 2. The regime wins and continues its dictatorship and severe suppression. (Much depends in this respect on whether or not the Western and Arab Gulf countries that have supported the opposition will accept such a de facto situation, or whether they will yet keep supporting the opposition in an effort to help effectuate regime change.) 3. Opposition groups win, with the possibility of an Islamist dictatorship establishing itself. (Much depends in this case on whether or not the main allies of the Syrian regime are prepared to allow this to happen.) 4. A combination whereby the country is (temporarily or not) split up into different areas where different, more or less authoritarian factions dominate. 5. A political compromise, which seems to be preferable to all these cases.

Documenting all war crimes in Syria is an important task that should not be neglected. Finding a political solution should have priority, however. There should be a political solution first and justice after; it cannot be the other way around.

According to the Geneva Communiqué (2012) there should be a continuity of governmental institutions and qualified staff. Some of these institutions, and particularly the army and security institutions, are to a great extent packed by regime supporters. State institutions and regime supporters are interconnected to such an extent that 'regime change' could lead to a collapse of particularly those state institutions on which the regime has always depended to stay in power (like the army and the security services, the Ministries of Defence and Interior), unless the regime is fully willing to cooperate, which is doubtful. In the case of the regime being removed, the main state institutions that are linked to its power, therefore, would not be fully kept intact, but would need time to come to full capacity again after having been thoroughly reorganised.

During the war in Syria, people and organisations generally have become more radicalised due to extreme circumstances. Some existing alliances have shifted from moderate to more radical. Whereas Western countries originally only supported peaceful, and particularly also supposedly secular opposition forces, they later expanded their support to include various Islamist armed groups, like Ahrar al-Sham and Jaysh al-Islam, after these organisations had subscribed to the idea of a political solution as formulated in the Riyadh Declaration of the High Negotiations Council (2015). It is doubtful, however, that the Islamist groups that have subscribed to the Riyadh principles would be prepared to bring them into practice if they were able to seize power. Implementing the Riyadh principles would only be possible if the same signatory groups were really willing to share power, once the occasion arose.

Some Western countries, on pragmatic grounds and for the sake of the struggle against the Islamic State, made military alliances with radical forces, like the Kurdish PYD, which, under different situations, would have been rejected.

As long as no political compromise can be found, the Syrian War is bound to continue, and Syria may be divided into various zones of influence, until a political solution transpires.

In November 2016, Bashar al-Asad declared that he planned to remain president until at least 2021, when his third seven-year term would end, and that he would rule out any political changes before winning the war.[5] If this statement is taken seriously, which I think it should be, this would imply that there will likely not be any serious negotiations between the regime and the opposition in the foreseeable future, and that developments will go further in the direction of a military solution, unless al-Asad can be convinced by his main supporters and opponents (both foreign and domestic) to make some necessary concessions.

Serious efforts should be continued to help achieve a political solution. Miracles only happen if one keeps believing in them.

# NOTES

All translations, unless stated otherwise, are the author's own.

## PREFACE

1 Nikolaos van Dam, *The Struggle for Power in Syria: Politics and Society under Asad and the Ba'th Party*, 4th edn (London, 2011).

## INTRODUCTION

1 Wherever the name of 'Greater Syria' is used here, it refers to Bilad al-Sham.

2 Otto Jastrow, *Die mesopotamisch-arabischen qeltu-Dialekte*, 2 Vols (Wiesbaden, 1978–81).

3 Clifford Edmund Bosworth, *The New Islamic Dynasties: A Chronological and Genealogical Manual* (Edinburgh, 1996).

4 President Hafiz al-Asad has argued that if foreign powers had implemented the Fertile Crescent project, by unifying Bilad al-Sham and Mesopotamia, then there would now have been a large unified eastern Arab state, from which foreign domination would have disappeared in due course. Faruq al-Shar', *Al-Riwayah al-Mafqudah* ('The missing account') (Doha, 2015), p. 156. Former Syrian Ba'thist minister 'Abd Allah al-Ahmad distinguished two types of colonialism: 'divisive' and 'unifying colonialism'. The Arab world had, according to him, become the victim of divisive colonialism, whereas the Indonesians, for example, had been united, 'thanks to the so-called unifying colonialism' of the Dutch. In fact, colonial policies were generally inspired mainly by self-interest, not by the idea of acting in the interest of the

colonised peoples. See 'Abd Allah al-Ahmad, 'Ila al-Safir Nikolaos van Dam', *al-Safir*, 8 June 1995 and Nikolaos van Dam, 'Dutch unifying colonialism', *The Jakarta Post*, 3 December 2007.

The Fertile Crescent plan was promoted by the Hashemite monarchy in Iraq. Various Syrian politicians were in favour of it, but Syrian military and others were against it as long as Iraq was a monarchy. After the fall of the Hashemite monarchy in Iraq in 1958, the Fertile Crescent plan was no longer promoted.

5  See Muhammad 'Ali Zarqah, *Qadiyat Liwa' al-Iskandarunah. Watha'iq wa Shuruh*, 3 Vols (Beirut, 1993–4).

6  See Stefan Winter, *A History of the 'Alawis: From Medieval Aleppo to the Turkish Republic* (Princeton, 2016), pp. 262–8.

7  Lamia Rustum Shehadah, 'The name of Syria in ancient and modern usage', *Al-Qantara*, January 1994, pp. 285–96. See also Steve Tamari, 'Territorial consciousness in the 17th century: Bilad al-Sham among Syrian Christians and Muslims', in *Cohabitation et conflits dans le Bilad al-Cham à l'époque ottomane* (Beirut, 2009), p. 64.

8  See Patrick Seale, *The Struggle for Arab Independence: Riad al-Solh and the Makers of the Modern Middle East* (Cambridge, 2010).

9  Philip S. Khoury, *Syria and the French Mandate: The Politics of Arab Nationalism, 1920–1945* (London, 1987), pp. 100–2, 515.

10  Leila Al-Shami and Robin Yassin-Kassab, *Burning Country: Syrians in Revolution and War*, Kindle edn (London, 2016), p. 117.

11  Albert H. Hourani, *Minorities in the Arab World* (London, 1949), p. 14.

12  The members of the extended Ba'thist Military Committee were: Muhammad 'Umran, Salah Jadid, Hafiz al-Asad, 'Uthman Kan'an and Sulayman Haddad (all five Alawis); 'Abd al-Karim al-Jundi and Ahmad al-Mir (both Isma'ilis); Salim Hatum and Hamad 'Ubayd (both Druzes); six Sunnis, among whom three from Hawran: Musa al-Zu'bi, Mustafa al-Hajj 'Ali and Ahmad Suwaydani; two from Aleppo: Amin al-Hafiz and Husayn Mulhim, and one from Latakia: Muhammad Rabah al-Tawil. See also Mustafa Talas, *Mir'at Hayati, al-'Aqd al-Thani, 1958–1968* (Damascus, 1995), pp. 156–8, who

mentions Munir Jirudi as being a member of the original highest leadership of the Military Committee before it was extended. Jirudi did not play a visible role thereafter. He was apparently arrested in 1966 on accusation of being involved in the aborted coup attempt led by Druze officers Fahd al-Sha'ir and Salim Hatum. See Nikolaos van Dam, *The Struggle for Power in Syria*, pp. 52–61. According to Hanna Batatu, Jirudi was a Sunni from the village of Jirud in the Qalamun region. Hanna Batatu, *Syria's Peasantry, the Descendants of Its Lesser Rural Notables, and Their Politics* (Princeton, 1999), pp. 146–7. Marwan Habash also mentions Tawfiq Barakat as member of the extended Military Committee.

Earlier, various Ba'thist officers had been transferred to Egypt, after a list with their names had been given to the Egyptian military attaché in Damascus by Ba'thist colonel Mustafa Hamdun on the basis of a promise that they would be given 'sensitive' posts in Syria, but they were deceived. Once in Cairo, these officers formed a first Military Committee, consisting of Bashir Sadiq (as its leader), Mazyad Hunaydi, Mamduh Shaghuri, 'Abd al-Ghani 'Ayyash and Muhammad 'Umran. After some time, they were all posted in the diplomatic service abroad, with the exception of Muhammad 'Umran, who then formed a new, in fact second, Military Committee, which finally took over power in Syria in March 1963. See Marwan Habash, 'Hawl al-Lajnah al-'Askariyah', in *Qadaya wa Ara'* (Damascus, 2010), pp. 17–20.

13 It should be noted that there are no reliable contemporary statistics, only rough estimates. Church registers reportedly provide very low numbers. A general survey is not available.

14 Michel 'Aflaq, 'Fi Dhikra al-Rasul al-'Arabi' ('Commemorating the Arab Prophet'), in *Fi Sabil al-Ba'th* (Beirut, 1963), pp. 50–61. Towards the end of his life, Michel 'Aflaq converted to Islam, and he was buried in Baghdad as a Muslim in 1989.

15 Sami al-Jundi, *al-Ba'th* (Beirut, 1969), p. 38.

16 Mounir Mushabik Mousa, *Etude sociologique des 'Alaouites ou Nusaïris* (Thèse Principale pour le Doctorat d'Etat) (Paris, 1958), pp. 924–6.

17  Jacques Weulersse, *Paysans de Syrie et du Proche Orient* (Paris, 1946), p. 77. Cf. Jacques Weulersse, *Le Pays des Alaouites* (Tours, 1940), pp. 49, 73, 288.

18  Samir 'Abduh, *Taryif al-Madinah wa Madnanat al-Rif* ('Ruralising the city and urbanising the countryside') (Damascus, 1989).

19  Stefan Winter, *A History of the 'Alawis: From Medieval Aleppo to the Turkish Republic* (Princeton, 2016), p. 6.

20  Al-Shaykh 'Abd al-Rahman al-Khayyir, *'Aqidatuna wa Waqi'una Nahnu al-Muslimin al-Ja'fariyin al-'Alawiyin*, 3rd edn (Damascus, 1992); *Min Turath al-Shaykh 'Abd al-Rahman al-Khayyir: Tarikh al-'Alawiyin* (Damascus, 1992); and *Min Turath al-Shaykh 'Abd al-Rahman al-Khayyir: Risalah Tabhath fi Masa'il Muhimmah hawl al-Madhhab al-Ja'fari: (Al-'Alawi)* (Damascus, 1994). For an extensive treatise on the so-called 'Shi'ization' of Alawis in Syria see *Al-Ba'th al-Shi'i fi Suriyah 1919–2007* ('The Shi'i Ba'th in Syria 1919–2007'), al-Ma'had al-Duwali lil-Dirasat al-Suriyah, n.p., n.d.

21  'Alawi clergy slams BBC claim that sect is "distancing itself" from Assad', *BBC*, 4 April 2016. Haytham Mouzahem, 'Are Syria's Alawites turning their backs on Assad?', *Almonitor*, 25 April 2016. For an analysis of the document of the Alawi Shaykhs concerned, see also 'Study of the document of Alawi initiative', *Jusoor for Studies*, December 2016. Available at http://jusoor.co/content_images/users/1/contents/315.pdf.

22  Stefan Winter, *A History of the 'Alawis*, p. 17.

23  This view is confirmed by Stefan Winter, who argues that far from being excluded on the basis of their religion, the Alawis were in fact fully integrated into the provincial administrative order.

24  Stefan Winter, *A History of the 'Alawis*, pp. 7–8, 17, 25, 41–2.

25  Henri Lammens, *La Syrie. Précis Historique*, 2 Vols (Beirut, 1921).

26  A.H. Hourani, *Minorities in the Arab World* (London, 1947), pp. 15–22; Nikolaos van Dam, *The Struggle for Power in Syria*, pp. 1–3.

27  Kamal Salibi, *A House of Many Mansions: The History of Lebanon Reconsidered* (London, 1988), pp. 130–50; and Stefan Winter, *A History of the 'Alawis*, p. 43.

28  Patrick Seale, *Asad: The Struggle for the Middle East* (London, 1988), p. 8, quoted by Stefan Winter, *A History of the 'Alawis*, p. 44.


# 1. A SYNOPSIS OF BA'THIST HISTORY BEFORE THE SYRIAN REVOLUTION (2011)

1  Munif al-Razzaz, *al-Tajribah al-Murrah* (Beirut, 1967), pp. 158–9.

2  Hizb al-Ba'th al-'Arabi al-Ishtiraki, al-Qutr al-Suri, al-Qiyadah al-Qutriyah, *Azmat al-Hizb wa Harakat 23 Shubat wa In'iqad al-Mu'tamar al-Qutri al-Akhir* (Damascus, 1966).

3  Mahmud Sadiq, *Hiwar hawl Suriyah* (London, 1993), pp. 5–6.

4  Muta' Safadi, *Hizb al-Ba'th: Ma'sat al-Mawlid Ma'sat al-Nihayah* (Beirut, 1965).

5  Ibid., p. 69.

6  Ibid., pp. 338–9.

7  For a detailed analysis of Muta' Safadi's book see Nikolaos van Dam, *De Rol van Sektarisme, Regionalisme en Tribalisme in de Strijd om de Politieke Macht in Syrië (1961–1977)* (Amsterdam, 1977), pp. 63–71.

8  Munif al-Razzaz, *al-Tajribah al-Murrah*, p. 102. *Muluk al-Tawa'if* refers to a period in the history of Andalusia, in which various Muslim rulers established their independent principalities, emirates or fiefdoms, after the dissolution of the central authority of the Umayyad Caliphate of Cordoba.

9  Hanna Batatu, *Syria's Peasantry, the Descendants of Its Lesser Rural Notables, and Their Politics* (Princeton, 1999), p. 374n29. Hanna Batatu, 'Some observations on the social roots of Syria's ruling military group and the causes for its dominance', *Middle East Journal* 35/3 (Summer 1981), pp. 340–3.

10  In May 1965, the Military Committee was officially dissolved and replaced by a Military Bureau, but most of its original members

kept control over their military networks. See Marwan Habash, 'Hawl al-Lajnah al-'Askariyah', in *Qadaya wa Ara'* (Damascus, 2010), p. 20.

11  Munif al-Razzaz, *al-Tajribah al-Murrah*, p. 160.

12  Mustafa Talas, *Mir'at Hayati, al-'Aqd al-Thani (1958–1968)* (Damascus, 1995), pp. 612–14. Marwan Habash, 'Muhawalat 'Usyan al-Ra'id Salim Hatum fi al-Suwayda' Yawm 8 Aylul 1966', in *al-Ba'th wa Thawrat Adhar* (Damascus, 2011), pp. 243–64.

13  *Filastin* (Jerusalem) and *al-Difa'* (Amman), 14 September 1966.

14  *Al-Hayat*, 15 September 1966.

15  Circular of the Organisational Bureau of the Syrian Regional Command of the Ba'th Party, 19 March 1967.

16  Patrick Seale, *Asad: The Struggle for the Middle East* (London, 1988), pp. 150–3.

17  Mustafa Talas, *Mir'at Hayati, al-'Aqd al-Thani, 1958–1968* (Damascus, 1995), p. 852n1. Khalil Mustafa, *Suqut al-Jawlan* (Amman, 1969), p. 104; and *Min Milaffat al-Jawlan* (Amman, 1970). Khalil Mustafa (Pseudonym for Khalil Barayyiz), a Syrian military officer, was kidnapped in Lebanon in 1971 and imprisoned in Syria. He was not released when his sentence expired in 1985.

18  Salah al-Din al-Bitar, "Afwuk Sha'b Suriyah al-'Azim' ('Forgiveness, Great People of Syria'), *al-Ihya' al-'Arabi*, 21 July 1980. See also *Tadmur, al-Majzarah al-Mustamirrah* ('Palmyra, the continuous slaughter'), n.p., n.d., 2nd edn, 1984.

19  Salah al-Din al-Bitar, ' "al-Mas'alah al-Suriyah": Suriyah Maridah Maridah wa ta'ish Mihnah wa Ma'sat' ('"The Syrian question": Syria is very very ill and lives through a tragedy'), *al-Ihya' al-'Arabi*, 25 April 1980.

20  Hazim Saghiyah, *Al-Ba'th al-Suri. Tarikh Mujaz* (Beirut, 2012), p. 159, gives an estimate of almost two million Ba'thists. Emile Hokayem, *Syria's Uprising and the Fracturing of the Levant*, Kindle edn (London, 2013), location 3404, gives an estimate of 2.5 million Ba'th Party members. According to the 'Organisational Report' (*al-Taqrir al-Tanzimi*) of the Eighth Syrian Regional Ba'th Party Congress (1985), the official number of Ba'th Party

members in October 1984, was 537,864. For details see Nikolaos van Dam, *The Struggle for Power in Syria*, p. 88.

21 *Jaysh al-Sha'b*, 25 April 1967.

22 *Al-Nadhir*, No. 6, 8 November 1979.

23 *Al-Nadhir*, No. 2, 21 September 1979.

24 *Al-Nadhir*, No. 10, 1 February 1980, p. 12. Cf. *Al-Nadhir,* No. 9, 8 January 1980.

25 Raphaël Lefèvre, *Ashes of Hama: The Muslim Brotherhood in Syria* (London, 2013), p. 105.

26 The widow of Ibrahim al-Yusuf later published a book about her late husband and her own experiences: 'Azizah Jallud, *Ibrahim al-Yusuf wa Safahat min Tarikh al-Tali'ah al-Muqatilah fi Suriya. Masirah wa Sirah wa Haqa'iq takshif al-Mastur*, n.p., 2016. She was apparently not aware of the Aleppo Artillery Academy massacre beforehand, but gives an account of her terrible experiences in prison thereafter, and relates how her husband – in the period before the Aleppo massacre – had complained about favouritism towards Alawi officers by way of promoting them after the October 1973 War, at the expense of other officers. Al-Yusuf was, according to his widow, also brought before a military court on accusation of devoting too much time to prayer. When al-Yusuf had objected by saying that he performed the ritual prayers during his time off, whereas others were drinking forbidden substances during their work time, the case against him was apparently dropped.

27 *Al-Film al-Watha'iqi 'Basamat al-Dam al-Ula' – Majzarat Madrasat al-Midfa'iyah fi Halab.* Available at https://www.youtube.com/watch?v=0TxhsOm0raE&feature=youtu.be.

28 See Yasin al-Hajj Salih, 'al-Ta'ifiyah wa al-Siyasah fi Suriyah', in Hazim Saghiyah (ed.), *Nawasib wa Rawafid. Munaza'at al-Sunnah wa al-Shi'ah fi al-'Alam al-Islami al-Yawm* (Beirut, 2010), p. 64, who describes the Aleppo massacre as a heinous event that 'separates two stages in Syrian history where the issue of sectarianism is concerned'.

29 Cf. *Al-Nadhir*, No. 4, 22 October 1979, p. 3.

30  Raphaël Lefèvre, *Ashes of Hama*, p. 109.

31  Faruq al-Shar', *Al-Riwayah al-Mafqudah* ('The missing story') (Doha, 2015), pp. 62–3. According to Salah al-Din al-Bitar, the attack was carried out by members of the Military Police who were responsible for guarding the presidential guest house. Salah al-Din al-Bitar, "Afwuk Sha'b Suriyah al-'Azim' ('Forgiveness, Great People of Syria'), *al-Ihya' al-'Arabi*, 21 July 1980.

32  'Mawt Rajul al-Asadayn al-'Imad Shafiq Fayyad' ('The death of General Shafiq Fayyad … the Man of the Two Asads'), *Alarabiya.net*, 9 October 2015. Fayyad was one of the longest-serving hardline loyalist generals of the regimes of Hafiz and Bashar al-Asad. He may have advised President Bashar al-Asad that his 'Aleppo methods' could be effective once again in order to suppress the Syrian Revolution of 2011 onwards, but whatever the case, this turned out to be a serious mistake. His memoirs, *Hadatha Ma'i* (Damascus, 2009), thus far have not been published.

33  *Tadmur, al-Majzarah al-Mustamirrah* ('Palmyra, the continuous slaughter'), 2nd edn, n.p., 1984, pp. 26–7; al-Maktab al-I'lami lil-Ikhwan al-Muslimin, *Hamah, Ma'sat al-'Asr* ('Hama, the tragedy of the century'), n.p., n.d., pp. 19–21.

34  Thomas Friedman, *From Beirut to Jerusalem* (London, 1989), pp. 100–1.

35  Nur al-Mudi' Murshid, *Lamahat hawl al-Murshidiyah* (*Dhikrayat wa Mushahadat wa Watha'iq*) (Beirut, 2008), pp. 360–5.

36  Muhammad Ibrahim al-'Ali, *Hayati wa al-I'dam* (*'My Life and Execution'*), Vol. 2, pp. 241–74. Mustafa Talas, *Mir'at Hayati (1978–1988)* (*'The Mirror of my Life'*), Vol. 4, pp. 345–9.

37  See Lisa Wedeen, *Ambiguities of Domination: Politics, Rhetoric, and Symbols in Contemporary Syria* (Chicago, 1999), on the 'as if culture' in Syria.

38  Patrick Seale, *Asad: The Struggle for the Middle East* (London, 1988).

39  Patrick Seale, *The Struggle for Syria: A Study of Post-War Arab Politics (1945–1958)* (London, 1965).

40 Raymond H. Hinnebusch, 'Class and State in Ba'thist Syria', in Richard T. Antoun and Donald Quataert (eds), *Syria: Society, Culture and Polity* (New York, 1991), pp. 46–7.

## 2. COULD THE WAR IN SYRIA HAVE BEEN AVOIDED?

1 The Syrian Revolution can also be traced to an earlier date, for instance to the anti-government protests in the Hariqah quarter of Damascus on 17 February 2011, or to 26 January 2011, when a Syrian man by the name of Hasan 'Ali 'Aqlah poured petrol over himself and set himself alight in al-Hasakah, in protest against government policies, similar to the protest action by the Tunisian Bouazizi, whose self-immolation on 17 December 2010 triggered the Arab Spring. See for instance Carsten Wieland, *Syria – A Decade of Lost Chances: Repression and Revolution from Damascus Spring to Arab Spring* (Seattle, 2012), pp. 16–19. Charles R. Lister, *The Syrian Jihad: Al-Qaeda, The Islamic State and the Evolution of an Insurgency* (London, 2015), p. 12. David W. Lesch, *Syria: The Fall of the House of Assad* (London, 2012), p. 92. Although the book title suggests that it is about the fall of the house of al-Asad, Lesch at the time was among the few who explicitly took account of the possibility that the regime might stay on for a long time. See also Carsten Wieland, *Syria – A Decade of Lost Chances*, pp. 289–91.

2 According to 'I Am Syria', the death count in Syria had reached 450,000 in December 2016. Available at http://www.iamsyria.org/death-tolls.html.

3 *The Syrian Refugee Crisis and its Repercussions for the EU*, September 2016. Available at http://syrianrefugees.eu. A substantial number of Syrians fled also to the regions of Latakia and Tartus, which were considered to be relatively safe under regime control.

4 Nikolaos van Dam, *The Struggle for Power in Syria*, pp. 134–5.

5 Kevin W. Martin, *Syria's Democratic Years* (Bloomington, IN, 2015). Sami M. Moubayed, *Damascus Between Democracy and Dictatorship* (Lanham, MD, 2000).

6 According to Sadiq Jalal al-'Azm, half of the Syrian opposition would have been silenced if Riyad Sayf had been included in al-Asad's new government in the spring of 2011. Interview of Carsten Wieland with al-'Azm, quoted in *Syria – A Decade of Lost Chances*, p. 188.

7 Nour Samaha describes the basic regime's strategy as 'survival on its own terms wrapped in the blanket of "long breath"'. Nour Samaha, 'Survival is Syria's strategy', *Report Syria*, The Century Foundation, 8 February 2017.

8 Nikolaos van Dam, 'Syria: The dangerous trap of sectarianism', *Syria Comment*, 14 April 2011.

9 Charles R. Lister, *The Syrian Jihad*, p. 29.

10 See Peter Behnstedt, *Sprachatlas von Syrien, Kartenband*, Maps 9 and 10; Nikolaos van Dam, book review of '*Language Atlas of Syria*' by Peter Behnstedt, *Sprachatlas von Syrien*, Wiesbaden, 1997, in *ALL4SYRIA*, 17 June 2008; and *Syria Comment*, 19 June 2008. See also Stephen Starr, *Revolt in Syria: Eye-Witness to the Uprising* (London, 2012), pp. 183–4.

11 See *Syrian Opinions and Attitudes Towards Sectarianism in Syria – Survey Study*, The Day After, 22 February 2016.

12 According to Al-Shami and Yassin-Kassab, *Burning Country: Syrians in Revolution and War*, pp. 111–12, 169, 212–21, a number of 'state-directed' massacres took place. On 25 May 2012, 108 people were murdered in Hulah, a village with a Sunni population surrounded by Alawi villages. On 6 June 2012, between 78 and 100 people were murdered in al-Qubayr, again a Sunni farming area surounded by Alawi villages. On 10 July 2012, between 68 and 150 people – both civilians and opposition military – were killed at Tremseh. The Shabbihah, accompanied by the army, were reportedly responsible for most of these massacres. On 2 and 3 May 2013, at least 248 Sunni civilians were murdered in Bayda' and Banyas. These killings were sectarian-tinted as well. On 25 August 2012, 245 people were massacred by the regime's army in Daraya. Sectarian-tinted provocations of the Shabbihah against Sunnis in the coastal region have been extensively described by

Samar Yazbek, *A Woman in the Crossfire: Diaries of the Syrian Revolution* (London, 2012). Being an Alawi woman in the opposition, Yazbak was being dealt with by the regime as a traitor.

According to the study of Tim Anderson, *The Dirty War on Syria: Washington, Regime Change and Resistance*, Global Research (Montréal, 2016), most of these massacres were most probably 'false flag operations' in which the regime was made responsible for the massacres, whereas in reality it would have been the work of units of the Free Syrian Army. See also Robert Fisk, 'Inside Daraya – how a failed prisoner swap turned into a massacre', *The Independent*, 29 August 2012. Fisk was criticised by the opposon for reporting while being embedded in the Syrian Arab Army. For an account of a massacre of Alawis by Sunni Islamist radicals (of Jabhat al-Nusrah and IS) see Jonathan Steele, 'Syria: massacre reports emerge from Assad's Alawite heartland', *Guardian*, 2 October 2013.

13   According to Raphaël Lefèvre, *Ashes of Hama: The Muslim Brotherhood in Syria*, p. 184, in 2012 there were already reports 'suggesting that over 10,000 local Christians – or 90 per cent of the city's Christian community – have fled Homs for fear that the predominantly Sunni rebels might take revenge for their tacit support of the regime'.

14   In a survey study carried out by The Day After Association, it has been suggested that the Syrian regime may have been using truce agreements to effect a 'pre-planned demographic shift':

> Most of the interviewees said that there are outsiders (civilians from other sects or fighters loyal to the regime [i.e. Alawis or other members of minorities]) who came to their areas and lived there, and a considerable percentage said that they seized stores and homes whose owners fled, this figure reaching its peak in al-Bayada, Homs.

See The Day After, *Local Truces and Demographic Change in Syria*, 31 January 2017.

It should be noted that Sunni Islamist radical opposition forces in several cases followed a similar line.

15 'Opposition-regime swap deal in Syria frozen until further notice', *Lebanon Pulse, Almonitor*, 15 September 2015.

16 'The Displacement Agreement from Aleppo. How it happened? And how it has been done?', *Jusoor for Studies*, 26 December 2016. Available at http://jusoor.co/content_images/users/1/contents/312.pdf.

For an analysis of the military groups that participated in the battle for Aleppo in December 2016, see Cody Roche, 'Battle "Break the siege of Aleppo"' [July 2016 to December 2016]. Available at https://medium.com/@badly_xeroxed/battle-break-the-siege-of-aleppo-final-atgm-statistics-c56c6b83084f#.il6k7isxu, 5 January 2017.

17 Arond Lund, 'A voice from the shadows', *Syria in Crisis*, Carnegie Middle East Center, 25 November 2016. Interview by Robert Fisk with General Jamil Hasan: 'Tougher tactics would have ended Syrian war, claims the country's top intelligence general', *The Independent*, 27 November 2016. Jamil Hasan claimed that his military colleague Suhayl Hasan 'had been in action against Islamist suicide bombers in Idlib province in Syria in 2005 – six years before the world realised the extent of the government's war against its armed opponents'.

18 Interview of Riyad Hijab with *Al Jazeera*, 30 September 2016.

19 Sami Moubayed, *Under the Black Flag: At the Frontier of the New Jihad* (London, 2015), pp. 63–4. Raphaël Lefèvre, *Ashes of Hama: The Muslim Brotherhood in Syria* (London, 2013), pp. 204–5, has described how numerous Muslim Brotherhood fighters, after the Hama massacre of 1982, stopped sympathising with the Brotherhood leadership, which had decided not to continue the military struggle against the regime. Instead, they joined the Mujahidin in Afghanistan, 'waiting for the right time to return to Syria to settle scores, once and for all with the Ba'ath'. Lefèvre adds that 'perhaps the best explanation for the Brotherhood's historical comeback at the forefront of Syrian politics and society lies in the group's unique organisational capabilities'.

20  Patrick Cockburn, *The Jihadis Return: ISIS and the New Sunni Uprising* (London, 2014), p. 73, has noted that returning Jihadists are finding that their home route is not always an easy one, because 'their native governments, for example Saudi Arabia or Tunisia, which may have welcomed their departure as a way of exporting dangerous fanatics, are now appalled by the idea of battle-hardened Salafists coming back'.

21  Not all EU countries withdrew their ambassadors from Damascus. Ambassadors of, for instance, the Czech Republic, Hungary and Romania remained in place, and a restricted number of other EU ambassadors based in Beirut kept visiting Damascus from time to time. The European Union also maintained an office in Damascus.

22  See Bassam Haddad, *Business Networks in Syria: The Political Economy of Authoritarian Resilience* (Stanford, 2012), for the economic situation prior to the Syrian Revolution, and its prospects at the time.

23  Charles Lister, *The Syrian Jihad*, p. 54.

24  See Line Khatib, *Islamic Revivalism in Syria: The Rise and Fall of Ba'thist Secularism* (London, 2011); Thomas Pierret, *Religion and State in Syria: The Sunni Ulama from Coup to Revolution* (Cambridge, 2013); and Annabelle Böttcher, *Syrische Religionspolitik unter Asad* (Freiburg, 1998).

25  Ehsani2, 'How will the Syrian crisis end?', *Syria Comment*, 10 October 2016.

    According to former Syrian parliamentarian Muhammad Habash, the regime 'drove Salafists and Sufis to violence. Ideology was part of the reason, but let me tell you: if Ghandi spent three months in Syria, he would be a jihadi extremist.' Quoted in Michael Weiss and Hassan Hassan, *ISIS: Inside the Army of Terror* (New York, 2015), p. 145.

26  Reinoud Leenders, 'Repression is not "a stupid thing"', in Michael Kerr and Craig Larkin (eds), *The Alawis of Syria* (London, 2015), pp. 261, 339n86.

27  'Gunfire in locked-down Syrian city', *Al Jazeera*, 19 April 2016; Charles Lister, *The Syrian Jihad*, p. 53.

28  David W. Lesch, *Syria: The Fall of the House of Assad*, p. 106.

29  Stephen Starr, *Revolt in Syria: Eye-Witness to the Uprising*, p. 32, reports about the fears of Christians during the Syrian Revolution, who 'disowned elements of their communities that have displayed anti-regime rhetoric'.

30  Haytham Al Maleh, *Syria: Legalizing Crime*, n.p., 2012, p. 82.

31  On Buthayna Sha'ban see Bouthaina Shaaban, *Damascus Diary: An Inside Account of Hafez Al-Assad's Peace Diplomacy, 1990–2000* (London, 2013).

32  Faruq al-Shar', *Al-Riwayah al-Mafqudah* ('The missing account') (Doha, 2015), pp. 456–7. On the issue of 'family succession' see Roger Owen, *The Rise and Fall of Arab Presidents for Life* (London, 2012), pp. 139–52.

33  David W. Lesch, *Syria: The Fall of the House of Assad*, p. 66.

34  Saghiyah, Hazim, *Al-Ba'th al-Suri. Tarikh Mujaz* (Beirut, 2012), pp. 140–1.

35  President Bashar al-Asad in a meeting with the Dutch Minister of Foreign Affairs, Bernard Bot, *Achteraf Bezien. Memoires van een Politieke Diplomaat* (Amsterdam, 2015), pp. 371, 428.

36  David W. Lesch, *Syria: The Fall of the House of Assad*, p. 212.

37  Ibid., p. 19.

38  See for instance Mustafa Khalifa, *al-Qawqa'ah, Yawmiyat Mutalassis* (translated as Moustafa Khalifé, *La Coquille: Prisonnier politique en Syrie*) (Paris, 2012), various other memoirs of political prisoners, and the reports concerned of Amnesty International and Human Rights Watch.

39  See also Miriam Cooke, *Dancing in Damascus: Creativity, Resilience, and the Syrian Revolution* (London, 2016), for a comprehensive analysis of the dramatic voices of 'artist-activists' and others struggling to be heard through the Syrian Revolution. Cooke identifies reasons why the terrible events in Syria are leaving the world numb, or worse, indifferent, and what should be done to communicate the messages of the revolution effectively.

40  See for instance the interview with Father Frans van der Lugt, 'Bij defaitisme is niemand gebaat', *Mediawerkgroep Syrië*,

13 January 2012. Father van der Lugt was assassinated in Homs on 7 April 2014. Available at https://mediawerkgroepsyrie.wordpress.com/2012/01/13/bij-defaitisme-is-niemand-gebaat/; and Tim Anderson, *The Dirty War on Syria: Washington, Regime Change and Resistance*, Global Research (Montréal, 2016), pp. 15–22.

41  Ehsani2, 'Who is to blame for Syria's nightmare?', *Syria Comment*, 31 July 2016.

42  Charles Lister, *The Syrian Jihad*, p. 52.

43  See also Sami Moubayed, *Syria and the USA: Washington's Relations with Damascus from Wilson to Eisenhower* (London, 2012); and Robert F. Kennedy Jr, 'Why the Arabs don't want us in Syria', *Politico.EU*, 16 September 2016.

44  According to various sources the drought started in 2006, long before the Syrian Revolution began.

45  Robin Yassin-Kassab, 'Revolutionary culture', *Critical Muslim*, 11, *Syria*, July–September 2014, p. 25.

46  Patrick Cockburn, *The Jihadis Return: ISIS and the New Sunni Uprising*, pp. 83–97.

47  Stefan Winter, *A History of the 'Alawis: From Medieval Aleppo to the Turkish Republic* (London, 2016), p. 2, has, on the basis of his research, come to the conclusion that the widespread notion of 'historical persecution' of the Alawis is not borne out by historical evidence. According to Winter, the

> focus on confessional difference … is not only unsatisfying in scholarly terms but also undefensible in light of the sectarianist myths being mobilized on all sides of the civil war in Syria. Numerous sources exist that point to the 'Alawis' integration in wider Syrian society throughout history.

Winter's study focuses on the period before Syrian independence. The idea of the Alawis taking 'refuge in the mountains' as a persecuted minority has been a myth, at least in the past. See the Introduction to this book.

48  Peter Harling and Robert Malley, 'How the Syrian regime is ensuring its own demise', *Washington Post*, 1 July 2011.

49 After Professor Muhammad al-Fadil, rector of Damascus University and a prominent Alawi, was assassinated in 1977 by Mujahidin, his eldest son Nebras had to decide whether his father was to be buried in Damascus or in the Latakia mountains. Burying him in Damascus was considered an important symbolic act, because it confirmed that Alawis should have a formal place in Damascus, just like other Syrians.

50 Fabrice Balanche, 'Go to Damascus my son', in Michael Kerr and Craig Larkin (eds), *The Alawis of Syria* (London, 2015), pp. 90, 103. Kheder Khaddour, 'Assad's Officer Ghetto: Why the Syrian Army Remains Loyal', *Regional Insight*, 4 November 2015, Carnegie Middle East Center. Available at http://carnegie-mec.org/2015/11/04/assad-s-officer-ghetto-why-syrian-army-remains-loyal-pub-61449.

51 According to Fouad Ajami, *The Syrian Rebellion* (London, 2012), pp. 186–7, 'There is no likelihood of reviving the state of the Alawites. The vision of the Alawi barons and security officers quitting Damascus and taking up agricultural work in villages where the land had long been annulled is pure fantasy.'

52 Fabrice Balanche, *Parcours personnel* (Vol. 2), Diplôme d'habilitation à diriger des recherches. Université Lumière Lyon 2, 2013–14, pp. 33–5; Fabrice Balanche, *La région alaouite et le pouvoir syrien*, and 'The work of Fabrice Balanche on Alawites and Syrian Communitarianism' reviewed by Nikolaos van Dam, *Syria Comment*, 30 November 2013.

53 See for instance Mordechai Kedar, 'Assad's grandfather's 1936 letter predicts Muslims' slaughter of minorities, praises Zionists', *The Jewish Press*, 20 September 2012; Shlomo Avineri, Director General of Foreign Ministry, 'Conditions for Achieving Peace in the Middle East: Recognition of its Pluralist Character', Government Press Office (Tel Aviv), 2 August 1976; John Kimche, *The Second Arab Awakening* (London, 1973), p. 238 (with an imaginative map titled 'The Middle East of the 1970s', incuding a 'Druze Neutral Zone', a 'Kurdish Neutral Zone', a 'Sinai–Israel–Levant

Confederation' including parts of Lebanon, and a 'Syrian–Palestine Republic', including Syria, Jordan and a part of the West Bank). Nikolaos van Dam, 'Israel and Arab National Integration. Pluralism versus Arabism', *Asian Affairs*, June 1979, pp. 144–50.

54  John McHugo, *Syria: A Recent History* (London, 2015), 253–4.

55  For details concerning the possible falsification see Stefan Winter, *A History of the 'Alawis*, pp. 257–62; Stefan Winter, 'The Asad Petition of 1936: Bashar al-Asad's grandfather was pro-Unionist', *Syria Comment*, 14 June 2016; and Hassan Husseini, 'Watha'iq al-Khiyanah al-Ta'ifiyah. Risalat Sulayman al-Asad al-Maz'umah ila Faransa, 1–2' ('Documents of sectarian treason. The alleged letter of Sulayman al-Asad to France'), *Syrian Virtual Society*, 1–2 September 2012. Available at https://www.facebook.com/ SVS.Syria/posts/451091191602159, http://strategic-review.yolas-ite.com/modern-syrian-history.php, and https://www.facebook. com/SVS.Syria/posts/450497591661519.

Hassan Husseini's theory about the 'separatist' petition supposedly signed by Sulayman Asad is 'that it was created by French officers working in Syria, in an attempt to maintain their privileges and positions overseas, as long as they could'.

For the text of the so-called 'separatist' petition see, for instance, Harakat Ahrar al-'Alawiyin in their statement 'This is the betrayal of the al-Wahash [i.e. al-Asad] Family with the French' *(Hadhihi Khiyanat 'A'ilat al-Wahash ma' Faransa)*. Available at https:// twitter.com/jojohm7/status/737423989908373504.

56  *Syria: Opinions and Attitudes on Federalism, Decentralization, and the Experience of the Democratic Self-Administration*, The Day After, 26 April 2016.

## 3. CONFRONTATION BETWEEN THE MILITARY OF THE REGIME AND THE OPPOSITION

1  Charles Lister, *The Syrian Jihad*, p. 54. For some vivid accounts of defections see Husam Wafaei, *Honorable Defection* (Victoria, BC, 2012).

2   Available at https://www.hrw.org/news/2011/07/09/syria-defectors-describe-orders-shoot-unarmed-protesters.

3   Cody Roche, 'Syrian opposition factions in the Syrian Civil War', *Bellingcat*, 13 August 2016. Available at https://www.bellingcat.com/news/mena/2016/08/13/syrian-opposition-factions-in-the-syrian-civil-war/.

4   Harakat Ahrar al-'Alawiyin, @jojohm7. The tweets of Harakat Ahrar al-'Alawiyin portray the struggle within the Alawi community as a struggle between tribal federations and subgroups. The al-Asad family and its main allies like the families of Makhluf and Shalish are portrayed to belong to the Klaziyah, whereas their 'opponents' are considered to belong to the *'Haydariyin, Makhusin, Murshidiyin, Ja'fariyin'* and other groups. It makes a confusing and inconsistent impression. As I argued in *The Struggle for Power in Syria,* pp. 124–5, the Alawi officers loyal to the regime belonged to all tribal confederations. Tribal subsections have been of importance, and extended families even more, but these could not be considered as politically homogeneous.

5   Charles Lister, *The Free Syrian Army: A Decentralized Insurgent Brand*, The Brookings Project on U.S. Relations with the Islamic World, Analysis Paper | No. 26, November 2016, p. 3.

6   Charles Lister, *The Syrian Jihad*, p. 210.

7   Ibid., p. 2.

8   Thomas Pierret, 'States sponsors and the Syrian insurgency: The limits of foreign influence', in *Inside Wars: Local Dynamics of Conflict in Syria and Libya* (European University Institute, 2016), pp. 22–8.

9   Patrick Cockburn, *The Jihadis Return*, p. 72.

10  Sami Moubayed, *Under the Black Flag*, p. 81.

11  Charles Lister, *The Syrian Jihad*, p. xii.

12  Members of Da'ish are called Dawa'ish (which is the plural of Da'ish).

13  Yaron Friedman, *The Nusayri-Alawis: An Introduction to the Religion, History and Identity of the Leading Minority in Syria* (Leiden, 2010), pp. 62–4, 146, 188–99; and Stefan Winter, *A History of the 'Alawis*, pp. 56–61. See also Patrick Cockburn, *The Jihadis*

*Return*, pp. 83–4, for the execution by ISIS of Alawi truck drivers on religious grounds.

14  Charles Lister, *The Syrian Jihad*, p. 216. Sami Moubayed, *Under the Black Flag*, pp. 142–4.

15  For a comparison of the number killed by government forces, armed opposition actions, Russian forces, IS, unidentified international coalition forces, Kurdish autonomous forces, Jabhat Fath al-Sham and unidentified groups, see Syrian Network for Human Rights, 'The six main parties that kill civilians in Syria and the death toll percentage distribution among them from March 2011 until November 2016'. Available at http://sn4hr. bmetrack.com/c/v?e=A54204&c=9DF04&t=0&l=48F63B57&e-mail=lQsadv0Y9rbPEXJUHKvlzxaIw4W6c2hcNyIeD9VsXLU%3D.

The numbers produced by the Syrian Network for Human Rights are strongly disputed by Tim Anderson, *The Dirty War on Syria: Washington, Regime Change and Resistance*, Global Research (Montréal, 2016). See pp. 9–11, 19, 60, 64–5.

16  Christopher Phillips, *The Battle for Syria: International Rivalry in the New Middle East* (New Haven, 2016), pp. 202–6.

17  Christopher Phillips, *The Battle for Syria*, quoting Patrick Cockburn, *The Rise of the Islamic State: ISIS and the New Sunni Revolution* (London, 2015). Patrick Cockburn, *The Jihadis Return: ISIS and the New Sunni Uprising* (London, 2014), pp. 83–97.

18  Charles Lister, *The Syrian Jihad*, pp. 2, 390. For a detailed compilation of military opposition organisations see *The Syrian Opposition Guide*, by Jennifer Cafarella and Genevieve Casagrande, Institute for the Study of War, 7 October 2015. Available at http://understandingwar.org/backgrounder/syrian-opposition-guide, and https://en.wikipedia.org/wiki/List_of_armed_groups_in_the_ Syrian_Civil_War, where over 300 groups and units are mentioned, including of the regime. See also the detailed study of Cody Roche, 'Syrian opposition factions in the Syrian Civil War', *Bellingcat*, 13 August 2016, who distinguishes some 350 military opposition groups.

19  See the maps produced by Thomas van Linge and distributed by Pieter van Ostaeyen: https://pietervanostaeyen.com/category/maps/ and @arabthomness; and those published by *Jusoor for Studies*: http://jusoor.co/.

20  Available at http://www.mediafire.com/convkey/04ed/dpwvmu qv8aa7qsqzg.jpg.

21  Rojava in Kurdish refers to 'Western Kurdistan'.

22  Charles Lister, *The Syrian Jihad*, p. 80, interview with Amjad Farekh, January 2015.

23  Charles Lister, *The Syrian Jihad*, p. 8.

24  Nikolaos van Dam, 'Syrian future scenarios', *Syria Comment*, 27 November 2011; and 'How to solve or not to solve the Syrian crisis', *Orient*, III–2012, pp. 31–7.

25  Hicham Bou Nassif, '"Second-class": The grievances of Sunni officers in the Syrian armed forces', *Journal of Strategic Studies*, 5 August 2015, p. 11.

26  Of the 23 mentioned commanders of the Syrian Armed Forces on the eve of the 2011 uprising, 20 were Alawis and three Sunni. The eight directors of Syrian intelligence agencies in charge of controlling the armed forces have all been Alawis. The seven commanders of the Republican Guard and the 4th Armoured Division have all been Alawis. Of the seven commanders of the Special Forces and the Airborne Special Forces, six have been Alawis and one Sunni. Of the six Commanders of the Air Force and the Air Defence, three were Alawi and three Sunni. The 13 subcommanders of the Special Forces were all Alawis. Of the seven subcommanders of the Airborne Special Forces, five were Alawis and two Sunni.

27  Hicham Bou Nassif, '"Second-class": The grievances of Sunni officers in the Syrian armed forces', *Journal of Strategic Studies*, 5 August 2015, p. 7.

28  Ibid., pp. 14–15.

29 Hazim Saghiyah, *Al-Ba'th al-Suri. Tarikh Mujaz* (Beirut, 2012), pp. 145–6, notes that Generals Ghazi Kan'an and Hikmat al-Shihabi, together with Vice-President 'Abd al-Halim Khaddam, had been linked to an abortive coup attempt against Bashar al-Asad. Khaddam, who had had ambitions to succeed Hafiz al-Asad as president, subsequently went into exile.

30 Arond Lund, 'The death of Rustum Ghazaleh', *Syria in Crisis*, 30 April 2015. Available at http://carnegie-mec.org/diwan/59953.

31 According to Michael Weiss and Hassan Hassan, *ISIS: Inside the Army of Terror*, p. 107, 'new evidence had emerged suggesting that this assassination may have been an inside job, waged by Iranian-backed hardliners against Shawkat, who advocated negotiating with the anti-al-Assad opposition'. It appears strange, however, that Iran, being one of the main allies of the Syrian regime, would be behind such an operation. According to Ehsani, it was someone linked to the opposition who had been behind the assassination of Shawkat, and later informed the regime that they wanted 'to convince President Assad and his generals that they should come to a political agreement with the opposition and leave Syria because the opposition could assassinate them as surely as it has assassinated Assef Shawkat'. Ehsani2, 'Is Assad the author of ISIS? Did Iran blow up Assef Shawkat?', *Syria Comment*, 5 December 2016.

32 Arond Lund, 'Mikhail Bogdanov and the Syrian Black Box', *Syria in Crisis*, 18 March 2014. Available at http://carnegie-mec.org/diwan/55006?lang=en.

33 Joseph Holliday, 'The Assad Regime: From counterinsurgency to Civil War', *Middle East Security Report 8,* Washington, DC: Institute for the Study of War, 2013, p. 27, quoting *The Military Balance 2011*, p. 330. Cody Roche gives an estimate of 300,000 before the start of the Syrian Revolution in 2011: 'Assad regime Militias and Shi'ite Jihadis in the Syrian Civil War', *Bellingcat*, 30 November 2016. Available at https://www.bellingcat.com/news/

mena/2016/11/30/assad-regime-militias-and-shiite-jihadis-in-the-syrian-civil-war/.

34 Hicham Bou Nassif, ' "Second-class": The grievances of Sunni officers in the Syrian armed forces', *Journal of Strategic Studies*, 5 August 2015, p. 19.

35 Interview of Robert Fisk with Suhayl Hasan, 'An audience with "the Tiger" – Bashar al-Assad's favourite soldier', *The Independent*, 8 June 2014. In October 2016, the Tiger Forces issued an urgent call for new recruits, indicating a shortage of men. Available at https://twitter.com/FSAPlatform/status/789792256274362368/photo/1.

36 Tobias Schneider, 'The decay of the Regime is much worse than you think', *War on the Rocks*, 31 August 2016. Available at http://warontherocks.com/2016/08/the-decay-of-the-syrian-regime-is-much-worse-than-you-think.

37 Yezid Sayigh, Carnegie Endowment for International Peace, 'Syria's strategic balance at a tipping point', 7 June 2013.

38 For a survey of articles on pro-Asad militias, published by Aymenn Jawad Al-Tamimi in *Syria Comment*, 30 August 2016 see http://www.aymennjawad.org/2016/08/bibliography-pro-assad-militias.

    For an extensive survey of 'Assad regime militias and Shi'ite Jihadis in the Syrian Civil War' see Cody Roche, *Bellingcat*, 30 November 2016. Available at https://www.bellingcat.com/news/mena/2016/11/30/assad-regime-militias-and-shiite-jihadis-in-the-syrian-civil-war/.

39 Tobias Schneider, 'The decay of the Regime is much worse than you think'.

40 See the detailed article by Cody Roche, 'Assad regime Militias and Shi'ite Jihadis in the Syrian Civil War'.

41 See Chapter 1.

42 Interview by *Al Jazeera* with Shaykh Abu Muhammad al-Jawlani, 27 May 2015.

43 Raymond Hinnebusch has argued that even if a ceasefire were to be reached, the sectarian animosity and distrust created by

years of killing would likely be an intractable obstacle to power-sharing, needed to create enough stability to overcome the security dilemma in a failed state like Syria. 'Whole new generations that have grown up under civil war have adopted sectarian identities and rival politicians would not be likely to resist the temptation to use sectarianism to mobilize support'. Raymond Hinnebusch, 'The sectarian revolution in the Middle East', *Revolutions: Global Trends & Regional Issues*, 4/1 (2016), pp. 120–52.

44 See the maps of the predominantly Kurdish areas in Harriet Allsop, *The Kurds of Syria* (London, 2015); and in Jordi Tejel, *Syria's Kurds: History, Politics and Society* (London, 2011).

45 For a survey of Iraqi Shi'i groups fighting on the side of the Syrian regime see Cody Roche, 'Assad regime Militias and Shi'ite Jihadis in the Syrian Civil War'.

## 4. THE AMBIVALENT WESTERN APPROACH TO THE SYRIA CONFLICT

1 See also Emile Hokayem, *Syria's Uprising and the Fracturing of the Levant*, Kindle edn (London, 2013), locations 2629, 2643, 2673, 2689. Hokayem quotes (the otherwise well-informed) senior US official Fred Hof as saying in December 2011 that 'Assad was a dead man walking'.

2 When the French academic Fabrice Balanche, during an interview in France in 2011, commented on the situation in Syria by saying that the regime was not 'ripe' to fall and that the country was going straight in the direction of a civil war, he was categorised as a 'defender of the Asad regime'. When in mid-2012 he continued to declare that the regime should not be expected to fall soon, his interview was published under the title of '*L'interview qui fâche*' ('The interview that makes you angry'). See 'The work of Fabrice Balanche on Alawites and Syrian communitarianism reviewed by Nikolaos van Dam', *Syria Comment*, 30 November 2013.

3 Sami Moubayed, *Under the Black Flag: At the Frontier of the New Jihad*, p. 70.

4 Nikolaos van Dam, 'Syrian future scenarios', *Syria Comment*, 27 November 2011. Lecture for the panel discussion on the future of Syria, Berlin, Akademie der Konrad Adenauer Stiftung, 23 November 2011.

5 Peter Ford, who was the British ambassador to Syria from 2003 to 2006, declared in an interview with the BBC on 21 December 2016 that Britain's policy on Syria had been 'wrong every step of the way'. According to Ford, the United Kingdom 'had made matters worse by not putting troops on the ground and instead encouraging rebel groups to mount a doomed campaign ... The situation had led to hundreds of thousands of civilian casualties, which could have been foreseen.' Ford said the United Kingdom should have put forces onto the battlefield or refrained from encouraging the launch of the opposition campaign. He noted: 'We have made the situation worse ... It was eminently foreseeable to anyone who was not intoxicated with wishful thinking.'

Whether putting foreign forces onto the battlefield would have solved the conflict or would only have made things worse (which is my opinion), is another matter. Various countries undoubtedly have excellent Syria experts, but it is the politicians who finally decide. See Nikolaos van Dam, 'The (ir)relevance of academic research for foreign policy making', in Jan Michiel Otto and Hannah Mason (eds), *Delicate Debates on Islam* (Leiden, 2011), pp. 31–9.

6 Richard Haass, 'Aleppo's sobering lessons', *Project Syndicate – The World's Opinion Page*, 23 December 2016.

7 See also Noam Chomsky and Ilan Pappé, *On Palestine* (London, 2015), p. 78, where Chomsky argues:

You have to ask what is going to help them [in this case the Syrian opposition], not what is going to make me feel good. Call it pragmatic if you like, but I would call it ethical. You are concerned with the effects of your actions on the people you are standing in solidarity with.

8  Sami Khiyami, *Virtues of Nomination in Indoctrinated Nations*, pp. 3–4, June 2016 (unpublished). See also his interview on the subject: http://www.all4syria.info/Archive/323515.

9  Patrick Seale, 'Assad family values. How the son learned to quash a rebellion from his father', *Foreign Affairs*, 20 March 2012.

10  David W. Lesch, *Syria: The Fall of the House of Assad*, pp. 143, 213. In an interview with Reese Erlich in 2006, President Bashar al-Asad similarly indicated that putting foreign pressure on Syria to encourage the regime to allow the formation of opposition parties would be counterproductive. Reese Ehrlich, *Inside Syria: The Backstory of Their Civil War and What the World Can Expect* (New York, 2016), p. 74.

11  Peter Harling, 'The Syrian trauma', *Synaps*, 28 September 2016. Available at http://www.synaps.network/the-syrian-trauma.

12  Christopher Phillips, *The Battle for Syria: International Rivalry in the New Middle East* (New Haven, 2016), pp. 79, 249, in an interview with Robert Ford in March 2015.

Charles Glass, *Syria Burning: ISIS and the Death of the Arab Spring*, Kindle edn (London, 2015), p. 1117, quotes former US ambassador Robert Ford as having said during a conference in Washington in 2015: 'The people we have backed have not been strong enough to hold their ground against the Nusra Front.' If the United States could not achieve its goals in Syria, Ford reportedly added, 'then we have to just walk away and say there's nothing we can do about Syria'. Apparently, it took some time for Robert Ford to openly distantiate himself from the official United States policies he earlier had been obliged to defend, although he may not have agreed to these policies personally (as had been the case with prematurely calling for President Bashar al-Asad's departure).

13  Christopher Phillips, *The Battle for Syria*, pp. 80–2.

14  David W. Lesch, *Syria: The Fall of the House of Assad*, p. 155.

15  Bert Koenders, 'Aleppo must not become synonymous with global inaction', *The Independent*, 31 July 2016.

16  Tristan Quinalt Maupoil, 'Syrie: Fillon veut mettre le régime d'Assad autour de la table des négociations', *Le Figaro*, 15 December 2016.

17  Christopher Phillips, *The Battle for Syria*, p. 171, interview with Basma Qadmani, 2015.

18  Christopher Phillips, *The Battle for Syria*, p. 171.


## 5. INTRA-SYRIAN TALKS BUT NO NEGOTIATIONS

1  Available at http://www.un.org/apps/news/story.asp?NewsID= 41144&Cr=Syria&Cr1.

2  For details of the six-point plan concerned see http://www. un.org/News/Press/docs/2012/sc10583.doc.htm.

3  In 2016, Egypt was no longer accepted as part of the 'London 11' by the other member countries, apparently because its relations with the Syrian regime were considered as being too close. Facing its own IS-led insurgency in the Sinai Peninsula, Egypt started to consider Syria as a credible partner in its war against terrorism, and therefore was keen to cooperate with the Syrian army. See Nour Samaha, 'Survival is Syria's strategy', *Report Syria*, The Century Foundation, 8 February 2017.

4  'Asharat al-Muthaqqafin al-Suriyin yutliquna Mubadarat "Nida' min ajl Suriya" li-Tamthil Haqiqi lil-Thawrah wa I'adat Hayka-liyat al-I'tilaf' ('Tens of Syrian Intellectuals launch an "Appeal for Syria" for a real representation of the Revolution and a Revision of the Coalition's Structure'), *Al-Sultah al-Rabi'ah*, 25 November 2016. Available at http://alsulta-alrabi3a.com/2016/11/8381. html.

5  Later, in April 2015, Lu'ayy Husayn and his deputy Dr Muna Ghanim fled from Syria after having given up hope that they could bring political change from within the country.

6  Human Rights Watch, 'If the dead could speak. Mass deaths and torture in Syria's detention facilities', 16 December 2015. See also *'It Breaks the Human': Torture, Disease and Death in Syria's Prisons*, Amnesty International, 18 August 2016.

7  See *Humanitarian Slaughterhouse: Mass Hangings and Extermination at Saydnaya Prison, Syria*, Amnesty International, 7 February 2017.

8  Available at http://www.diplomatie.gouv.fr/en/country-files/syria/events/article/final-statement-of-the-conference-of-syrian-revolution-and-opposition-forces.

9  Available at http://www.newscenter.news/ar/news/view/15040.html. The complete list was: Ahmad al-Jarba (SOC), Ahmad al-'Asrawi (NCC), Bashar Manla, Bakkur Salim, George Sabra, Husam Hafiz, Hasan Ibrahim, Khalid Khoja (SOC President), Riyad Hijab, Riyad Na'san Agha, Ziyad Watfah, Salim al-Muslit, Samir Habbush, Suhayr al-Atasi, Safwan 'Akkash, 'Abd al-Hakim Bashar (Kurdish National Council), 'Abd al-'Aziz al-Shallal, 'Abd al-Latif al-Hawrani, Faruq Tayfur (Muslim Brotherhood), Labib Nahhas (Ahrar al-Sham), Lu'ayy Husayn (Building the Syrian State), Muhammad Jum'ah 'Abd al-Qadir, Hasan Hajj 'Ali, Muhammad Hijazi, Muhammad Mustafa 'Allush (Jaysh al-Islam), Muhammad Mansur, Mu'adh al-Khatib, Mundhir Makhus, Munir Bitar, Hind Qabawat, Walid al-Zu'bi, Yahya Qadmani and Iyad Ahmad.

Mu'adh al-Khatib (first president of the SOC), who was also on the list, let it be known that he was not to be considered a member of the HNC. Others, like Lu'ayy Husayn (BSS), later withdrew from the HNC because they did not agree with its policies and personalities. Some of those who were invited, like Haytham Manna' (Qamh), declined to come.

10  Harriet Allsopp, *The Kurds of Syria* (London, 2015), pp. 201–4.

11  Arond Lund, 'Syria's opposition conferences: Results and expectations', Carnegie Middle East Center, *Syria in Crisis*, 11 December 2015. Available at http://carnegie-mec.org/diwan/62263?lang=en.

12  The full negotiations delegation was composed of: George Sabra, Muhammad 'Allush, Suhayr al-Atasi, As'ad al-Zu'bi, Muhammad al-Sabra, Ahmad al-Hariri, Fu'ad 'Aliko, 'Abd al-Basit Tawil, Muhammad 'Abbud, Basma Qadmani, 'Abd al-Majid Hamo, Khalaf Dahud, Muhammad 'Attur, Nadhir Hakim, Alice Mafraj, Khalid al-Mahamid.

13  Interview of President Bashar al-Asad with *Komsomolskaya Pravda*, 12 October 2016.

14 Interview of Bashar al-Ja'fari with ABC News, 16 March 2016. Available at http://www.abc.net.au/news/2016-03-16/interview:-dr-bashar-jaafari,-syrian-ambassador-to/7252962.

15 Available at http://syrianobserver.com/EN/News/30748/Geneva_Regime_Delegation_Sidesteps_Political_Transition_Demands_Recovery_of_Golan; http://www.alhayat.com/m/story/14620254.

16 *The Tower*, 3 October 2016. Available at http://www.thetower.org/syrian-rebels-leader-assad-is-the-main-enemy-not-israel/.

17 Available at http://etilaf.org/images/reports/hnc.geneva2012.pdf, https://gallery.mailchimp.com/91f7a2c8b39d32e7ac9968d75/files/HNC_Executive_Summary_English.pdf.

18 Intra-Syrian Track-2 meetings were organised between various Syrian opposition personalities by organisations like the Brookings Center Doha with Salman Shaikh (later the Shaikh Group), the Carter Center, the Center for Humanitarian Dialogue, and others, in Stockholm, Istanbul, Zurich, Geneva, Amsterdam and elsewhere.

19 By way of an example, the famous Muslim leader Salah al-Din al-Ayyubi from Tikrit was a Kurd.

20 Fabrice Balanche, 'Go to Damascus my son', in Michael Kerr and Craig Larkin (eds), *The Alawis of Syria* (London, 2015), p. 90.

21 Interview of the author with the Kurdish Democratic Party leader Mustafa Barzani, Hajj 'Umran, Iraq, 15 August 1971.

22 In academic literature, minorities are generally defined as being dominated by others within the same state; they generally differ culturally from the dominant group (in which religion and/or language may be the most relevant); they are usually smaller in number than the dominant group, *but not always*; in their relation with the dominant group they usually want to abolish their unequal status. See Leonard C. Biegel, *Minderheden in het Midden-Oosten* ('Minorities in the Middle East') (Amsterdam, 1972), pp. 13–19.

23 Nikolaos van Dam, 'Middle Eastern political clichés: "Takriti" and "Sunni rule" in Iraq; "Alawi rule" in Syria. A critical appraisal', *Orient*, 21/1 (January 1980).

24 Yassin Al-Haj Saleh, 'Majoritarian Syria: Justice in conflict resolution', *al-Jumhuriya* (English), 20 October 2016. Available at http://aljumhuriya.net/en/syrian-revolution/majoritarian-syria-justice-in-conflict-resolution.

25 Peter Harling, 'The Syrian trauma', *Synaps*, 28 September 2016. Available at http://www.synaps.network/the-syrian-trauma.

## CONCLUSIONS

1 Interview of *Al Jazeera* with Riyad Hijab, 30 September 2016.

2 See Bente Scheller, *The Wisdom of Syria's Waiting Game: Foreign Policy under the Assads* (London, 2013), pp. 209–17.

3 Nour Samaha, 'Survival is Syria's strategy', *Report Syria*, The Century Foundation, 8 February 2017. For similar reasons various foreign (including Russian) text proposals for a new Syrian Constitution have been rejected because of their origin.

4 On 29 April 2011, opposition personalities issued a declaration stating that 'the only institution that has the capability to lead the transition period would be the military, and especially the current Minister of Defense General Ali Habib and the Chief of Staff General Dawud Rajha.' *Souria Houria*, 30 April 2011. Rajihah was assassinated in July 2012 and Habib was reported dead in August 2011, but the opposition claimed that he left the country. Habib reportedly was acceptable to the opposition at the time because he supposedly was against using violence against the peaceful demonstrators.

5 *New York Times*, 1 November 2016.

# BIBLIOGRAPHY

Ajami, Fouad, *The Syrian Rebellion* (Stanford, 2012).

Allsop, Harriet, *The Kurds of Syria* (London, 2015).

Amnesty International, *'It Breaks the Human': Torture, Disease and Death in Syria's Prisons*, 18 August 2016.

——, *Humanitarian Slaughterhouse: Mass Hangings and Extermination at Saydnaya Prison, Syria*, 7 February 2017.

Anderson, Tim, *The Dirty War on Syria: Washington, Regime Change and Resistance*, Global Research, Montréal, 2016.

Avineri, Shlomo, Director General of Foreign Ministry, *Conditions for Achieving Peace in the Middle East: Recognition of its Pluralist Character*, Government Press Office (Tel Aviv), 2 August 1976.

Balanche, Fabrice, *La région alaouite et le pouvoir syrien* (Paris, 2006).

——, *Parcours personnel* (Vol. 2), Diplôme d'habilitation à diriger des recherches. Université Lumière Lyon 2, 2013–14.

——, 'Go to Damascus my son', in Michael Kerr and Craig Larkin (eds), *The Alawis of Syria* (London, 2015).

Batatu, Hanna, 'Some observations on the social roots of Syria's ruling military group and the causes for its dominance', *Middle East Journal* 35/3 (Summer 1981).

——, *Syria's Peasantry, the Descendants of Its Lesser Rural Notables, and Their Politics* (Princeton, 1999).

Behnstedt, Peter, *Sprachatlas von Syrien*, 2 Vols (Wiesbaden, 1997).

Biegel, Leonard C., *Minderheden in het Midden-Oosten* ('Minorities in the Middle East') (Amsterdam, 1972).

Bosworth, Clifford Edmund, *The New Islamic Dynasties: A Chronological and Genealogical Manual* (Edinburgh, 1996).

Bot, Bernard, *Achteraf Bezien. Memoires van een Politieke Diplomaat* (Amsterdam, 2015).

Böttcher, Annabelle, *Syrische Religionspolitik unter Asad* (Freiburg, 1998).

Bou Nassif, Hicham, ' "Second-class": The grievances of Sunni officers in the Syrian armed forces', *Journal of Strategic Studies*, 5 August 2015.

Cafarella, Jennifer and Genevieve Casagrande, *The Syrian Opposition Guide*, Institute for the Study of War, 7 October 2015.

Chomsky, Noam and Ilan Pappé, *On Palestine* (London, 2015).

Cockburn, Patrick, *The Jihadis Return: ISIS and the New Sunni Uprising*, Kindle edn (London, 2014).

Cooke, Miriam, *Dancing in Damascus: Creativity, Resilience, and the Syrian Revolution* (London, 2016).

Dam, Nikolaos van, *De Rol van Sektarisme, Regionalisme en Tribalisme in de Strijd om de Politieke Macht in Syrië (1961–1977).* (Amsterdam, 1977).

———, 'Israel and Arab National Integration. Pluralism versus Arabism', *Asian Affairs*, June 1979, pp. 144–50.

———, 'Middle Eastern political clichés: "Takriti" and "Sunni rule" in Iraq; "Alawi rule" in Syria. A critical appraisal', *Orient*, 21/1 (January 1980).

———, 'Dutch unifying colonialism', *The Jakarta Post*, 3 December 2007.

———, Book review of *Language Atlas of Syria* by Peter Behnstedt, *Sprachatlas von Syrien*, Wiesbaden, 1997, in *ALL4SYRIA*, 17 June 2008; *Syria Comment*, 19 June 2008.

———, 'Syria: The dangerous trap of sectarianism', *Syria Comment*, 14 April 2011.

———, 'Syrian future scenarios', *Syria Comment*, 27 November 2011.

———, 'The (ir)relevance of academic research for foreign policy making', in Jan Michiel Otto and Hannah Mason (eds), *Delicate Debates on Islam* (Leiden, 2011), pp. 31–9.

———, *The Struggle for Power in Syria: Politics and Society under Asad and the Ba'th Party*, 4th edn (London, 2011).

———, 'How to solve or not to solve the Syrian crisis', *Orient*, III–2012.

———, 'The work of Fabrice Balanche on Alawites and Syrian Communitarianism', *Syria Comment*, 30 November 2013.

Day After, The, *Syrian Opinions and Attitudes Towards Sectarianism in Syria – Survey Study*, 22 February 2016.

———, *Syria: Opinions and Attitudes on Federalism, Decentralization, and the Experience of the Democratic Self-Administration*, 26 April 2016.

———, *Local Truces and Demographic Change in Syria*, 31 January 2017.

Ehrlich, Reese, *Inside Syria: The Backstory of Their Civil War and What the World Can Expect* (New York, 2016).

Ehsani2, 'Who is to blame for Syria's nightmare?', *Syria Comment*, 31 July 2016.

———, 'How will the Syrian crisis end?', *Syria Comment*, 10 October 2016.

———, 'Is Assad the author of ISIS? Did Iran blow up Assef Shawkat?', *Syria Comment*, 5 December 2016.

Fisk, Robert, 'Inside Daraya – how a failed prisoner swap turned into a massacre', *The Independent*, 29 August 2012.

———, 'An audience with "the Tiger" – Bashar al-Assad's favourite soldier', *The Independent*, 8 June 2014.

———, Interview with General Jamil Hasan: 'Tougher tactics would have ended Syrian war, claims the country's top intelligence general', *The Independent*, 27 November 2016.

Ford, Peter, 'Britain "got Syria wrong every step of the way"', Interview with the BBC, 23 December 2016.

Friedman, Thomas, *From Beirut to Jerusalem* (London, 1989).

Friedman, Yaron, *The Nusayri-Alawis: An Introduction to the Religion, History and Identity of the Leading Minority in Syria* (Leiden, 2010).

Glass, Charles, *Syria Burning: ISIS and the Death of the Arab Spring*, Kindle edn (London, 2015).

Haass, Richard, 'Aleppo's sobering lessons', *Project Syndicate – The World's Opinion Page*, 23 December 2016.

Haddad, Bassam, *Business Networks in Syria: The Political Economy of Authoritarian Resilience* (Stanford, 2012).

Harling, Peter, 'The Syrian trauma', *Synaps*, 28 September 2016. Available at http://www.synaps.network/the-syrian-trauma.

Harling, Peter and Robert Malley, 'How the Syrian regime is ensuring its own demise', *Washington Post*, 1 July 2011.

Hinnebusch, Raymond H., 'Class and State in Ba'thist Syria', in Richard T. Antoun and Donald Quataert (eds), *Syria: Society, Culture and Polity* (New York, 1991), pp. 29–47.

———, 'The Sectarian Revolution in the Middle East', *Revolutions: Global Trends & Regional Issues*, 4/1 (2016), pp. 120–52.

Hokayem, Emile, *Syria's Uprising and the Fracturing of the Levant*, Kindle edn (London, 2013).

Holliday, Joseph, 'The Assad Regime: From counterinsurgency to Civil War', *Middle East Security Report 8*, Washington DC: Institute for the Study of War, 2013.

Hourani, A.H. *Minorities in the Arab World* (London, 1947).

Human Rights Watch, *If the Dead Could Speak: Mass Deaths and Torture in Syria's Detention Facilities*, 16 December 2015.

Jastrow, Otto, *Die mesopotamisch-arabischen qeltu-Dialekte*, 2 Vols (Wiesbaden, 1978–81).

*Jusoor for Studies*, 26 December 2016, 'The Displacement Agreement from Aleppo. How it happened? And how it has been done?' Available at http://jusoor.co/content_images/users/1/contents/312.pdf.

———, December 2016. 'Study of the document of Alawi initiative'. Available at http://jusoor.co/content_images/users/1/contents/315.pdf.

Kedar, Mordechai, 'Assad's Grandfather's 1936 letter predicts Muslims' slaughter of minorities, praises Zionists', *The Jewish Press*, 20 September 2012.

Kennedy Jr, Robert F., 'Why the Arabs don't want us in Syria', *Politico.eu*, 16 September 2016.

Khaddour, Kheder, 'Assad's Officer Ghetto: Why the Syrian Army remains loyal', *Regional Insight*, 4 November 2015, Carnegie Middle East Center.

Khalifé, Moustafa, *La Coquille: Prisonnier politique en Syrie* (Paris, 2012).

Khatib, Line, *Islamic Revivalism in Syria: The Rise and Fall of Ba'thist Secularism* (London, 2011).

Khiyami, Sami, *Virtues of Nomination in Indoctrinated Nations*, June 2016 (unpublished).

Khoury, Philip S., *Syria and the French Mandate: The Politics of Arab Nationalism, 1920–1945* (London, 1987).

Kimche, John, *The Second Arab Awakening* (London, 1970).

Koenders, Bert, 'Aleppo must not become synonymous with global inaction', *The Independent*, 31 July 2016.

Lammens, Henri, *La Syrie. Précis Historique*, 2 Vols (Beirut, 1921).

Leenders, Reinoud, 'Repression is not "a stupid thing"', in Michael Kerr and Craig Larkin (eds), *The Alawis of Syria* (London, 2015), pp. 245–73.

Lefèvre, Raphaël, *Ashes of Hama: The Muslim Brotherhood in Syria* (London, 2013).

Lesch, David, *Syria: The Fall of the House of Assad* (London, 2012).

Lister, Charles R., *The Syrian Jihad: Al-Qaeda, The Islamic State and the Evolution of an Insurgency* (London, 2016).

——, *The Free Syrian Army: A Decentralized Insurgent Brand*, The Brookings Project on U.S. Relations with the Islamic World, Analysis Paper | No. 26, November 2016.

Lugt, Father van der, 'Bij defaitisme is niemand gebaat', *Mediawerkgroep Syrië*, 13 January 2012. Available at https://mediawerkgroepsyrie. wordpress.com/2012/01/13/bij-defaitisme-is-niemand-gebaat/.

Lund, Arond, 'Mikhail Bogdanov and the Syrian black box', *Syria in Crisis*, 18 March 2014.

——, 'The death of Rustum Ghazaleh', *Syria in Crisis*, 30 April 2015.

——, 'Syria's opposition conferences: Results and expectations', Carnegie Middle East Center, *Syria in Crisis*, 11 December 2015.

——, 'A voice from the shadows', *Syria in Crisis*, Carnegie Middle East Center, 25 November 2016.

Maleh, Haytham Al, *Syria: Legalizing Crime*, n.p. (2012).

Martin, Kevin W., *Syria's Democratic Years* (Bloomington, Indiana, 2015).

Maupoil, Tristan Quinalt, 'Syrie: Fillon veut mettre le régime d'Assad autour de la table des négociations', *Le Figaro*, 15 December 2016.

McHugo, John, *Syria: A Recent History* (London, 2015).

Moubayed, Sami, *Damascus Between Democracy and Dictatorship* (Lanham, Maryland, 2000).

———, *Syria and the USA: Washington's Relations with Damascus from Wilson to Eisenhower* (London, 2012).

———, *Under the Black Flag: At the Frontier of the New Jihad* (London, 2015).

Mousa, Mounir Mushabik, *Etude sociologique des 'Alaouites ou Nusaïris* (Thèse Principale pour le Doctorat d'Etat) (Paris, 1958).

Mouzahem, Haytham, 'Are Syria's Alawites turning their backs on Assad?', *Almonitor*, 25 April 2016.

Owen, Roger, *The Rise and Fall of Arab Presidents for Life* (London, 2012).

Phillips, Christopher, *The Battle for Syria: International Rivalry in the New Middle East* (New Haven, 2016).

Pierret, Thomas, *Religion and State in Syria: The Sunni Ulama from Coup to Revolution* (Cambridge, 2013).

———, 'States sponsors and the Syrian insurgency: The limits of foreign influence', *Inside Wars: Local Dynamics of Conflict in Syria and Libya*, European University Institute, 2016.

Roche, Cody, 'Syrian opposition factions in the Syrian civil war', *Bellingcat*, 13 August 2016.

———, 'Assad regime Militias and Shi'ite Jihadis in the Syrian civil war', *Bellingcat*, 30 November 2016. Available at https://www.bellingcat.com/news/mena/2016/11/30/assad-regime-militias-and-shiite-jihadis-in-the-syrian-civil-war/.

———, 'Battle "Break the siege of Aleppo"' [July 2016 – December 2016]. Available at https://medium.com/@badly_xeroxed/battle-break-the-siege-of-aleppo-final-atgm-statistics-c56c6b83084f#.il6k7isxu.

Saleh, Yassin Al-Haj, 'Majoritarian Syria: Justice in conflict resolution', *al-Jumhuriya* (English), 20 October 2016. Available at http://

aljumhuriya.net/en/syrian-revolution/majoritarian-syria-justice-in-conflict-resolution.

Salibi, Kamal, *A House of Many Mansions: The History of Lebanon Reconsidered* (London, 1988).

Samaha, Nour, 'Survival is Syria's strategy', *Report Syria*, The Century Foundation, 8 February 2017.

Sayigh, Yezid, Carnegie Endowment for International Peace, *Syria's Strategic Balance at a Tipping Point*, 7 June 2013.

Scheller, Bente, *The Wisdom of Syria's Waiting Game: Foreign Policy under the Assads* (London, 2013).

Schneider, Tobias, 'The decay of the Regime is much worse than you think', *War on the Rocks*, 31 August 2016.

Seale, Patrick, *The Struggle for Syria: A Study of Post-War Arab Politics (1945–1958)* (London, 1965).

——, *Asad: The Struggle for the Middle East* (London, 1988).

——, *The Struggle for Arab Independence: Riad al-Solh and the Makers of the Modern Middle East* (Cambridge, 2010).

——, 'Assad family values. How the son learned to quash a rebellion from his father', *Foreign Affairs*, 20 March 2012.

Shaaban, Bouthaina, *Damascus Diary: An Inside Account of Hafez Al-Assad's Peace Diplomacy, 1990–2000* (London, 2013).

Shami, Leila Al-, and Robin Yassin-Kassab, *Burning Country: Syrians in Revolution and War*, Kindle edn (London, 2016).

Shehadah, Lamia Rustum, 'The name of Syria in ancient and modern usage', *Al-Qantara*, 1 January 1994, pp. 285–96.

Starr, Stephen, *Revolt in Syria: Eye-Witness to the Uprising* (London, 2012).

Steele, Jonathan, 'Syria: Massacre reports emerge from Assad's Alawite heartland', *Guardian*, 2 October 2013.

Tamari, Steve, 'Territorial consciousness in the 17th century: Bilad al-Sham among Syrian Christians and Muslims', *Cohabitation et conflits dans le Bilad al-Cham à l'époque ottomane* (Beirut, 2009).

Tamimi, Aymenn Jawad Al-, 'Survey of articles on pro-Asad militias', *Syria Comment*, 30 August 2016.

Tejel, Jordi, *Syria's Kurds: History, Politics and Society* (London, 2011).

Wafaei, Husam, *Honorable Defection* (Victoria, BC, 2012).

Wedeen, Lisa, *Ambiguities of Domination: Politics, Rhetoric, and Symbols in Contemporary Syria* (Chicago, 1999).

Weiss, Michael and Hassan Hassan, *ISIS: Inside the Army of Terror* (New York, 2015).

Weulersse, Jacques, *Le Pays des Alaouites* (Tours, 1940).

——, *Paysans de Syrie et du Proche Orient* (Paris, 1946).

Wieland, Carsten, *Syria – A Decade of Lost Chances: Repression and Revolution from Damascus Spring to Arab Spring* (Seattle, 2012).

Winter, Stefan, *A History of the 'Alawis: From Medieval Aleppo to the Turkish Republic* (Princeton, 2016).

——, 'The Asad Petition of 1936: Bashar al-Asad's grandfather was pro-Unionist', *Syria Comment*, 14 June 2016.

Yassin-Kassab, Robin, 'Revolutionary culture', *Critical Muslim* | 11, *Syria*, July–September 2014.

Yazbek, Samar, *A Woman in the Crossfire: Diaries of the Syrian Revolution* (London, 2012).

## WORKS IN ARABIC

'Abduh, Samir, *Taryif al-Madinah wa Madnanat al-Rif* ('Ruralising the city and urbanising the countryside') (Damascus, 1989).

'Aflaq, Michel, 'Fi Dhikra al-Rasul al-'Arabi' ('Commemorating the Arab Prophet'), *Fi Sabil al-Ba'th* (Beirut, 1963), pp. 50–61.

Ahmad, Abd Allah al-, 'Ila al-Safir Nikolaos van Dam', *al-Safir*, 8 June 1995.

*Alarabiya.net*, 9 October 2015, 'Mawt Rajul al-Asadayn al-'Imad Shafiq Fayyad' ('The death of Shafiq Fayyad … the man of the Two Asads').

'Ali, Muhammad Ibrahim al-, *Hayati wa al-I'dam*, 3 Vols (Damascus, 2007).

Bitar, Salah al-Din al-, *al-Ihya' al-'Arabi* (Paris, 1979–80).

Fayyad, Shafiq, *Hadatha Ma'i* (unpublished manuscript) (Damascus, 2009).

*Film al-Watha'iqi, al-, "Basamat al-Dam al-Ula"* – *Majzarat Madrasat al-Midfa'iyah fi Halab.* Available at https://www.youtube.com/watch?v=0TxhsOm0raE&feature=youtu.be.

Habash, Marwan, 'Hawl al-Lajnah al-'Askariyah', in *Qadaya wa Ara'* (Damascus, 2010), pp. 17–20.

——, 'Muhawalat 'Usyan al-Ra'id Salim Hatum fi al-Suwayda' Yawm 8 Aylul 1966', in *al-Ba'th wa Thawrat Adhar* (Damascus, 2011), pp. 243–64.

Hizb al-Ba'th al-'Arabi al-Ishtiraki, al-Qutr al-Suri, al-Qiyadah al-Qutriyah, *Azmat al-Hizb wa Harakat 23 Shubat wa In'iqad al-Mu'tamar al-Qutri al-Akhir* (Damascus, 1966).

Husseini, Hassan, 'Watha'iq al-Khiyanah al-Ta'ifiyah. Risalat Sulayman al-Asad al-Maz'umah ila Faransa' ('Documents of sectarian treason. The alleged letter of Sulayman al-Asad to France'), *Syrian Virtual Society,* 1–2 September 2012. Available at https://www.facebook.com/SVS.Syria/posts/451091191602159.

Jallud, 'Azizah, *Ibrahim al-Yusuf wa Safahat min Tarikh al-Tali'ah al-Muqatilah fi Suriya. Masirah wa Sirah wa Haqa'iq takshif al-Mastur,* n.p., 2016.

Jundi, Sami al-, *al-Ba'th* (Beirut, 1969).

Khalifa, Mustafa, *al-Qawqa'ah, Yawmiyat Mutalassis,* n.p. n.d.

Khayyir, Al-Shaykh 'Abd al-Rahman al-, *'Aqidatuna wa Waqi'una Nahnu al-Muslimin al-Ja'fariyin al-'Alawiyin,* 3rd edn (Damascus, 1992).

——, *Min Turath al-Shaykh 'Abd al-Rahman al-Khayyir: Tarikh al-'Alawiyin* (Damascus, 1992).

——, *Min Turath al-Shaykh 'Abd al-Rahman al-Khayyir: Risalah Tabhath fi Masa'il Muhimmah hawl al-Madhhab al-Ja'fari: (Al-'Alawi)* (Damascus, 1994).

Ma'had al-Duwali lil-Dirasat al-Suriyah, al-, *Al-Ba'th al-Shi'i fi Suriyah (1919–2007),* n.p., n.d.

Maktab al-I'lami lil-Ikhwan al-Muslimin, al-, *Hamah, Ma'sat al-'Asr* ('Hama, the tragedy of the century'), n.p., n.d.

Murshid, Nur al-Mudi', *Lamahat hawl al-Murshidiyah* (*Dhikrayat wa Mushahadat wa Watha'iq*) (Beirut, 2008).

Mustafa, Khalil (Pseudonym for Khalil Barayyiz), *Suqut al-Jawlan* (Amman, 1969).

——, *Min Milaffat al-Jawlan* (Amman, 1970).

*Nadhir, al-,* Newsletter of al-Tala'i' al-Muqatilah ('Fighting Vanguards'), 1980.

Razzaz, Munif al-, *al-Tajribah al-Murrah* (Beirut, 1967).

Sadiq, Mahmud, *Hiwar hawl Suriyah* (London, 1993).

Safadi, Muta', *Hizb al-Ba'th: Ma'sat al-Mawlid Ma'sat al-Nihayah* (Beirut, 1965).

Saghiyah, Hazim (ed.), *Nawasib wa Rawafid. Munaza'at al-Sunnah wa al-Shi'ah fi al-'Alam al-Islami al-Yawm* (Beirut, 2010).

——, *Al-Ba'th al-Suri. Tarikh Mujaz* (Beirut, 2012).

Saleh, Yasin al-Haj, 'al-Ta'ifiyah wa al-Siyasah fi Suriyah', in Hazim Saghiyah (ed.), *Nawasib wa Rawafid. Munaza'at al-Sunnah wa al-Shi'ah fi al-'Alam al-Islami al-Yawm* (Beirut, 2010), pp. 51–81.

Shar', Faruq al-, *Al-Riwayah al-Mafqudah* ('The missing account') (Doha, 2015).

Sultah al-Rabi'ah, al-, 25 November 2016, *'Asharat al-Muthaqqafin al-Suriyin yutliquna Mubadarat "Nida' min ajl Suriya" li-Tamthil Haqiqi lil-Thawrah wa I'adat Haykaliyat al-I'tilaf'* ('Tens of Syrian intellectuals launch an "Appeal for Syria" for a real representation of the Revolution and a revision of the coalition's structure').

*Tadmur, al-Majzarah al-Mustamirrah* ('Palmyra, the continuous slaughter'), n.p., 2nd edn (1984).

Talas, Mustafa, *Mir'at Hayati, al-'Aqd al-Awwal, 1948–1958*, 2nd edn (Damascus, 1991).

——, *Mir'at Hayati, al-'Aqd al-Thani, 1958–1968* (Damascus, 1995).

——, *Mir'at Hayati, al-'Aqd al-Rabi', 1978–1988* (Beirut, 2004), 2nd printing (Damascus, Dar Talas, 2007).

Zarqah, Muhammad 'Ali, *Qadiyat Liwa' al-Iskandarunah. Watha'iq wa Shuruh,* 3 Vols (Beirut, 1993–4).

# LIST OF ABBREVIATIONS

| | |
|---|---|
| BSS | Building the Syrian State |
| Da'ish | al-Dawlah al-Islamiyah fi al-'Iraq wa al-Sham ('The Islamic State in Iraq and Greater Syria') |
| FSA | Free Syrian Army |
| HNC | High Negotiations Council |
| HTS | Hay'at Tahrir al-Sham ('Council for the Liberation of al-Sham') |
| ICC | International Criminal Court |
| IS | Islamic State |
| ISI | Islamic State in Iraq |
| ISIS | Islamic State in Iraq and Greater Syria (or the Levant) |
| ISSG | International Syria Support Group |
| MOC | Military Operations Centre |
| MOM | Müşterek Operasyon Merkezi (Turkish for Joint Operations Centre) |
| NCC | National Coordination Committee for Democratic Change |
| PKK | Partiya Karkerên Kurdistanê – [Turkish] Kurdistan Workers Party |
| PYD | Partiya Yekîtiya Demokrat – [Syrian] Kurdish Democratic Union Party |
| SNC | Syrian National Council |
| SOC | Syrian Opposition Coalition (National Coalition of the Syrian Revolution and Opposition Forces) |
| SSNP | Syrian Social Nationalist Party |
| UNHCR | United Nations High Commissioner for Refugees |
| UNSC | United Nations Security Council |
| YPG | Yekîneyên Parastina Gel – [Kurdish] People's Protection Units |

# LIST OF MOVEMENTS AND FACTIONS

## SYRIAN REGIME

4th Armoured Division
Defence Companies (Saraya al-Difa')
Desert Hawks (Suqur al-Sahra')
National Defence Forces – Militia
Popular Committees – Militia
Presidential Guard
Republican Guard
Seventieth Armoured Brigade
Shabbihah ('Ghosts') – Militia
Special Forces (al-Quwwat al-Khassah)
Syrian Arab Army
Tiger Forces (Quwwat al-Nimr)

## ANTI-REGIME

*Civilian*

Building the Syrian State (BSS)
High Negotiations Council (HNC)
Kurdish Democratic Union Party (Partiya Yekîtiya Demokrat) (PYD)
Kurdish National Council
Muslim Brotherhood
National Coordination Committee for Democratic Change (NCC)

Qamh (Acronym for Qiyam Muwatanah Huquq – 'Values – Citizenship – Rights')

Syrian National Council (SNC)

Syrian Opposition Coalition (National Coalition of the Syrian Revolution and Opposition Forces) (SOC)

*Military*

Ahrar al-Sham (Harakat Ahrar al-Sham al-Islamiyah – 'The Islamic Movement of the Free Men of Greater Syria') – Islamist

Battalions of Ibrahim al-Yusuf, 'Adnan 'Uqlah and Husni 'Abu – Jihadist

Da'ish – Acronym for al-Dawlah al-Islamiyah fi al-'Iraq wa al-Sham ('The Islamic State in Iraq and Greater Syria') – Jihadist

Fath Halab ('The Victory of Aleppo'). Umbrella organisation for cooperation between Islamists and Jihadists, mainly in the Aleppo region

Fighting Vanguards (al-Tala'i' al-Muqatilah) – Jihadist

Free Officers' Movement

Free Syrian Army (FSA)

Hay'at Tahrir al-Sham (HTS – 'Council for the Liberation of al-Sham'). Umbrella organisation founded by Jabhat Fath al-Sham, formerly Jabhat al-Nusrah, linked to al-Qa'idah. Jihadist-Islamist

Islamic State

Islamic State in Iraq

Islamic State in Iraq and Greater Syria (ISIS or Da'ish)

Jabhat al-Fath ('Victory Front') – Umbrella organisation for cooperation between Islamists and Jihadists, mainly in the province of Idlib

Jabhat Fath al-Sham ('The Front for the Victory in Greater Syria', previously Jabhat al-Nusrah, linked to al-Qa'idah)

Jabhat al-Islamiyah, al- ('The Islamic Front') – Islamist

Jabhat al-Nusrah ('The Victory Front') – Jihadist, linked to al-Qa'idah

Jaysh al-Islam ('Islam Army') – Islamist

Liwa' al-Islam ('The Islam Brigade') – Islamist

Movement of Free Alawis (Harakat Ahrar al-'Alawiyin) – Alawi officers' movement

Mujahidin ('Strugglers') – Jihadist

People's Protection Units (Yekîneyên Parastina Gel) (YPG) – Kurdish

Qa'idah, al – Jihadist

Qa'idah fi al-'Iraq, al- ('al-Qa'idah in Iraq') – Jihadist

Syrian Democratic Forces – Umbrella organisation for cooperation between Kurdish forces of the PYD and others in the mainly Kurdish region in the north, called Rojava in Kurdish

# INDEX